IMAGES
of America

ELKIN

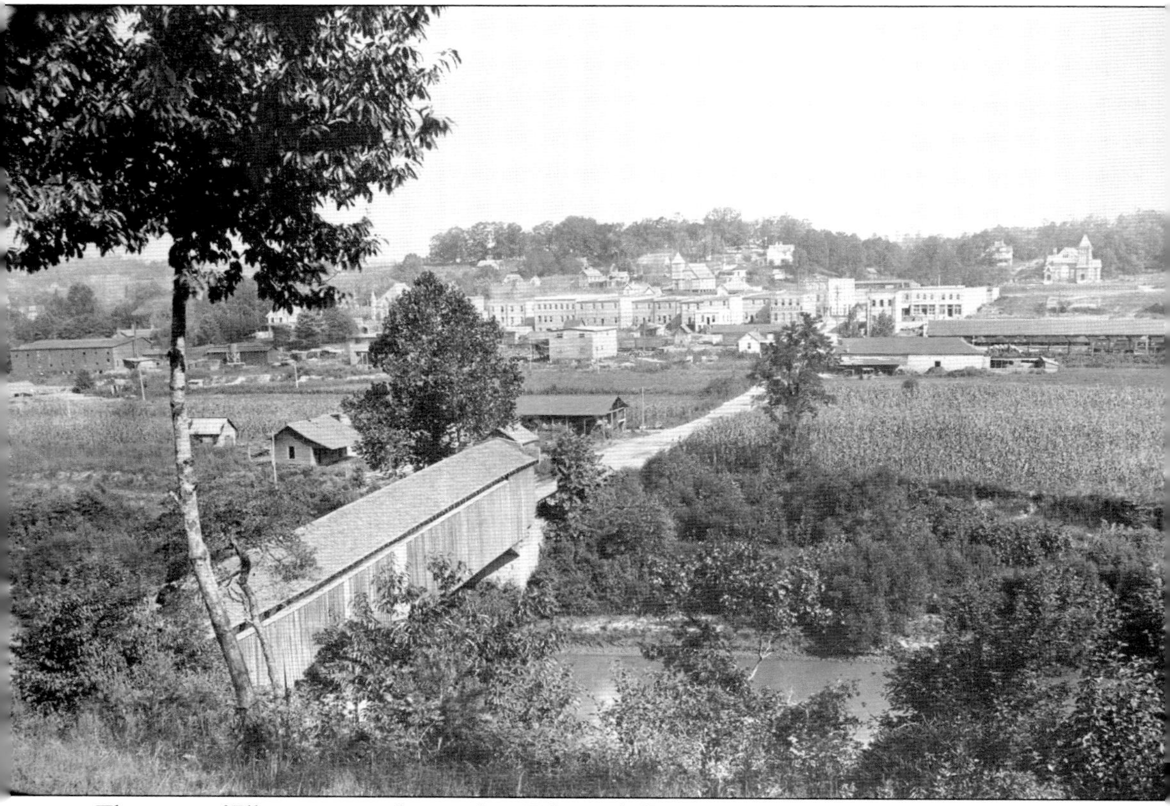

The town of Elkin is pictured around 1907 from a hill in Jonesville overlooking the Yadkin River. The covered bridge was located on South Bridge Street, where the Gwyn McNeil Bridge spans today. Initially built as a toll bridge, the crossing had become free by this time. The Methodist church buildings from 1905 and 1895 are at right in the picture. (Courtesy of James Partin.)

On the Cover: The Elkin bicycle club poses in front of the Elk Inn hotel in 1896. This building burned down in the great fire of 1898. The club members are, from left to right, Gordon Madison, Alonzo Reeves, Will M. Bell, Frank Tharp, W.O. Gilbert, ? Taylor, J.F. Hendren, Theodore Harris, Willie Click Biggs, Grace Gwyn Chatham, and Bertha Bell. (Courtesy of Elkin Historical Collection.)

IMAGES
of America

ELKIN

Dr. S. Jason Couch

ARCADIA
PUBLISHING

ISBN 978-0-7385-9210-7

Published by Arcadia Publishing
Charleston, South Carolina

Printed in the United States of America

Library of Congress Control Number: 2011933984

For all general information, please contact Arcadia Publishing:
Telephone 843-853-2070
Fax 843-853-0044
E-mail sales@arcadiapublishing.com
For customer service and orders:
Toll-Free 1-888-313-2665

Visit us on the Internet at www.arcadiapublishing.com

For Joshua and Laura, that they may learn to appreciate the history of their hometown

Contents

Acknowledgments

This book would not have been possible without the support and encouragement from my wife, Sherri, my parents, and my friends. Special thanks go to my friend and fellow collector Jack Partin, who, at the onset, offered his encouragement, his collection of negatives, and personal photographs. I also want to thank Judy Nance for proofreading the manuscript. This book has been a community effort, and my gratitude and thanks go to the numerous people who shared photographs, assisted with identifications, and answered many questions. Although all the pictures collected could not be included in the book, they are sincerely appreciated and will be preserved. Those who gave assistance are as follows: Gambill Aldridge; Al Banner; Tommy Benton; Deborah Boulware; Sarah Carter; Ed Chappell; Leroy Combs; Jimmy Darnell; Brad Howard; Theresa Knops; Mary Marsh; Cicely McCulloch; Melba Nance; Dr. Robert Nicks; Fred Norman; Randall Ray; Leon Reece; Martha Smith; Frank Transou; Joe Walker; Hubert Whittington; and Henry DeWolf Aerial Surveys of Rochester, New York; as well as those listed below whose photographs appear in the book. Special thanks to my acquisitions editors Lindsay Carter and James Wright at Arcadia, whose encouragement and assistance are greatly appreciated.

The images in this pictorial history appear courtesy of author S. Jason Couch (SJC), Rosy Beverley (RRB), David Brendle (DB), Bill Bruce (BB), Jean Bryan (JCB), Christine Burcham (CB), Gilmer Caudle (GC), Ralph Cooke (RC), Johnny Corder (JC), Dr. Bill H. Davis Jr. (BHD), the Elkin Historical Collection (EHC), the Elkin Jaycees (EJ), the Elkin Post Office (EPO), Graham Greene (GG), Paulette Gregory (PKG), Margaret Hinson (MCH), Teresa Howell (TH), Kay Hurt (KCH), Lula Johnson (LJ), Grace Laffoon (GL), Coolidge Layell (CL), Charles G. Mathis (CGM), *Our State* magazine (OSM), Craig Pardue (RCP), James Partin (JWP), Jim Poteat (JP), Suzanne Puckett (SP), Bill and Cissie Roth (BCR), Tom Roth (TR), Edwin Royall (ER), Bill Sams (BS), Kathleen Snyder (KCS), Graham W. Somers (GWS), Bonnie Stuart (BHS), Dr. Hal Stuart (HMS), John Sullivan (JS), Jackie Swaim (JRS), Evan Vestal (EV), Lucy Vestal (LHV), Tommy Wheeler (CTW), and Agri-Graphics (AG).

INTRODUCTION

In the southwest corner of Surry County, at the junction of Big Elkin Creek and the Yadkin River, lies the town of Elkin. The town was named after the creek, then known as the Elkin River, which was first identified on the 1770 map of North Carolina drawn by John Colet. Settlers began to apply for land grants and move into the area around 1752. One early resident was David Allen, who operated an ironworks somewhere along the Elkin Creek within his 2,482 acres. It was in operation as early as 1776, according to the Moravian records from Salem in Forsyth County, North Carolina. Rich iron ore deposits and timber provided the necessary resources for Allen to operate his furnace until December 1786, when he sold it to William Hill. The area was still sparsely populated and fairly untouched wilderness when Richard Gwyn, born in 1796 near Ronda, North Carolina, began purchasing land on Elkin Creek. He and his wife, Elizabeth Martin Hunt Gwyn, lived across the Yadkin River in Jonesville, where he was postmaster and ran a general store. In 1840, he moved his family across the river and built what is known as Elkin's first house, Cedar Point, which still stands today. Gwyn eventually bought around 6,000 acres of land. In the early 1840s, he constructed a gristmill on Elkin Creek near the present-day site of the Elkin Public Library. In 1847, he built an addition to the mill to house a small cotton mill and established the Elkin Manufacturing Company. He also erected a one-room building that was used as the community's first school and church around 1850. This structure, now known as the Richard Gwyn Museum, has been restored and preserved by the local Jonathan Hunt Chapter of the Daughters of the American Revolution (DAR). From these humble beginnings, Elkin began to grow.

In April 1865, during the final months of the Civil War, a group of Union cavalry, led by Maj. Gen. George Stoneman, passed through the Elkin area on a destructive raid through Western North Carolina and Virginia. The Elkin Manufacturing Company cotton mill was not destroyed, enabling the community to continue to prosper after the war. Before 1872, the only way to cross the Yadkin River between Elkin and Jonesville was by ferry; in May of that year, the covered bridge opened, providing an easy connection that facilitated commerce between the two settlements. At the time, it was said to be the longest wooden suspension bridge in the world. In 1866, Richard Ransome Gwyn, son of Elkin's founder, built a gristmill and store, called R.R. Gwyn & Company, in the community of Elkin Valley. It was located about one mile up the creek from the Elkin Manufacturing Company. He bartered for wool in exchange for goods, and in the mid-1870s bought a small wool carding machine to process the wool. In 1877, Thomas L. Gwyn, brother of Richard Ransome Gwyn, In 1877, Thomas L. Gwyn, brother of Richard Ransome Gwyn, and his brother-in-law Alexander Chatham bought the mill and small wool processing business called R.R. Gwyn & Company. They built a large addition to the mill, purchased more machinery, and founded the Elkin Valley Woolen Mill. In 1890, Thomas Gwyn sold his interest in the mill to Alexander Chatham, and it was reorganized as Chatham Manufacturing Company.

The town of Elkin was officially chartered by the North Carolina legislature on March 5, 1889. The population of the community at this time was 288. In 1890, Richard Ransome Gwyn sold the majority of his inherited property to the Elkin Land Company, owned by a group of investors from nearby Winston that included R.J. Reynolds. This group hired engineer J.L. Ludlow to draw a map of the town in 1891. The town of Elkin would develop from this plan, although with many modifications. The arrival of the Northwest North Carolina Railroad on April 8, 1890, was probably the single most important event in the growth of the community. In 1893, Chatham Manufacturing built a new plant east of town, adjacent to the railroad tracks. Other industries established around this time included the Elkin Shoe Company (1892); the Elkin Furniture Company (1896); the Baily Manufacturing Company (1896), makers of locust pins, brackets, and cross arms; and the Elkin Veneer Factory (1902).

On March 24, 1898, a large fire consumed most of the wooden buildings, including the post office, in the downtown area. The town rebuilt with brick structures, many of which are still present in the business district. The Yadkin River has flooded the town on three major occasions—in 1898, 1916, and 1940. The water level during the flood of 1916 crested at eight feet higher than the 1898 flood. The heavy floods of 1916 and 1940 left the river bottom in ruins and caused considerable damage to the town. The worst was the flood of 1940, when waters that rose and receded within 48 hours left over $500,000 in damage. The 1962 construction of the W. Kerr Scott Dam in Wilkesboro, North Carolina, prevented further flooding of similar magnitude.

As the industries of Elkin grew, so did the town, with the building of churches, schools, and additional downtown businesses. The first major newspaper to be published was the *Elkin Times*, begun in 1892 by R.L. Hubbard and John Roth. It eventually gave way to its competitor, *The Elkin Tribune*, which was started in 1911 by W.E. and H.G. Nichols and is still in business today. The 1911 opening of the Elkin & Alleghany (E&A) Railway brought much attention to Elkin, along with hope for the future. The goal of the railway was to connect to the Norfolk & Western line at Jefferson, North Carolina, in the Blue Ridge Mountains; however, it never made it beyond the foot of the mountain below Roaring Gap. Chatham Manufacturing Company continued to grow and became the largest blanket manufacturer in the world, providing millions of blankets for the armed services during both world wars. Thurmond Chatham, born in Elkin, became a naval commander, US congressman, and president of Chatham Manufacturing. He led the company through a period of growth and prosperity, which tremendously benefited the town. He was instrumental in building the original Hugh Chatham Memorial Hospital, as well as starting the YMCA, Elkin Jaycees, and Elkin Rescue Squad. His development of Klondike Farm, north of Elkin, would bring much interest in and prestige to the community in the 1930s; Klondike Iceberg, the most famous cow in the world at the time, was born near the Antarctic Circle in 1933. The positive effects that Chatham Manufacturing and the Chatham family have had on the town of Elkin are immeasurable.

While acknowledging, with respect and appreciation, the contributions of our founding fathers, it is the mill workers, factory workers, small-business owners, church members, educators, health care workers, civic organizations, and public servants who built Elkin into the town it has become, and they continue to sustain it. Today, Elkin is no longer the home of large textile and furniture factories. Its downtown area is listed in the National Register of Historic Places, and it is known for its quality schools and a first-class hospital. Located adjacent to Interstate 77 and minutes from the Blue Ridge Parkway, Pilot Mountain State Park, and Stone Mountain State Park, Elkin is still the "best little town in North Carolina."

One

Early Elkin through the 1920s

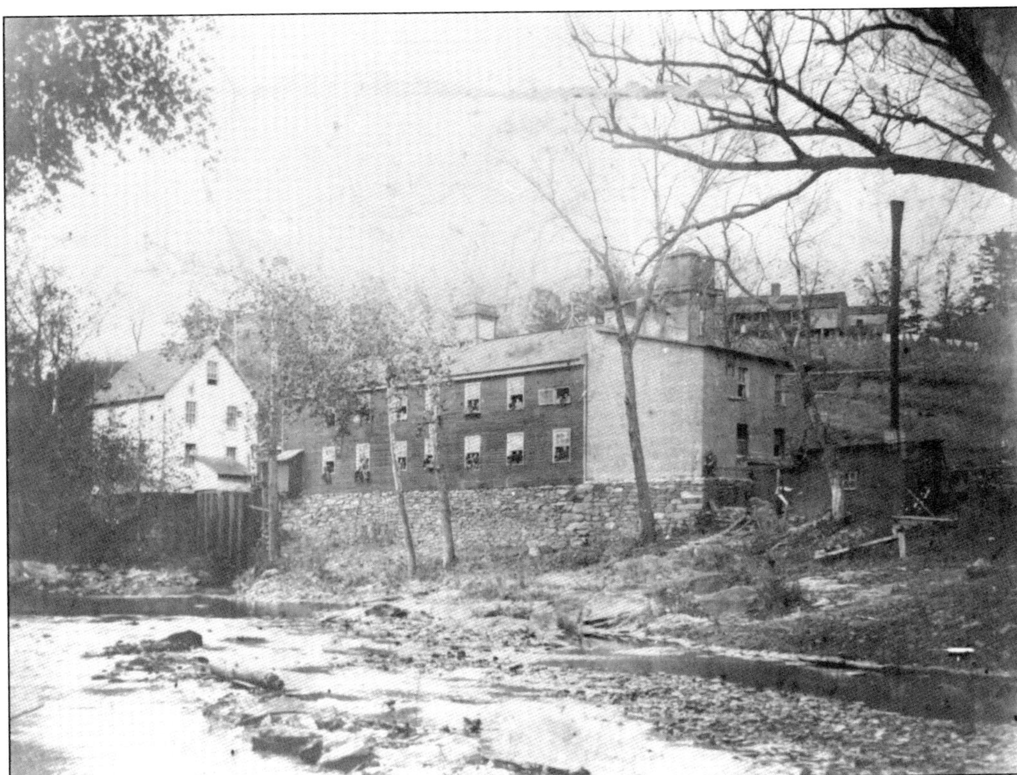

Richard Gwyn, referred to as the founding father of Elkin, built a gristmill, visible at left in the picture, on Elkin Creek in the early 1840s. He added a small cotton mill to the building in 1847 and formed the Elkin Manufacturing Company. It was incorporated in 1848 and operated until after 1903. The Elkin Public Library is currently located on this site. (JWP.)

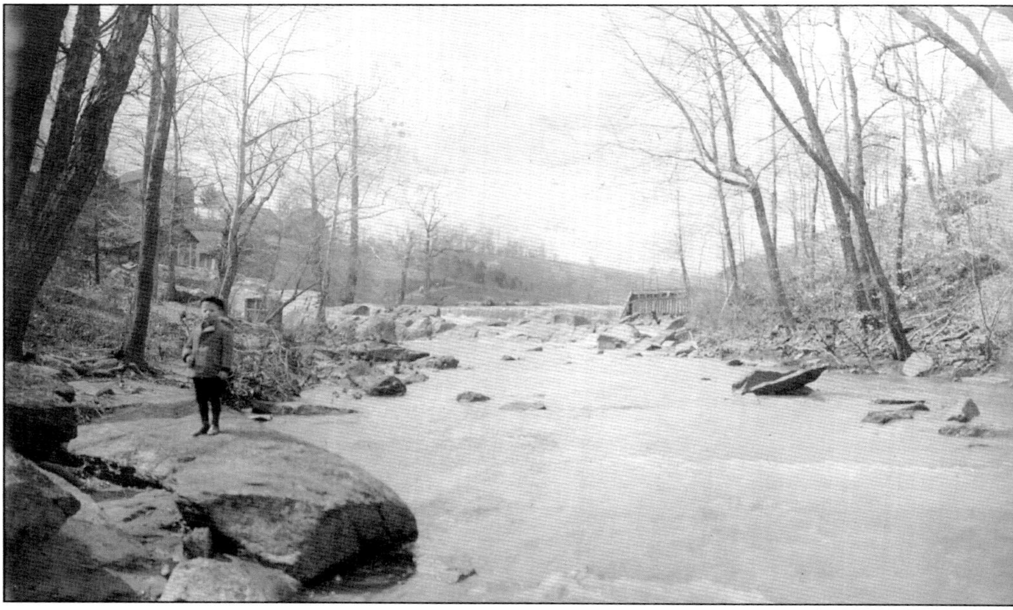

The first dam built on the Elkin Creek is shown around 1902; William Roth stands on the rock in the left foreground. The dam was constructed in the 1840s and was located between the existing library dam and the Elk Spur Street bridge. The wooden flume to the right of the dam furnished water for Richard Gwyn's gristmill and the Elkin Manufacturing Company's cotton mill. (RRB.)

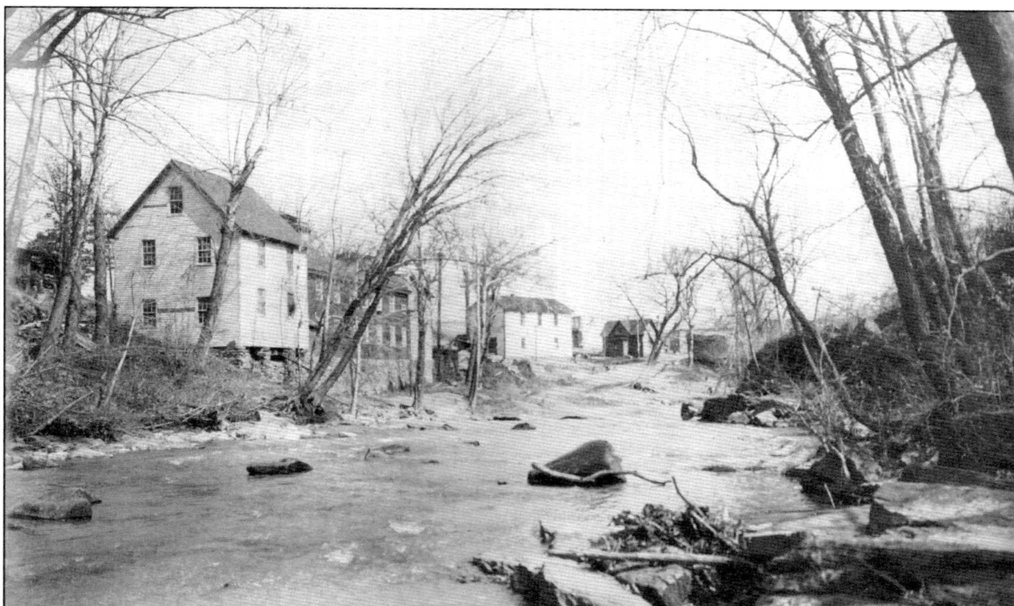

The Gwyn gristmill and Elkin Manufacturing Company are shown in this c. 1900 view looking south down Elkin Creek from upstream. The small building in the far right is the office for the Elkin Manufacturing Company, which was later used as the office for the Elkin & Alleghany Railway. (RRB.)

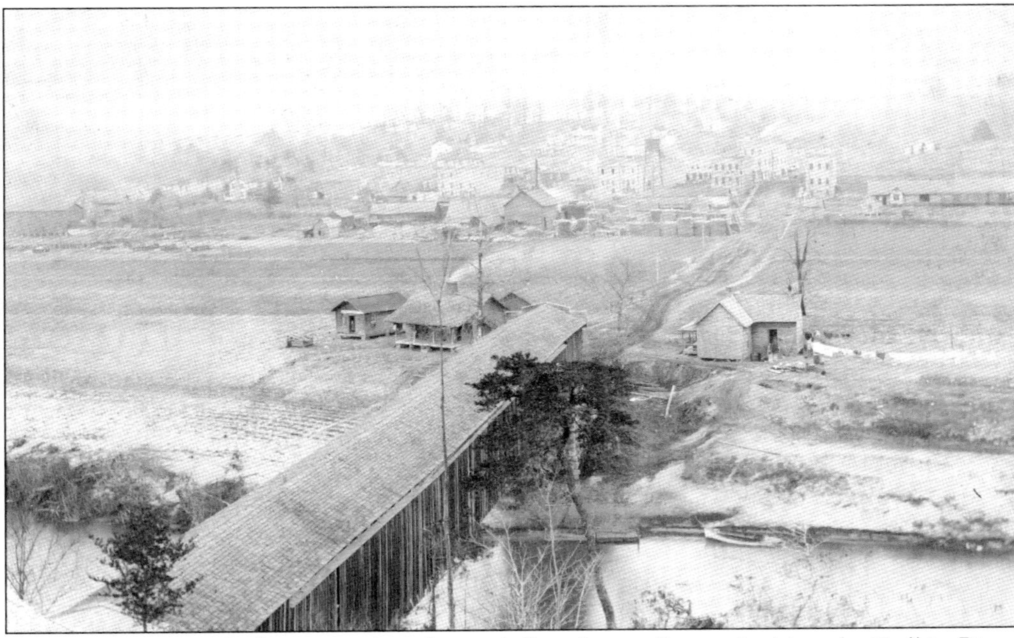

This c. 1901 view of Elkin was taken from a hill in Jonesville overlooking the Yadkin River. Fewer buildings existed on West Main Street, and the only structure cn East Main Street was the Holcomb Brothers Grocery. The railroad depot is the long building at right in the picture. The covered bridge operated as a toll bridge at this time. (SJC.)

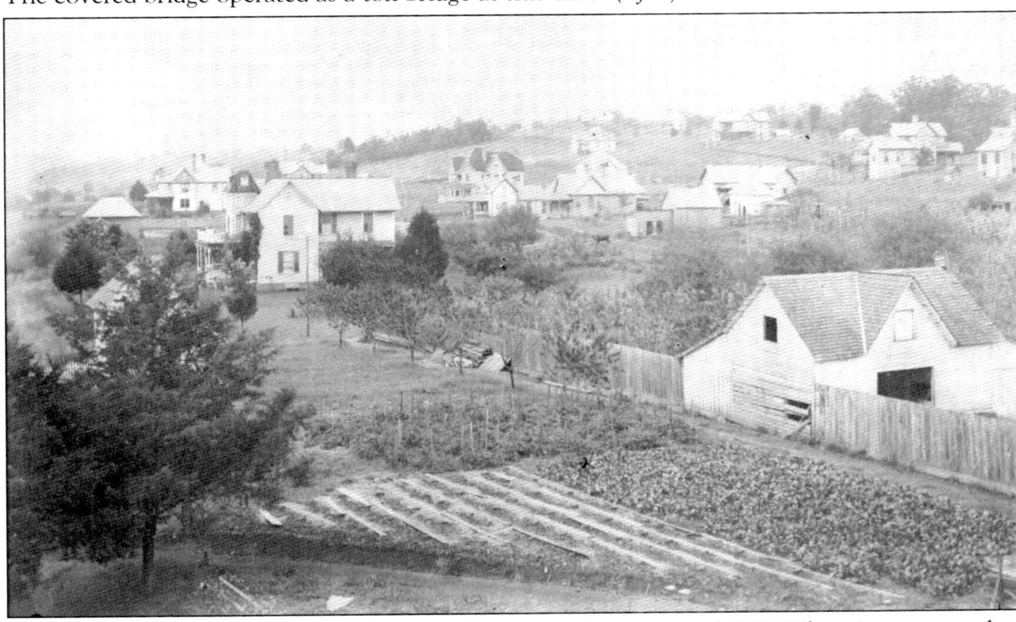

Houses along Surry Avenue and West Main Street are shown around 1900. This picture was taken from the backyard of the Gilvin T. Roth home on Terrace Avenue, looking west. The Robert L. Hubbard house is on the far left, and the John Roth house is in the left foreground. The Roth house originally faced the Yadkin River, but when Surry Avenue was built, a porch was added to the back. (TR.)

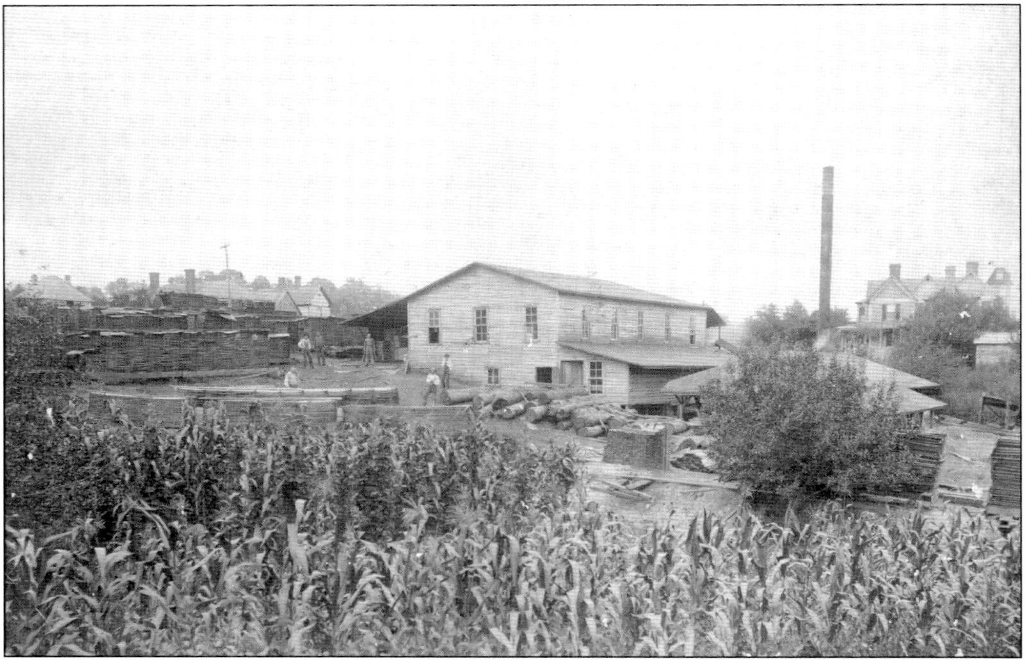

The Elkin Veneer Factory was located on Surry Avenue, west of the John Roth house (at right in the picture). Robert Lee Hubbard, W.E. Cooper, H.F. Gray, and William Bell established the factory in 1902. A.G. Click invested in the business soon after its founding. The factory made veneers used in furniture manufacturing and also made egg cases. It went out of business in 1920. (TR.)

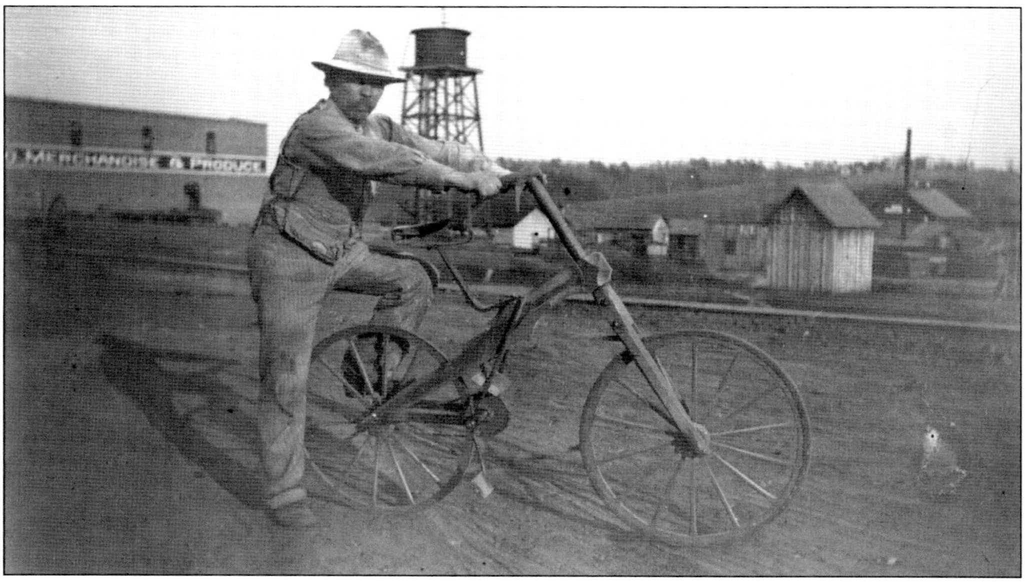

In this c. 1895 photograph, a man identified as possibly John Roth is pictured on an old wooden bicycle on West Main Street. This view, looking southeast, shows the Click and Company building on the left. In 1891, John F. Cooke built the town's first wooden sidewalks, which are visible in the background. Also pictured is the water tank used by the Northwest North Carolina Railroad, which came to Elkin in 1890. (BCR.)

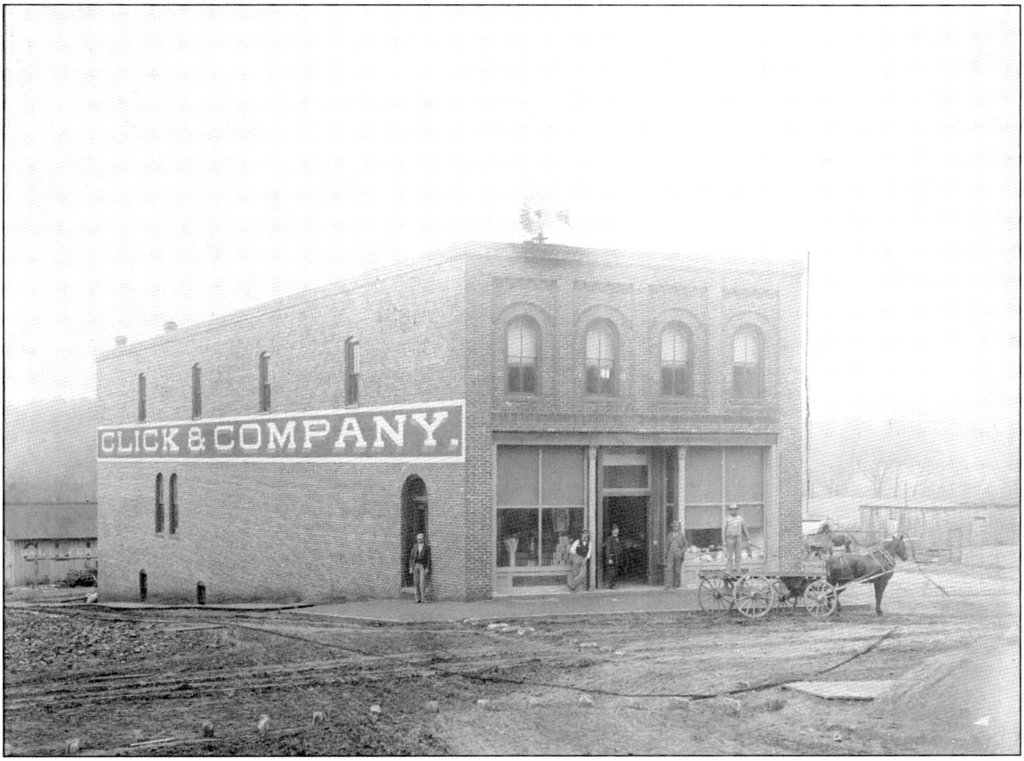

Click and Company was a general merchandise store in business prior to 1895. It was a partnership between A.G. Click and Chatham Manufacturing Company. This was one of the first buildings constructed in downtown Elkin, and it still stands today on the southwest corner of Main and Bridge Streets. (EHC.)

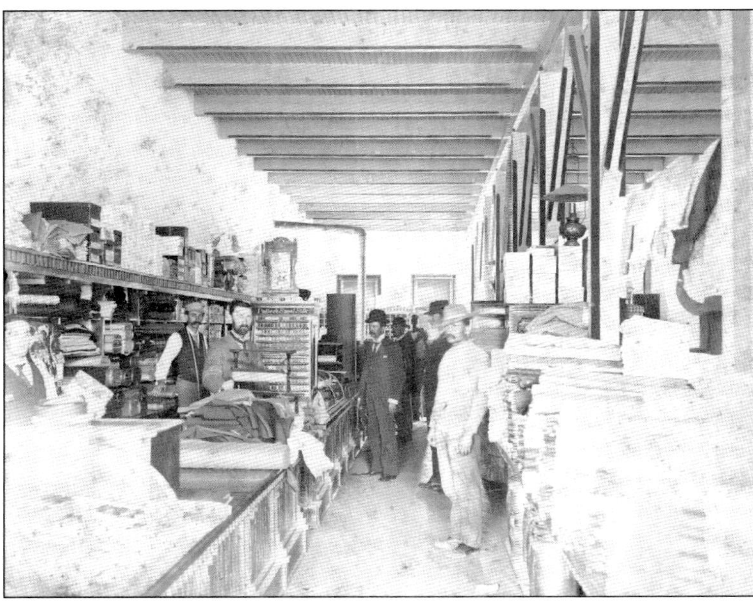

The interior of Click and Company is pictured around 1896. It sold dry goods, shoes, clothing, and general merchandise. From left to right are an unidentified man, Lytle Hickerson Hunt, owner A.G. Click, R.L. Hubbard, J.S. Roth, and three unidentified men. (EHC.)

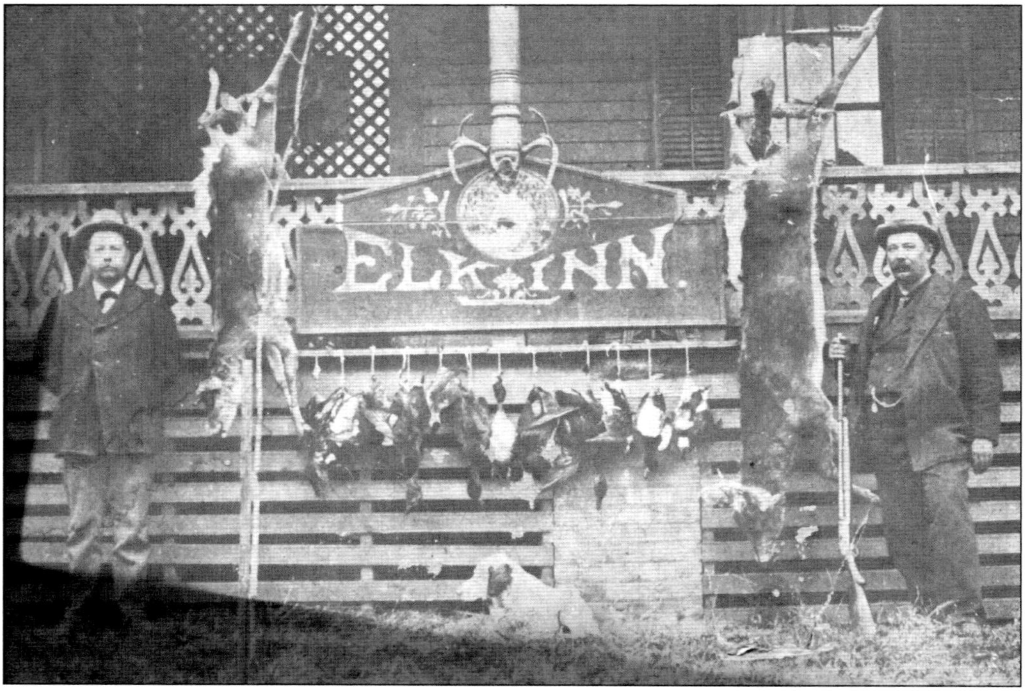

The Elk Inn, Elkin's first hotel, was built in 1883 by Charles H. Gwyn and was located on the northwest corner of West Main and Church Streets. Richard M. Chatham (right) and Charles H. Gwyn are pictured with their dog Scout in 1888. The hotel burned down in 1898 but was rebuilt. A four-foot-long elk antler was displayed over the dining room door. (EHC.)

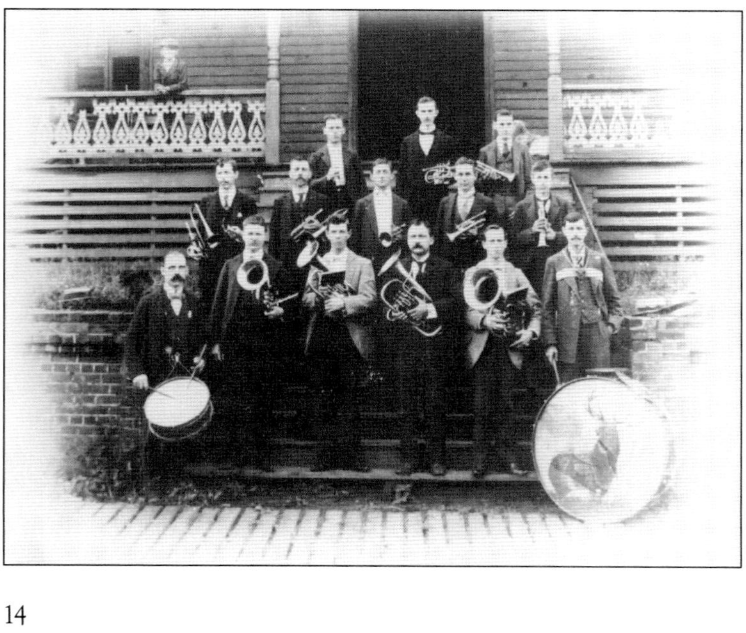

The Elkin Cornet Band is pictured around 1897 on the steps of the Elk Inn. Members of the group, some of whom are pictured here, included Mason Lillard, John Minish, Thede Harris, Joe Parris, Lon Reeves, John Roth, Gene Motsinger, Joe Chatham, J.E. Paul, Will Bell, Noah Tharp, and Jim Madison. They rehearsed in a room above Dr. J.W. Ring's drugstore. (EHC.)

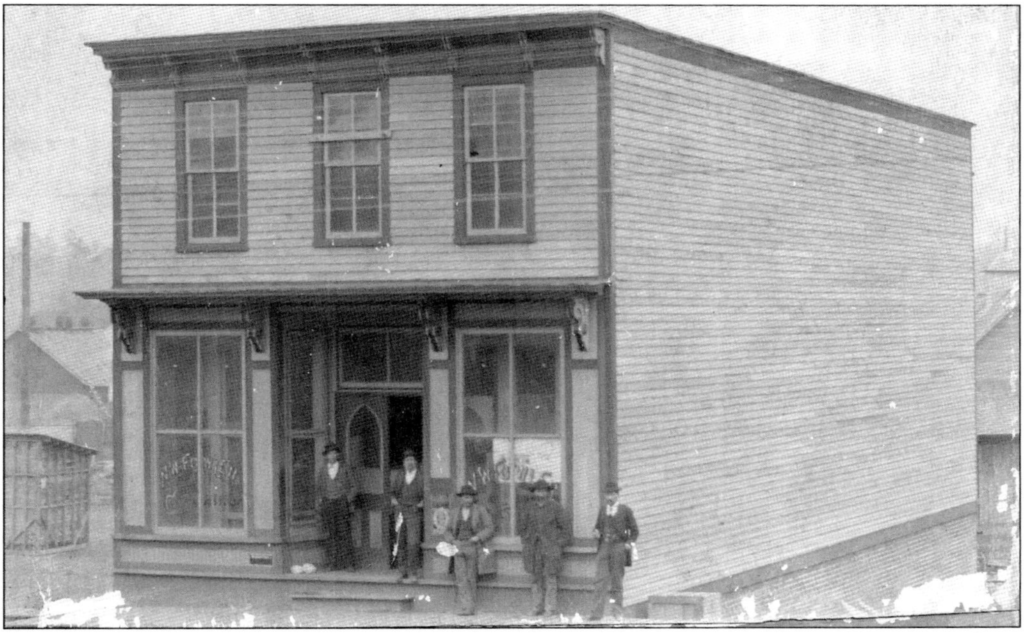

The N.W. Fowler clothing store was located on the south side of West Main Street, across from the Elk Inn. This wooden style was typical of many of the early downtown buildings that were destroyed in the great fire on March 24, 1898. Five stores, the original Elk Inn, the post office, J.F. Hendren's law office, and the home of A.G. Click were all consumed in the blaze. (BHD.)

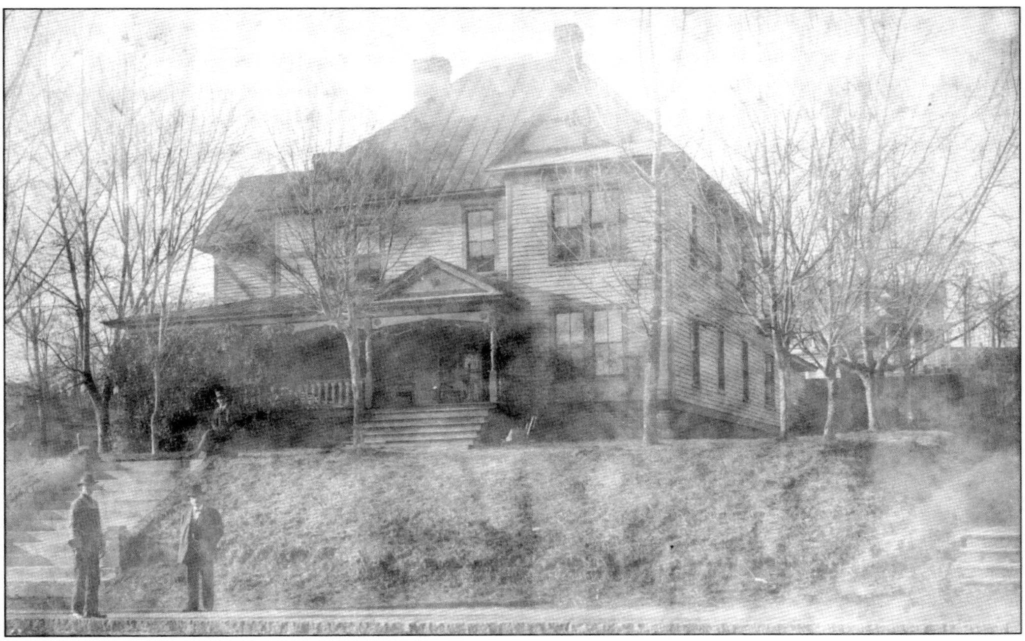

The new Elk Inn is pictured after being rebuilt following the fire of 1898. The original Elk Inn stood on the same site, at the northwest corner of West Main and Church Streets. This second hotel would burn down in 1927. Dr. Joseph W. Ring (right, standing on sidewalk) was Elkin's first doctor. He came to Elkin in 1872 and was the only doctor in town for over 10 years. (EHC.)

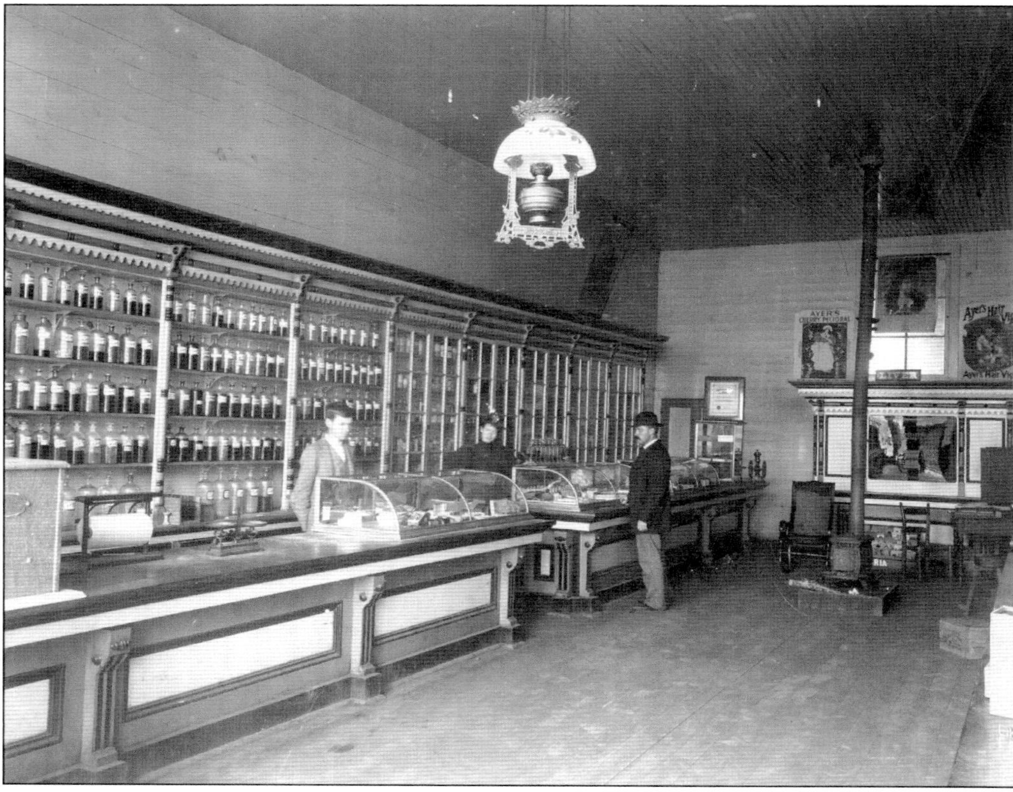

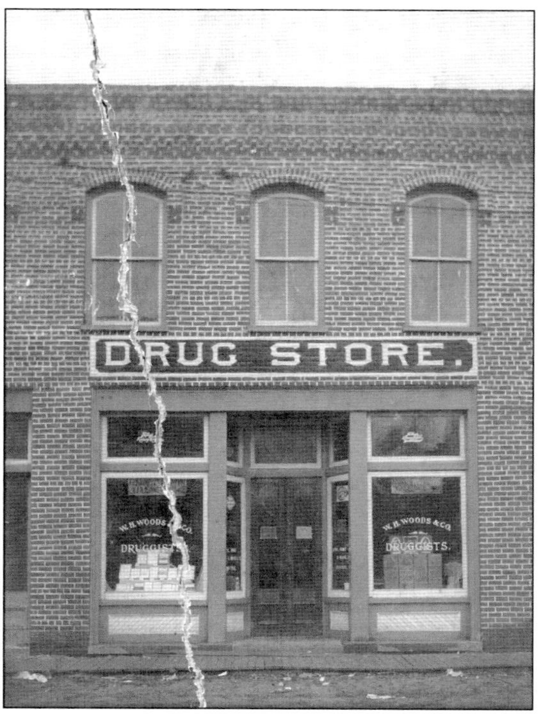

Dr. Joseph W. Ring came to Elkin in 1872 from Winston to practice as a physician and surgeon. He graduated from Jefferson Medical College in Philadelphia. He, along with Dr. L.J. Barker, opened the first drugstore in Elkin. The interior of Dr. Ring's drugstore is pictured around 1897; it burned down in the big fire on March 24, 1898. (EHC.)

In 1901, W.H. Woods and Company ran this drugstore, with the offices of Dr. J.W. Ring and Dr. Mosley upstairs. It was located at 109 West Main Street, the fifth store from the corner of Bridge Street. This structure, along with three others adjacent to it, burned down in 1912. Abernethy's Pharmacy was later located in a different building at this site. (EHC.)

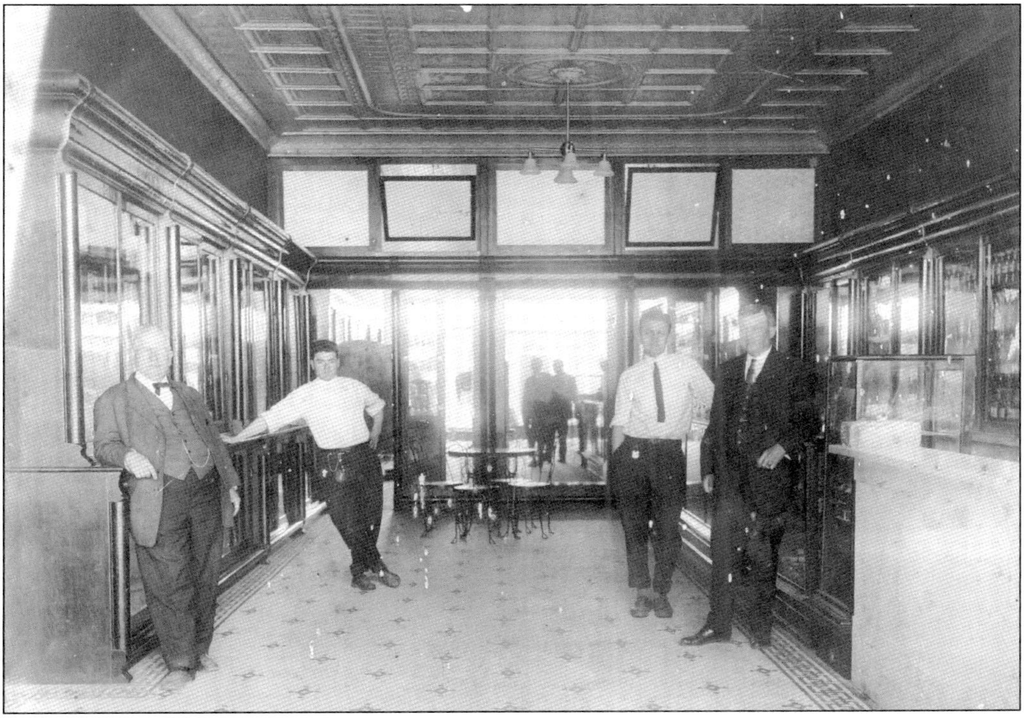

The interior of the Elkin Drug Company is shown after being remodeled in the early 1910s. The men pictured are, from left to right, Dr. J.W. Ring, R. Bob Lewis, Rom Llewellyn, and Dr. James Montgomery Reece. Dr. Ring organized the Elkin Drug Company in 1905. In 1914, Lewis was the druggist, and George Royall was a clerk in the store. (EHC.)

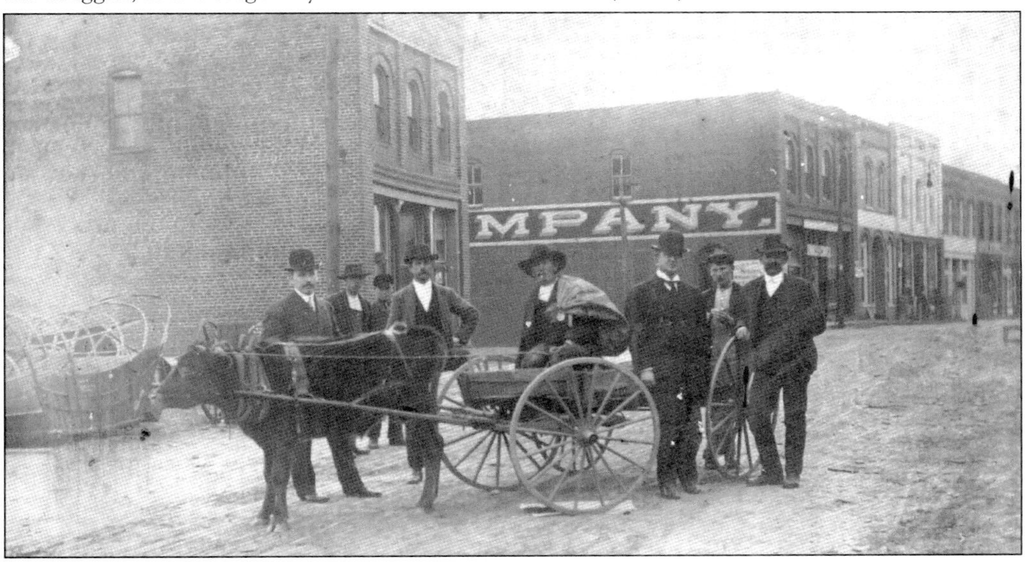

Frank Day is pictured sitting in his mail delivery oxcart around 1908; the other men are unidentified. Day was 14 years old when he lost his right arm at the Elkin Manufacturing Company cotton mill. He began delivering the mail in 1871. In 1887, he began carrying the mail between Elkin and Jonesville, making two round-trips per day. By 1910, he made three round-trips daily. (EHC.)

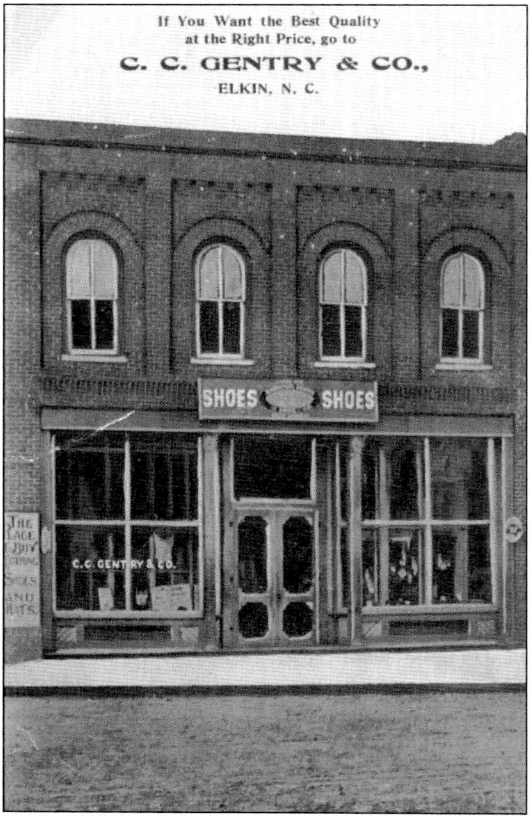

This postcard shows the front of the Click Building, located on the southwest corner of Main and Bridge Streets in 1908. Charles C. Gentry bought the business from A.G. Click in 1904 and renamed it C.C. Gentry & Company. It was purchased by S.H. Wilmoth in 1913 and reorganized as the Elkin Mercantile Company. Sydnor-Spainhour's department store opened in this building in 1926. (SJC.)

Crater and Sale was founded prior to 1903 and was located at 103 West Main Street, the second building from the corner of Bridge Street. Pictured around 1911, the business sold general merchandise, shoes, and millinery. Later, McDaniel's Department Store operated in this location for many years. Tharp's Hardware is located on the right in this picture. (EHC.)

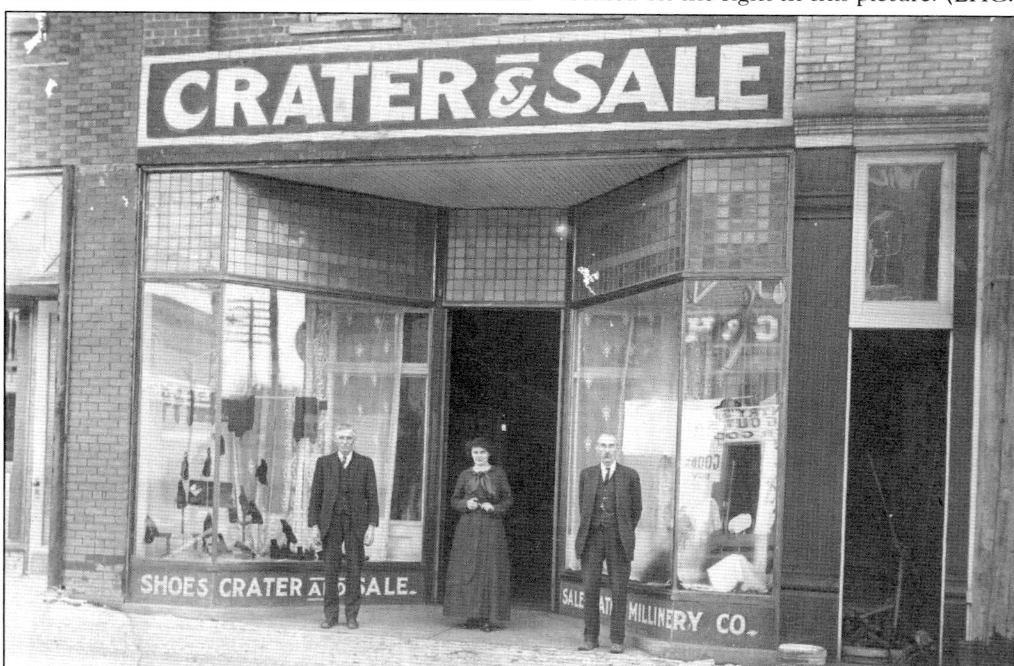

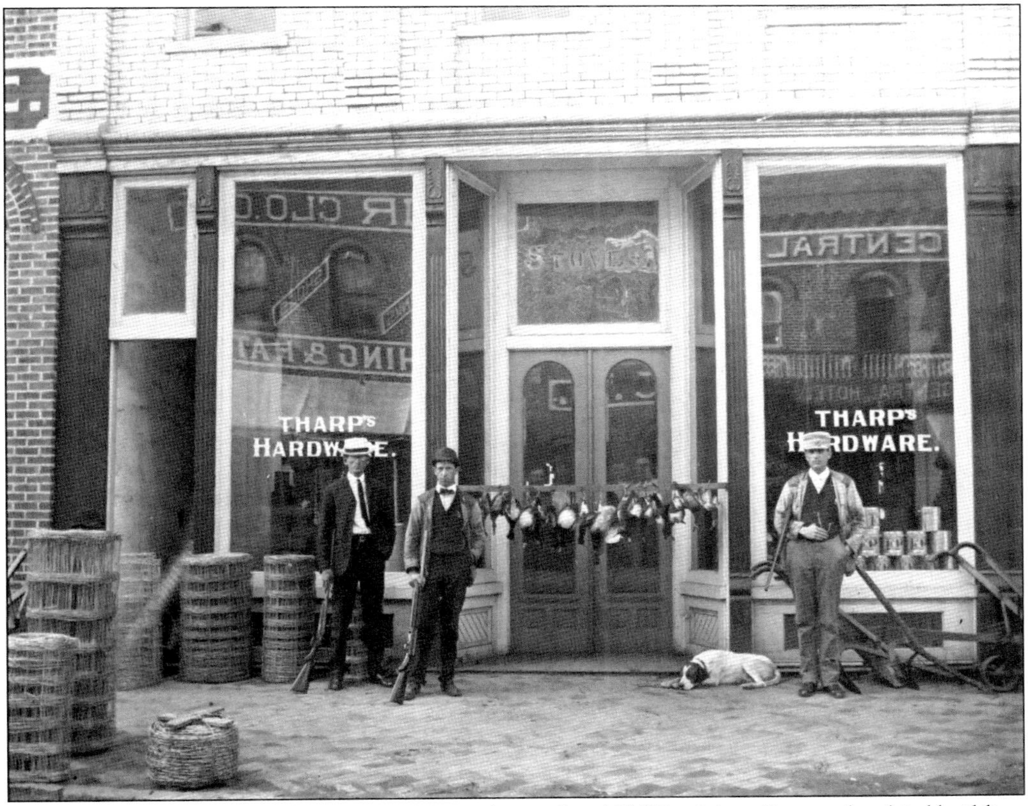

Tharp's Hardware, pictured prior to 1909, was located at 105 West Main Street, the third building from the corner of Bridge Street. It was founded in 1870 by Frank and Noah W. Tharp. They sold Carolina Canning outfits and large quantities of RFD mailboxes. In this image, Roy Bell (left), Noah Tharp (center), and William W. Whitaker are shown after a duck hunt. In 1915, this store was bought by J.R. Poindexter and became Surry Hardware, which was in business until 1977. (JWP.)

The Farmers' and Merchants' Bank was organized in 1908 by W.S. Reich. He moved to Elkin in 1900 and started the Reich-Walsh Furniture Company. The large, white brick bank building is still standing on the north side of West Main Street. The side of the M. Quiller Snow clothing store is visible at right. (RC.)

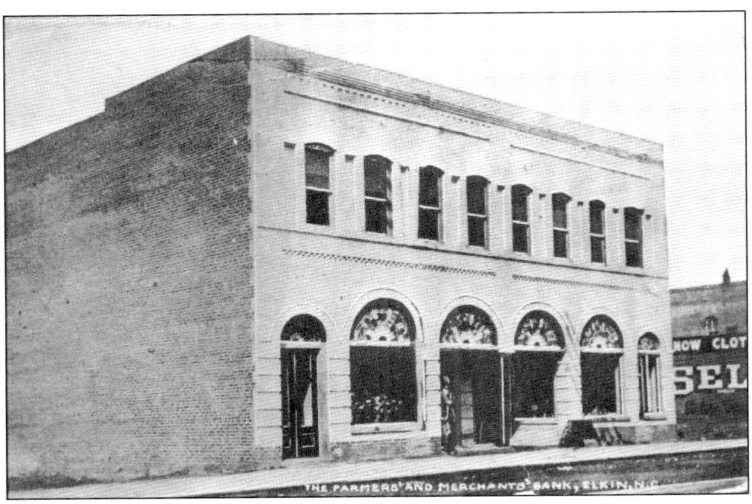

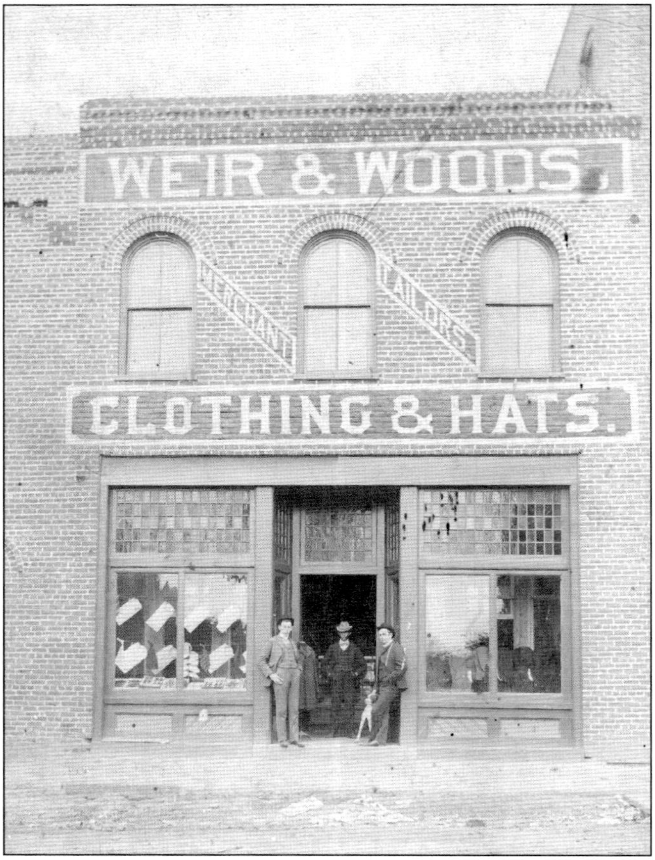

The Weir & Woods Clothing Company opened on February 1, 1898, and was located on the north side of West Main Street, adjacent to the Elkin National Bank. Around 1906, it was named the Elkin Clothing Company. From 1910 to 1913, it was owned by S.H. Wilmoth and called Wilmoth and Hayes. It was later bought by M.Q. Snow and operated until 1963. Lonnie Mathis is in the center of the doorway. (EHC.)

Elmer Fontaine McNeer (1867–1954) moved to Elkin in 1905 and bought the Hubbard and Roth hardware store. The name was changed to the Elkin Hardware Company, and it was located on the northeast corner of Main and Bridge Streets. This postcard from 1910 shows Bell Furniture on the right. By 1914, the Elk Printing Company, printers of the *Elkin Tribune*, was located in the furniture store building. (SJC.)

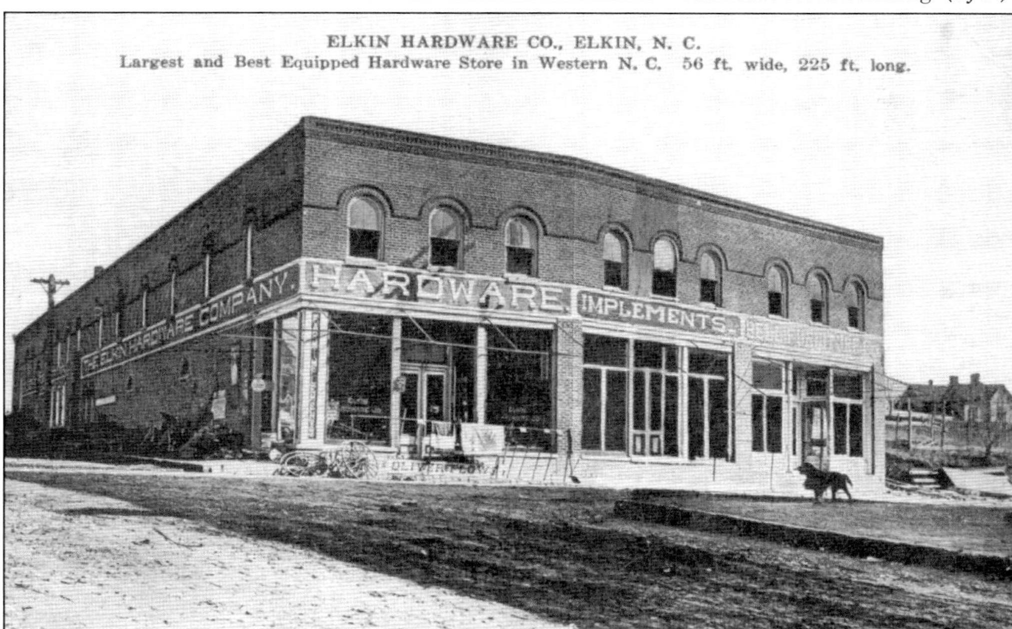

The Elkin National Bank was the first bank to open in town. It was organized on January 6, 1901, with Alexander Chatham as president. It was located on the northwest corner of Main and Bridge Streets. In this c. 1906 photograph, the Elkin Clothing Company is located to the left. This bank closed in 1932, during the Great Depression, and never reopened. The Bank of Elkin was relocated here from its East Main Street site in 1937. (JWP.)

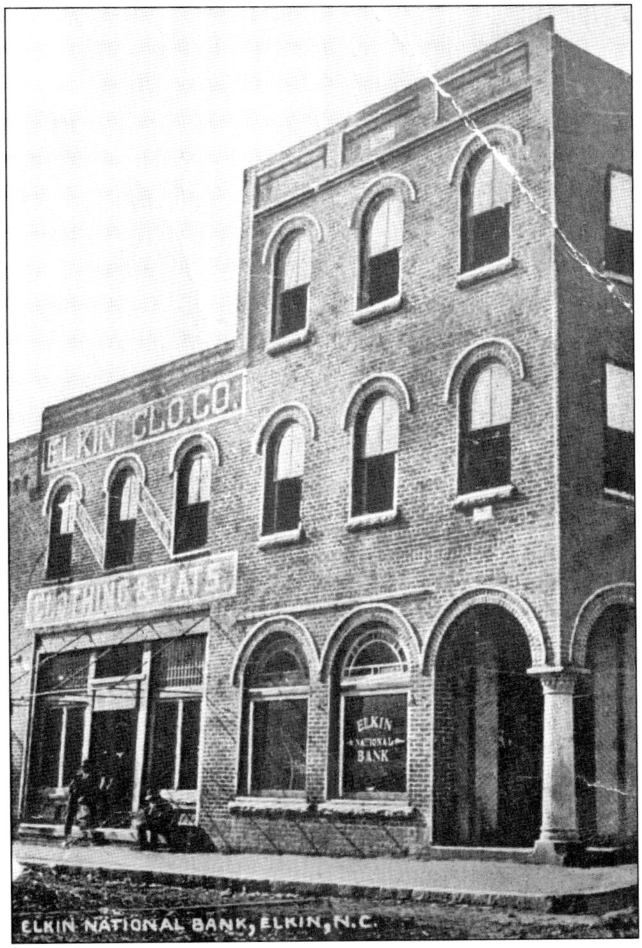

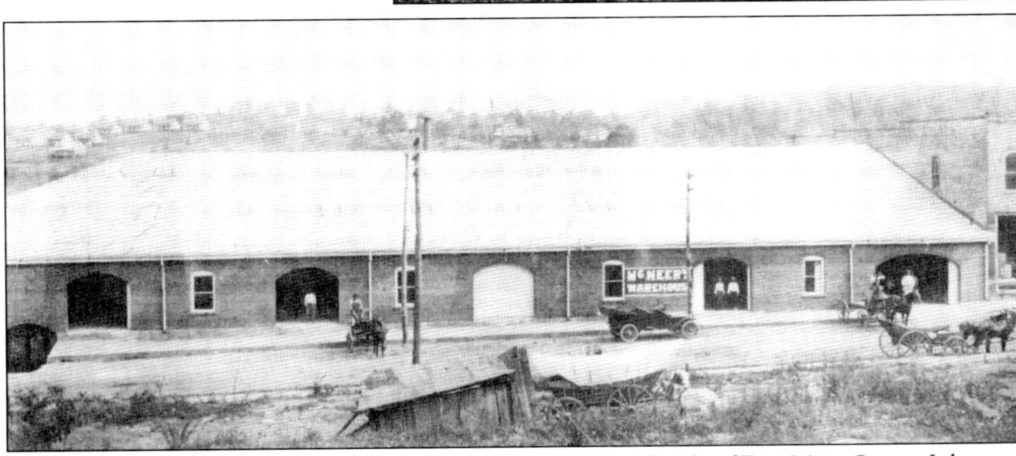

In 1914, E.F. McNeer built this tobacco warehouse on the south side of East Main Street. It burned down in 1919 and was replaced with a new structure that stood until the late 1930s. The Rev. Billy Sunday held a revival meeting there in the 1920s, and the first community fair was held there in 1932. It was also used for high school basketball games until a gymnasium was built. (CGM.)

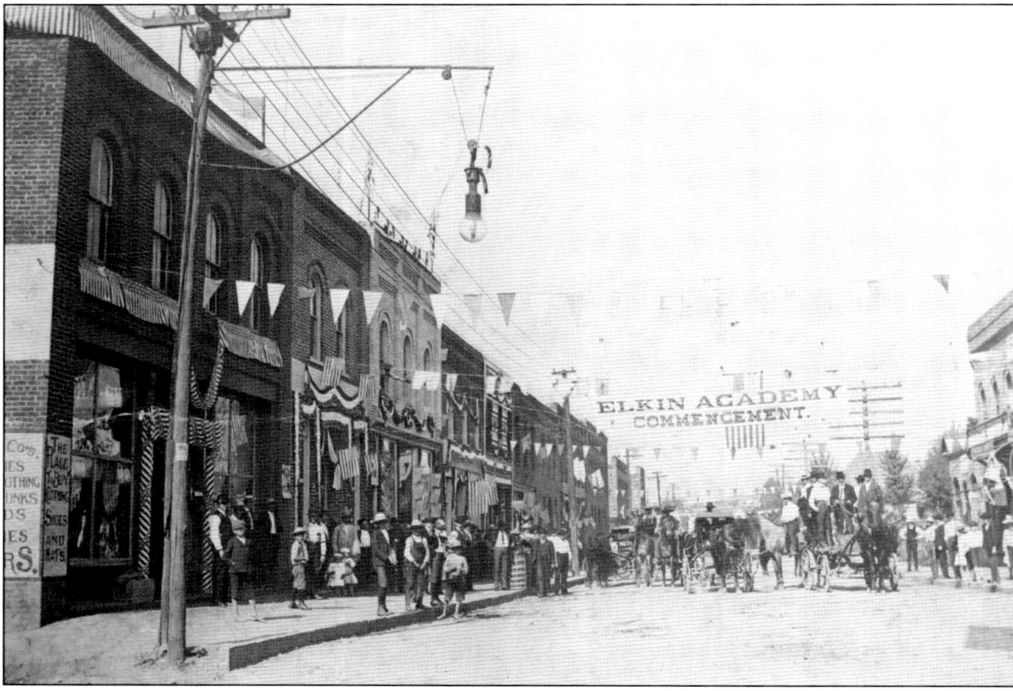

The Elkin Academy commencement day celebration on West Main Street is shown in 1908. The academy was a private school that opened its doors in September 1896. The first term had an enrollment of 125 students. Some of the subjects taught were Latin, Greek, French, German, higher mathematics, sciences, and music. (JWP.)

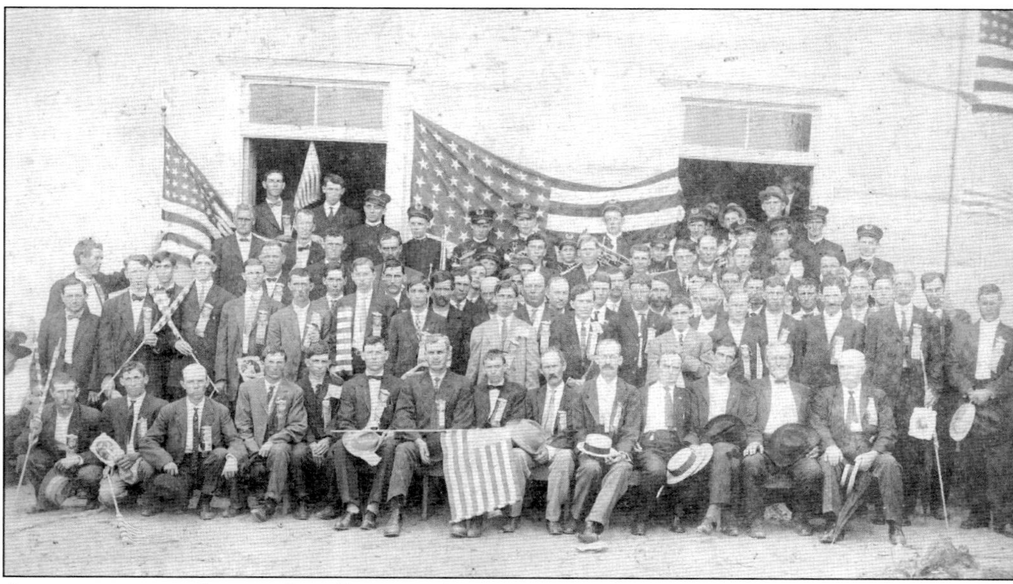

Commencement days at the Elkin Academy were grand occasions. In 1908, the governor of North Carolina, Robert Glenn (fourth from the right in the first row), attended. This group of local businessmen, band members, and others was photographed in front of what was possibly the academy building. J.H. Allen became principal of the school in 1906. (GWS.)

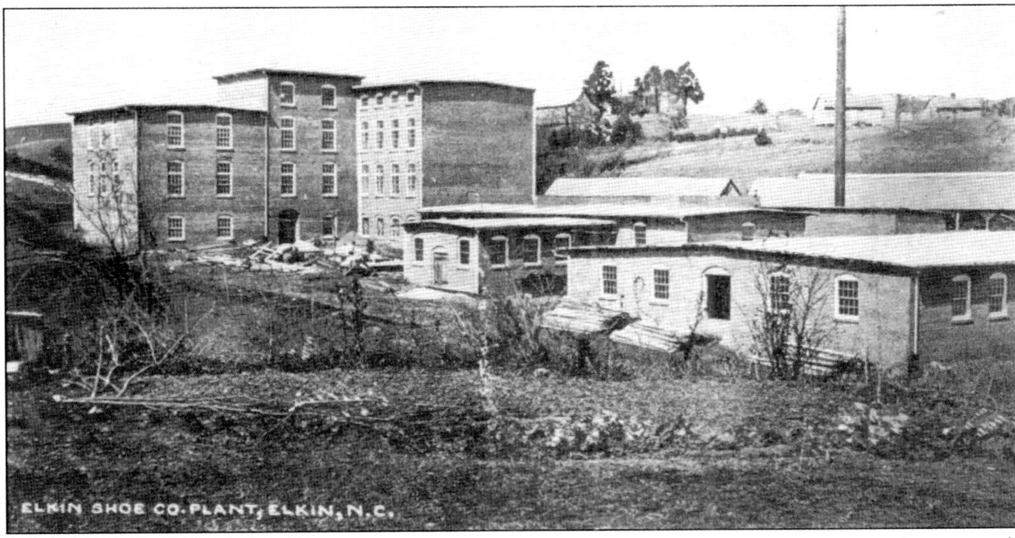

In this 1909 postcard, the Elkin Shoe Company is pictured at its second location, on the west side of the Elkin Creek, where the water treatment plant stands today. It was started by Alexander M. Smith (1866–1944) in 1892, and was moved into the Elkin Valley Woolen Mill building on the east side of the creek in 1896. At one time, the company employed 225 people and produced 1,500 pairs of shoes a day. It ceased operation in 1927. (SJC.)

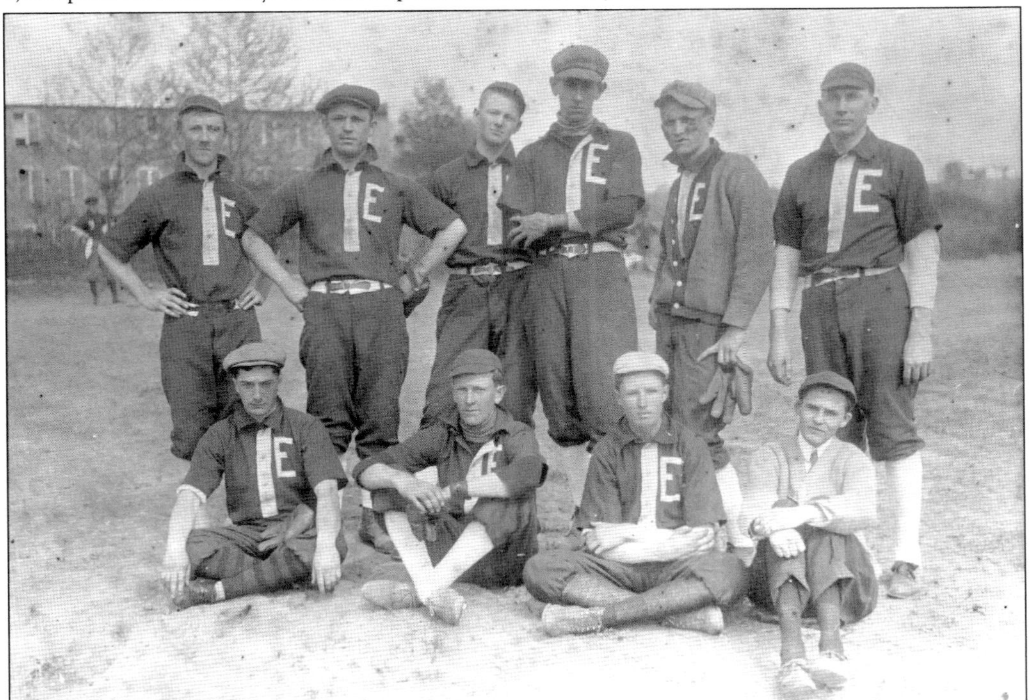

Members of the 1913 Elkin baseball team pictured here are, from left to right, (first row) Dr. L.C. Couch, Hal Bell, George Royall, and Walter Cherry; (second row) Dr. E.G. Click, Ernest Nichols, Jim Greenwood, Ab Bivins, Rom Llewellyn, and Grover Graham. The 1893 Chatham Mill is visible in the background. (EHC.)

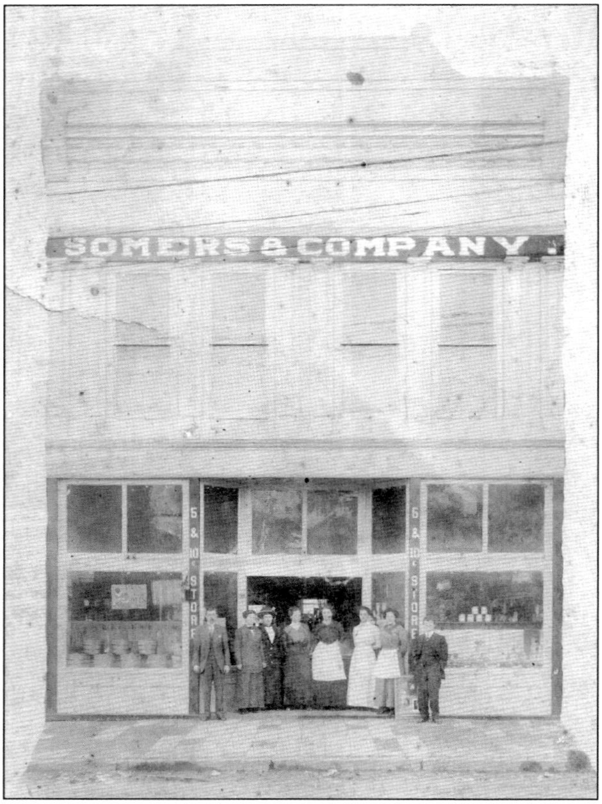

J.A. Somers and A.L. Reves organized the Somers and Company 5 & 10¢ Store in 1909. In 1911, the store moved into this building, with a metal facade, at 123 West Main Street. It sold dime-store merchandise, as well as stoneware, imported lace, and candy. The store's specialty products were Eastman Kodak cameras and supplies. (GWS.)

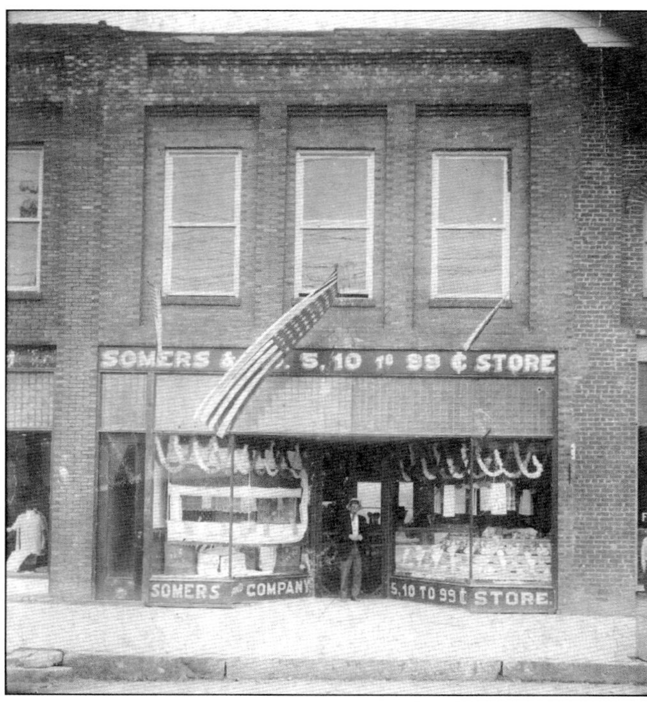

The second location of what had become Somers & Co. 5, 10, to 99¢ Store was to the right of Abernethy's Pharmacy at 111 West Main Street. Lonnie F. Walker began working for J.A. Somers in 1919 as an assistant manager. In 1931, he bought the store, renamed it Walker's 5 & 10, and operated it until his retirement in 1963. (GWS.)

This 1910 postcard shows the Atkinson Company, a wholesale grocery and dry goods business. It was the second building from the corner of Bridge Street on the south side of East Main Street. Organized by Jasper S. Atkinson (1876–1971) in 1907, the business bought large quantities of chickens, eggs, dried fruit, honey, beeswax, and other country produce to sell and ship to other communities. Currently, no building exists on this lot. (SJC.)

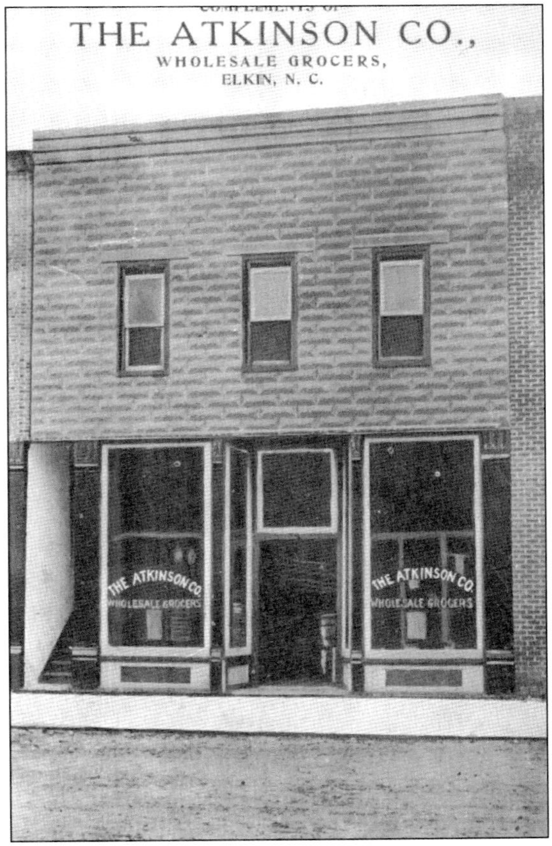

The Southern Railroad Depot is shown in this 1908 postcard. The depot was completed in 1891 and razed in the late 1980s for a parking lot. The first train arrived in Elkin on April 8, 1890, on the Northwest North Carolina Railroad. During the railroad's peak activity, at least two eastbound and two westbound trains, carrying both passengers and freight, came through Elkin daily. (SJC.)

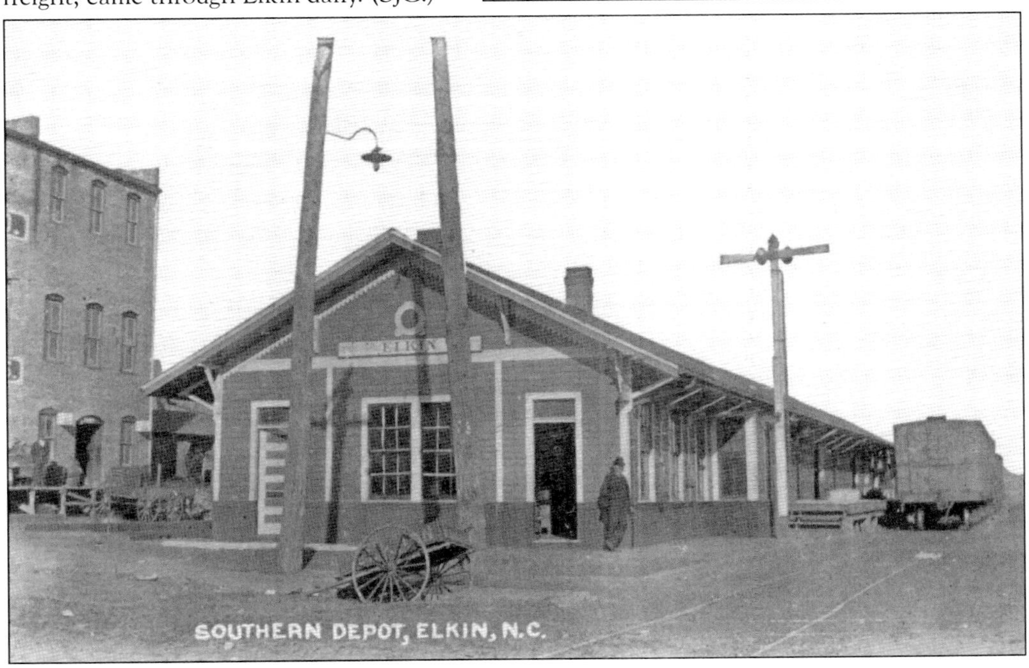

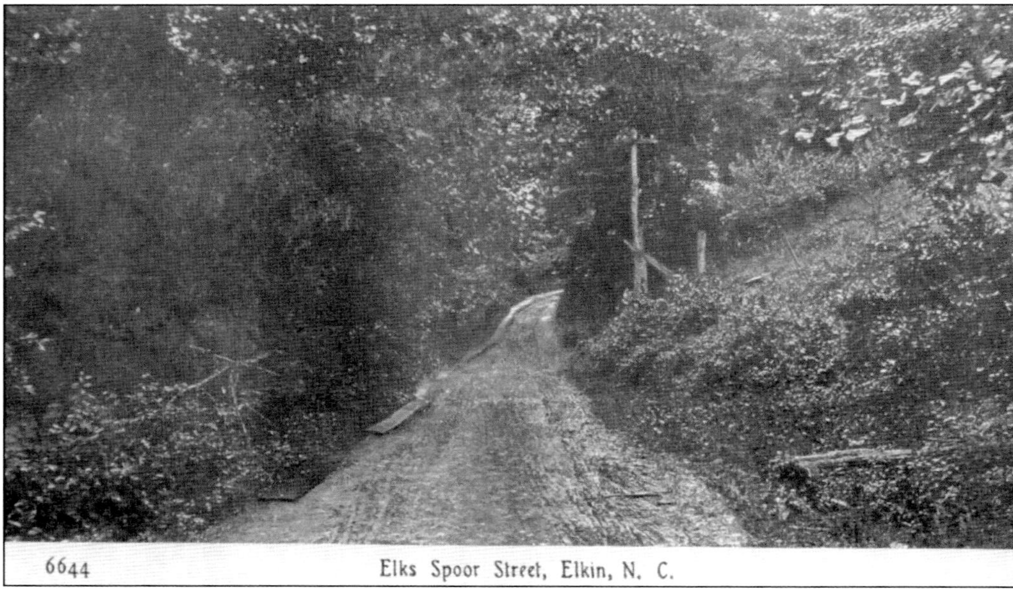

This 1906 postcard of Elk Spur Street shows the narrow dirt road leading south toward town. (Notice the spelling of the street name, Elks Spoor.) Previously, this road was referred to as the Old Traphill Road or Blue Ridge Avenue. The Galloway Memorial Episcopal Church is on the hill to the right, and Elkin Creek is on the left. The boards alongside the edge of the muddy road are there to assist pedestrians. (SJC.)

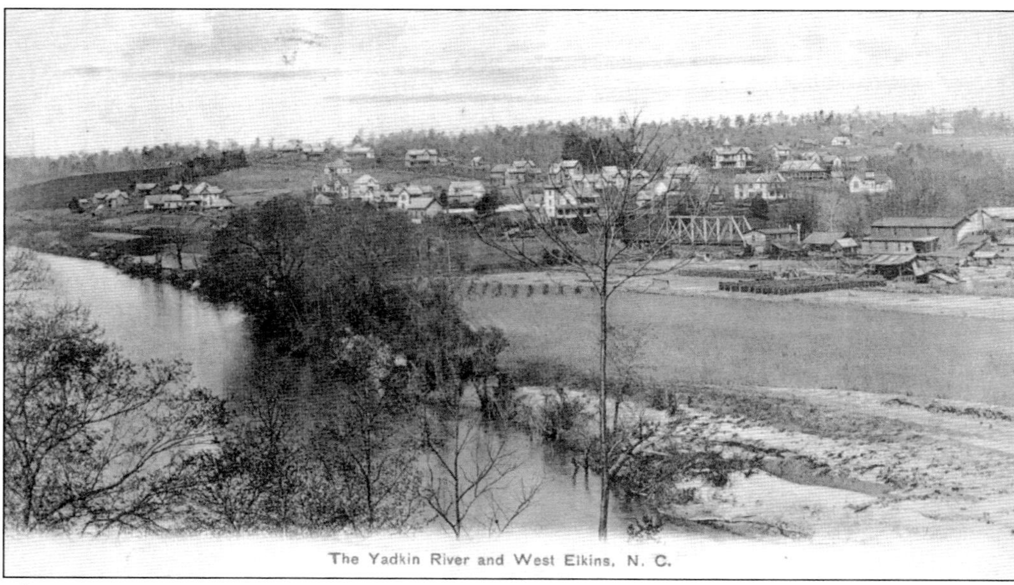

This 1907 postcard of Elkin shows the second train trestle to be built over Elkin Creek, along with many homes on West Main Street and Surry Avenue. Galloway Memorial Episcopal Church is on the far right in the picture; it is the white structure about halfway up the hill. The Yadkin River, which divides Surry and Yadkin Counties, is shown in the left of the picture. (SJC.)

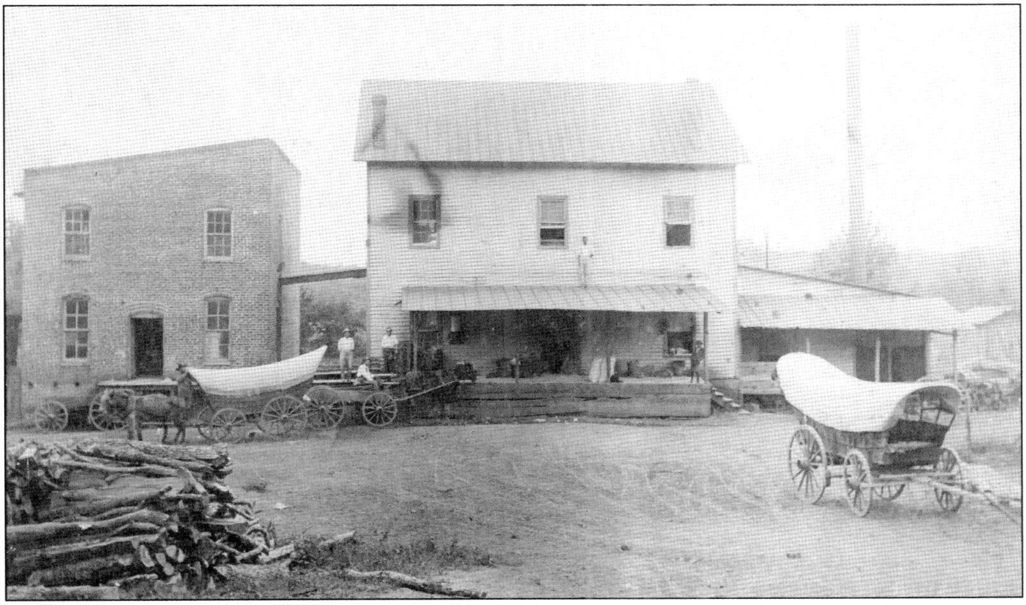

The Elkin Roller Mill was built in 1896 by Alexander and Hugh G. Chatham. It was located south of East Main Street, near the former location of the Hugh Chatham Bridge. It was purchased around 1900 by Lacy Jasper Bray and operated by him and his two sons, Abraham and James. The first electric power in Elkin came from a generator installed at the Roller Mill in 1898. (EHC.)

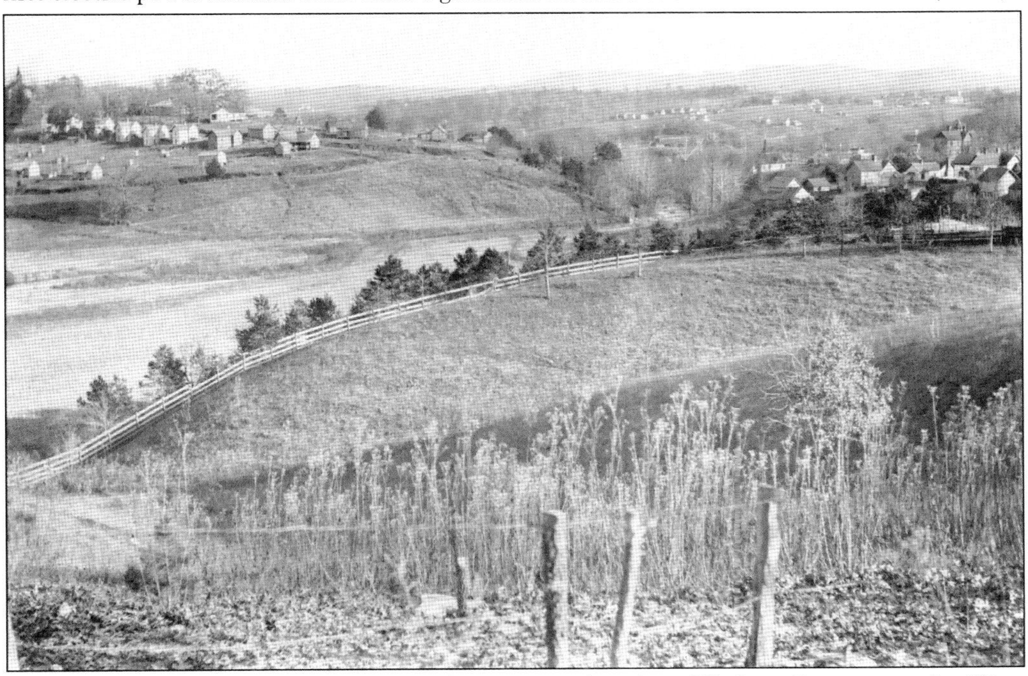

Cotton Mill Hill is shown in the left of this picture taken from Elk Spur Street, near the Elkin High School, around 1900. The Elkin Elementary School is currently located on this hill. Galloway Memorial Episcopal Church is at right in the picture, along with homes on West Main Street. Elkin Creek is in the valley below the hill on the far side of the fence. (TR.)

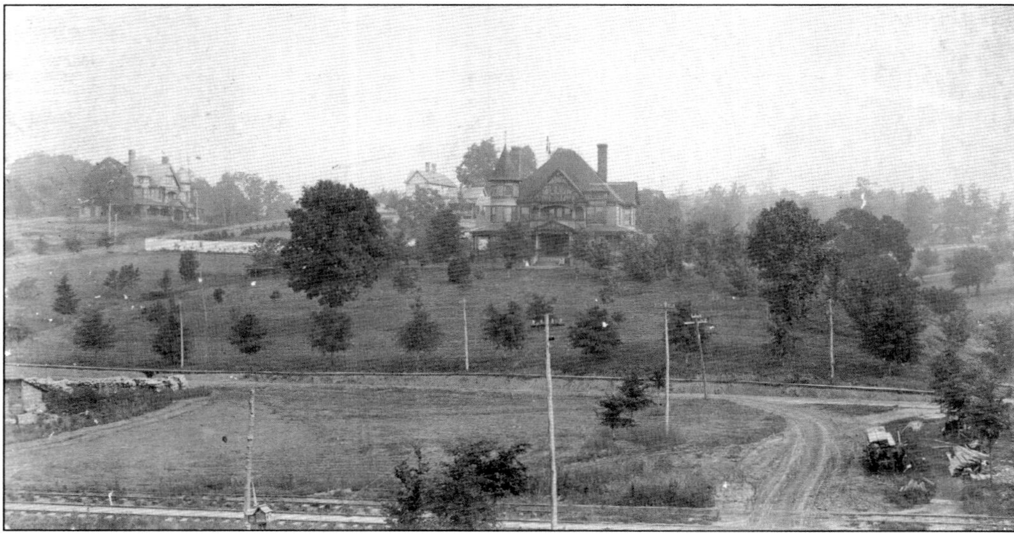

The Hugh Gwyn Chatham house, built in the 1890s, was located on Gwyn Avenue at the current site of the First Baptist Church. The house was the birthplace of US congressman Thurmond Chatham and was designed by George F. Barber, who sold prefabricated houses through a mail-order catalog. The home had walnut and oak patterned floors, as well as rooms trimmed in cherry, chestnut, oak, and forest pine. This was the first house in Elkin to have electricity. The Alexander M. Smith home in the far left background is also a Barber house. The Chatham house was razed in 1951 to make way for the new First Baptist Church. The details of this Queen Anne–style house are visible in the close-up view below. (Both, EHC.)

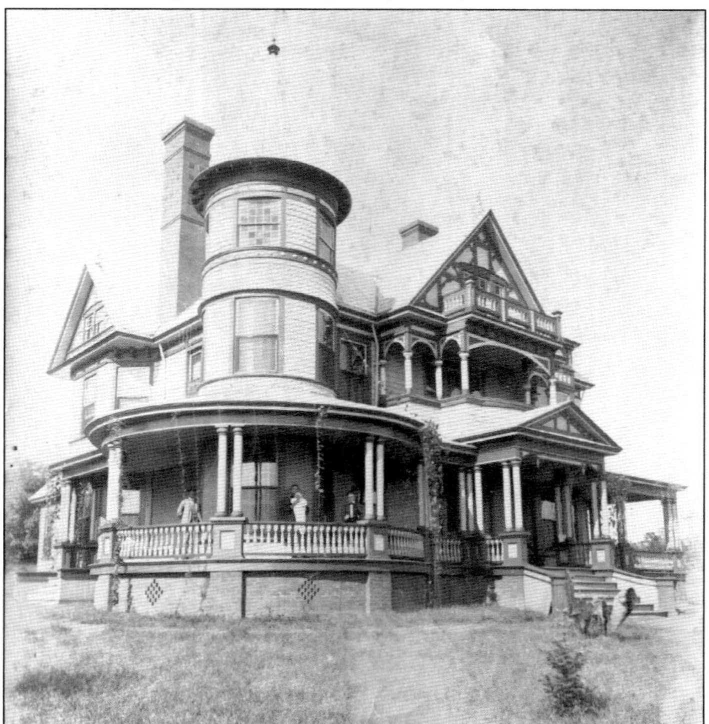

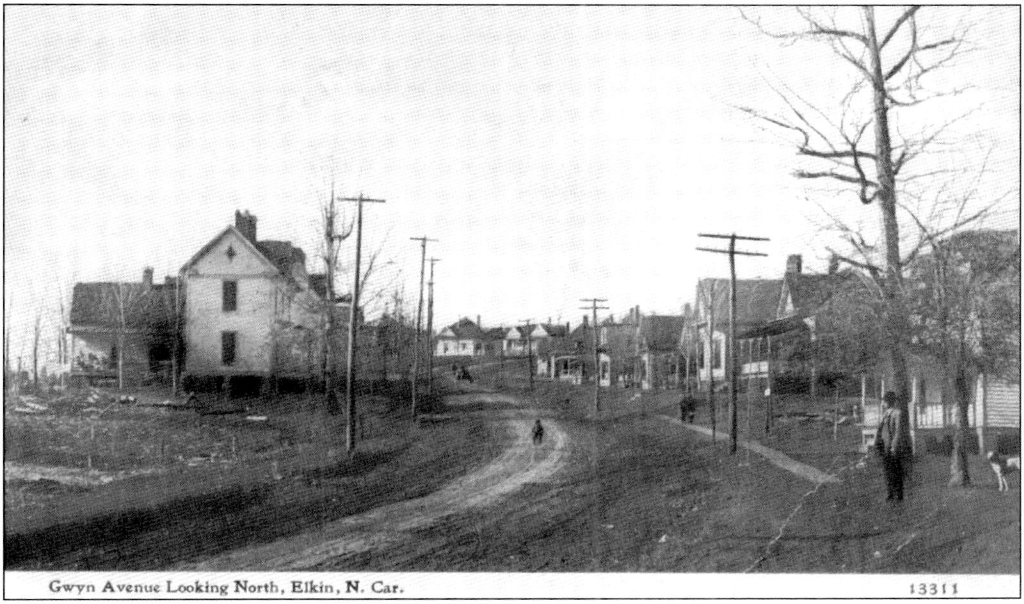

This c. 1911 postcard offers a northward view of Gwyn Avenue, one of the original streets on the 1891 Ludlow map of Elkin. Dr. L.R. Salmons's home is on the left. The house on the right, with the front porch, was the John F. Cooke residence, with the John Park family house behind. Features of note in this image are the dirt road, the small sizes of the trees, and the utility poles carrying power to the homes. (SJC.)

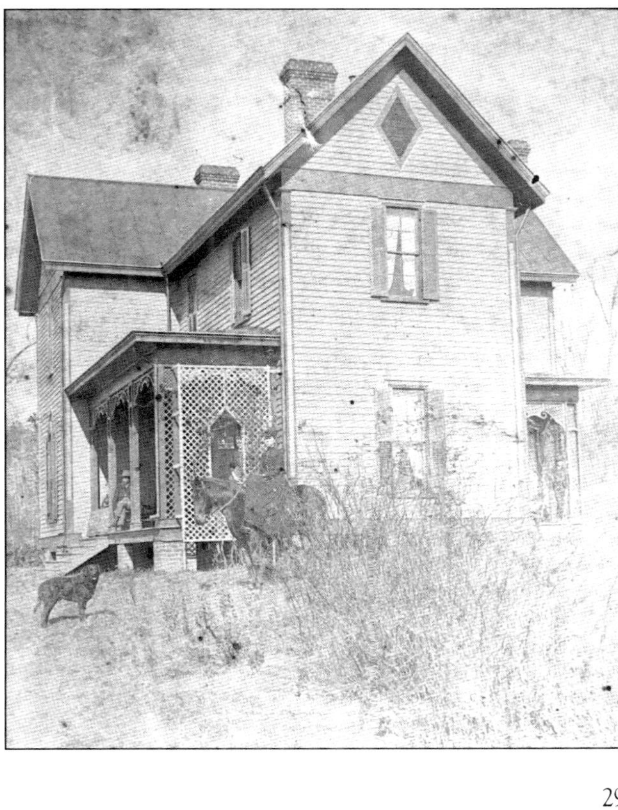

The home of Thomas Lenoir Gwyn, built around 1885, was located off Hillcrest Drive and North Carolina Highway 268 on the property formerly known as Neaves Park. The third Presbyterian church building was erected on this site in 1989. In this image, Thomas Gwyn sits on the porch while his daughter Sallie Gwyn Poindexter sits atop the horse. (EHC.)

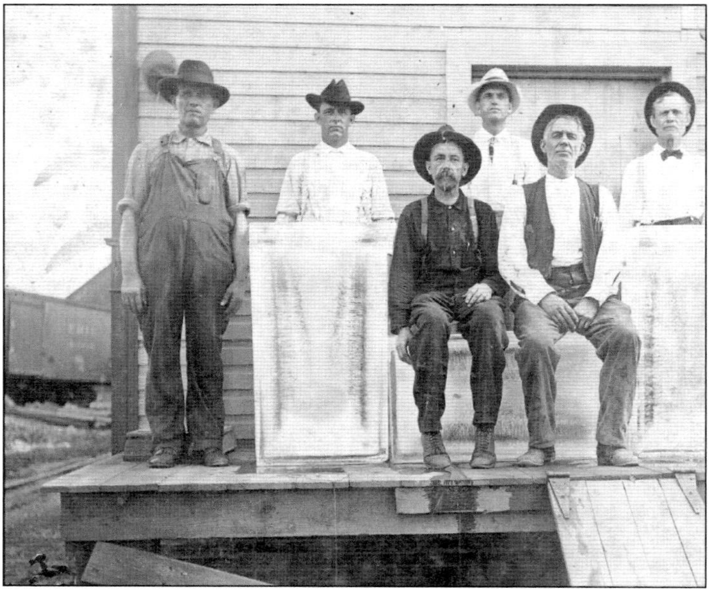

The Elkin Ice and Light Company was organized in 1912. It furnished electricity for Elkin until 1914. Pictured here are, from left to right, J.H. Allen, Sid Arnold, James W. Madison, William W. Whitaker, R.L. Poindexter, and W.S. Gough. The plant had a capacity of 10 tons of ice per day. It also made up to 25,000 clay bricks per day. The plant was located south of the railroad tracks on the east side of Bridge Street. It later became Carolina Ice and Fuel. (EHC.)

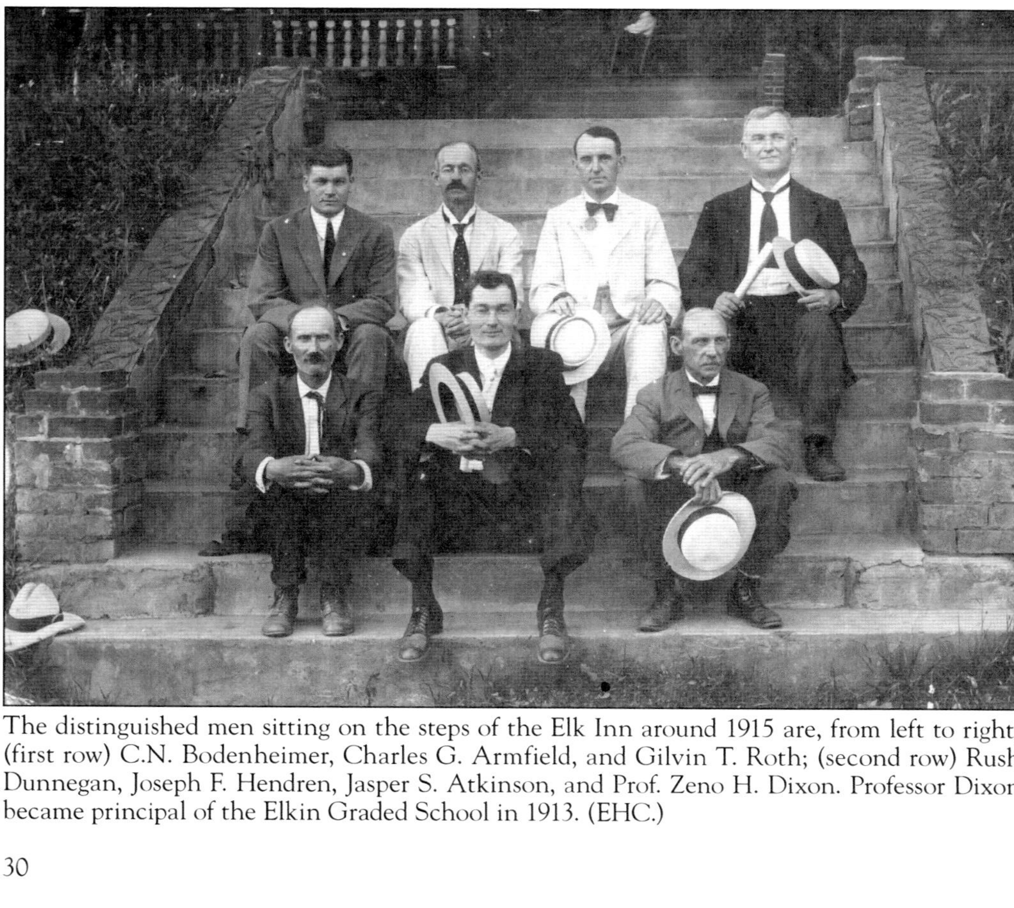

The distinguished men sitting on the steps of the Elk Inn around 1915 are, from left to right, (first row) C.N. Bodenheimer, Charles G. Armfield, and Gilvin T. Roth; (second row) Rush Dunnegan, Joseph F. Hendren, Jasper S. Atkinson, and Prof. Zeno H. Dixon. Professor Dixon became principal of the Elkin Graded School in 1913. (EHC.)

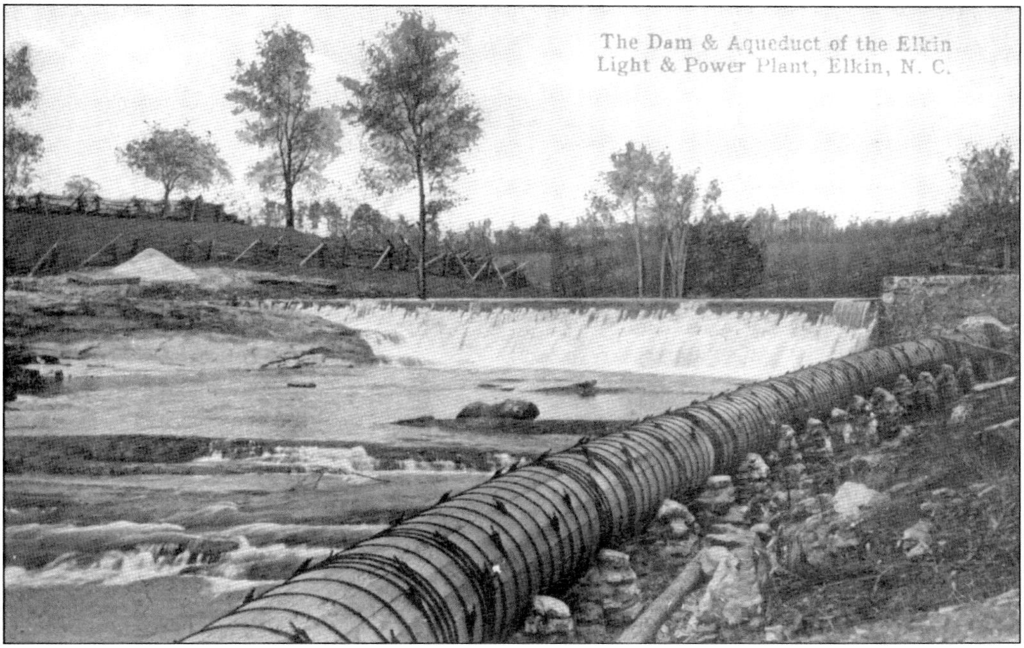

The postcard above shows the dam on the Elkin Creek at Carter Falls, about four miles north of Elkin. It was built in 1914 by the Carter Falls Power Company. The aqueduct was made of wooden boards joined together with steel bands to form a flume that carried water to the power plant downstream, which ran the 150-horsepower dynamo. Power poles carried the electricity to the town of Elkin. Carter Falls, shown below in 1911, were named for Barney Carter, who settled in the area around 1800. He owned several hundred acres of land in the Pleasant Ridge Community and has many descendants living in the area today. The falls were a popular destination for locals, as shown by the people sitting on the rocks near the waterfall. (Above, SJC; below, EHC.)

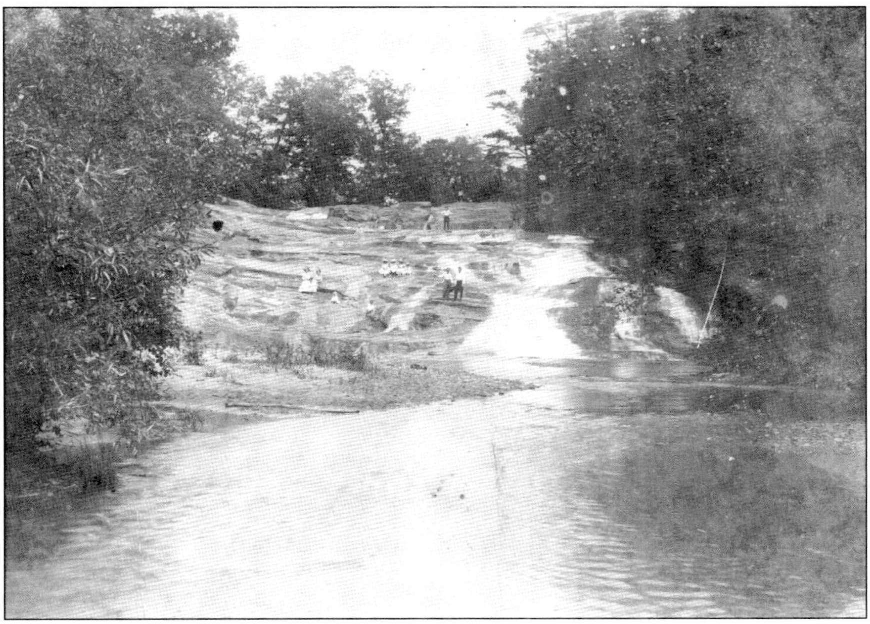

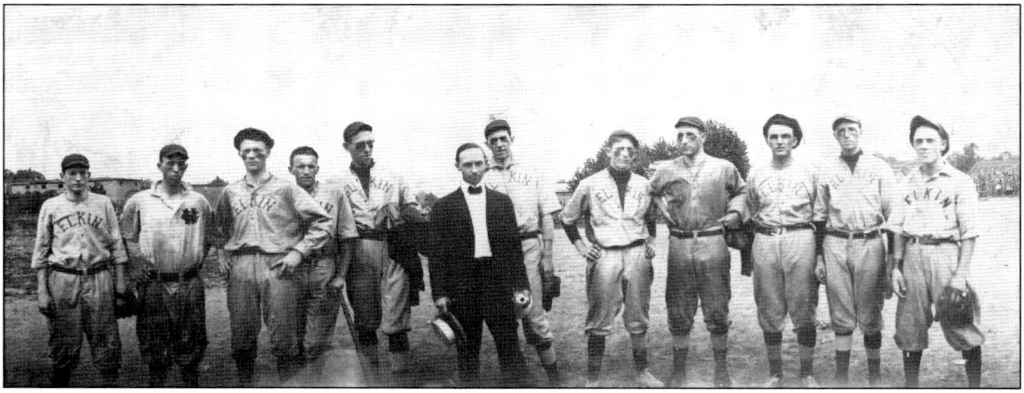

Members of the 1914 Elkin Baseball team are, from left to right, Ray Brandon, Frank Yow, Jim Greenwood, Rom Llewellyn, Ab Bivins, manager Joe Elam, Joe Bivins, Hal Bell, Charles Crater, Joe Bray, George Royall, and Edworth Harris. (EHC.)

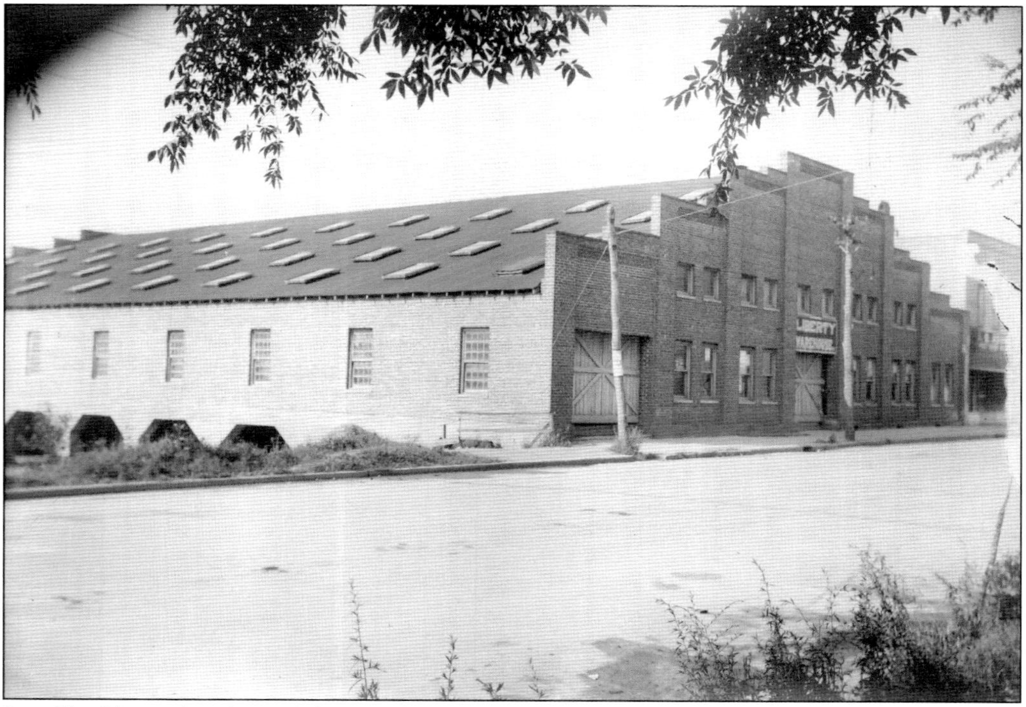

Local builder and architect John Bartlett Burcham constructed the Liberty Tobacco Warehouse, located on the south side of East Main Street, around 1917. Tobacco markets had such a positive impact on the local economy that the *Elkin Tribune* published a yearly "tobacco booster edition" to welcome farmers to town during market season. The Hugh Chatham Bridge was erected adjacent to this building in 1931, blocking the view from this angle. (CB.)

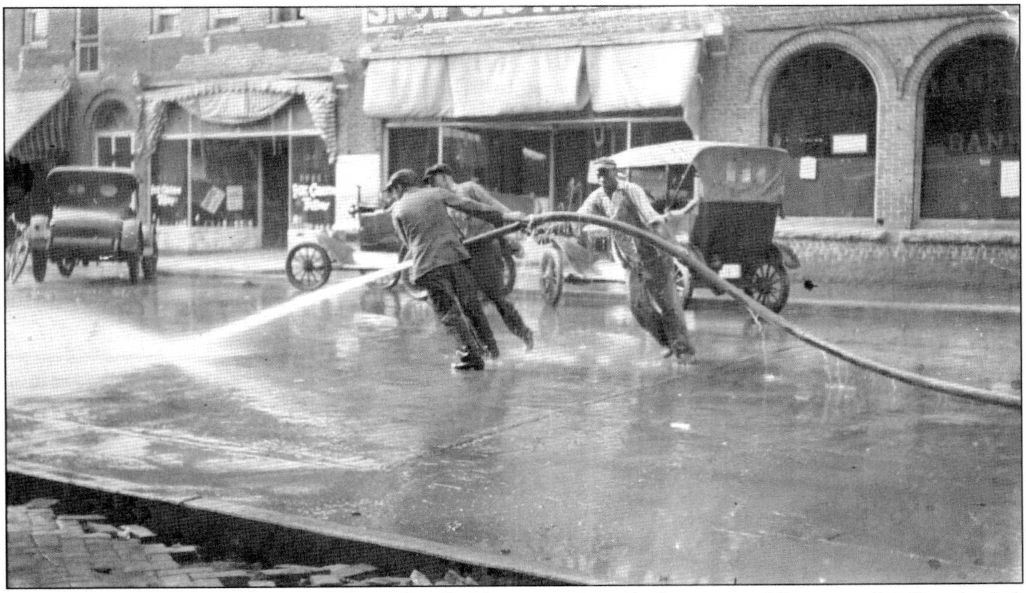

In this c. 1921 image, C.M. "Red" Saylor (left), an unidentified man, and Raymond Allen (right) wash Elkin's newly paved West Main Street with a fire hose. The businesses in the background are an ice cream parlor, M.Q. Snow Clothing, and the Elkin National Bank. The paving-brick sidewalk is being laid in the foreground. (EHC.)

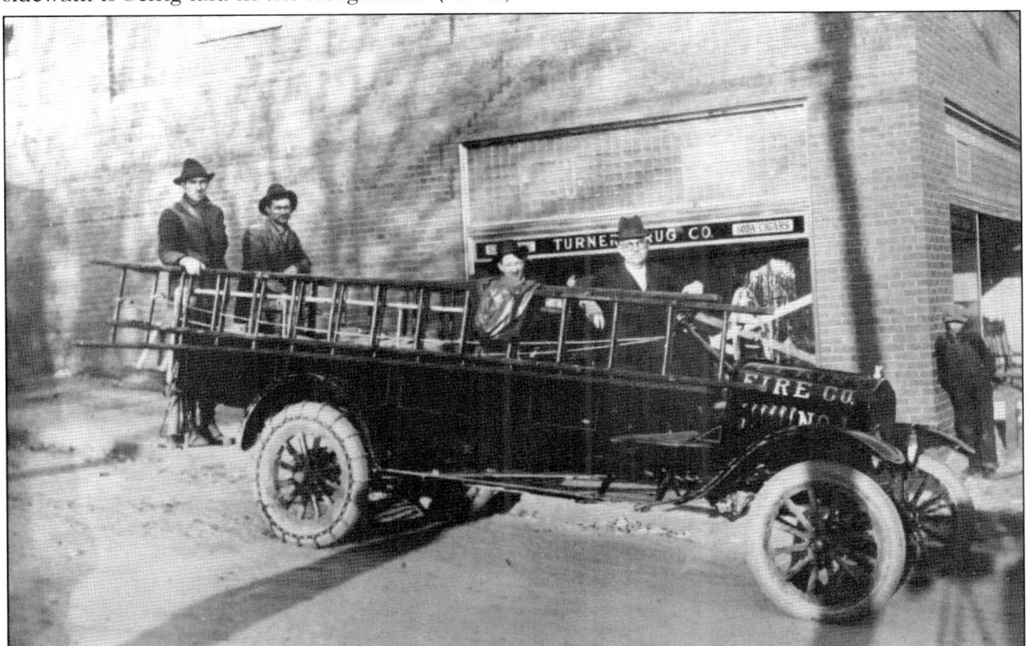

The first Elkin fire truck, a Model T Ford, is parked on the Church Street hill in this picture from 1925. It was purchased after the downtown fire of 1912. William W. Whitaker, the fire chief, is driving the truck. It was stored in the rear of W.W. Whitaker's store, located on West Main Street. The Salmons Building, erected in 1923, is in the background; it housed Turner Drug Company and Elkin's first hospital. (CTW.)

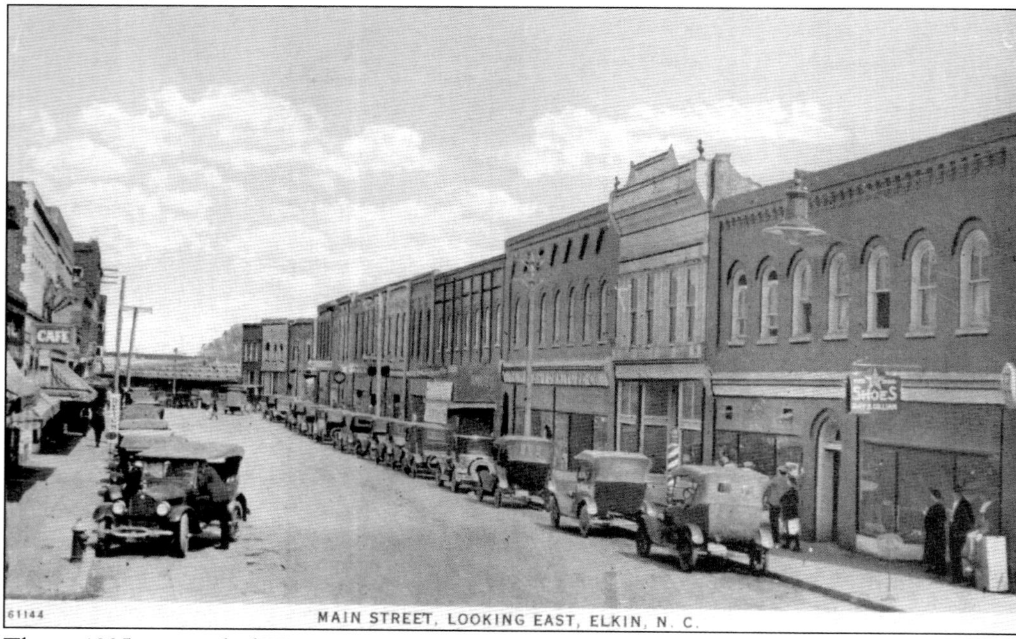

This c. 1925 postcard of West Main Street is looking east. Turner Drug is on the left, and behind it the Elkin Café. On the right, beginning in the foreground and heading toward the back of the image, are the Ray & Gilliam Shoe store, Somers 5 & 10¢ Store, T.L. Hayes Furniture, and the Amuzu (pronounced "amuse you") Theater, Elkin's first theater, run by Louis Mitchell. After the Amuzu ceased operation in the late 1920s, Eagle Furniture opened in the building. (SJC.)

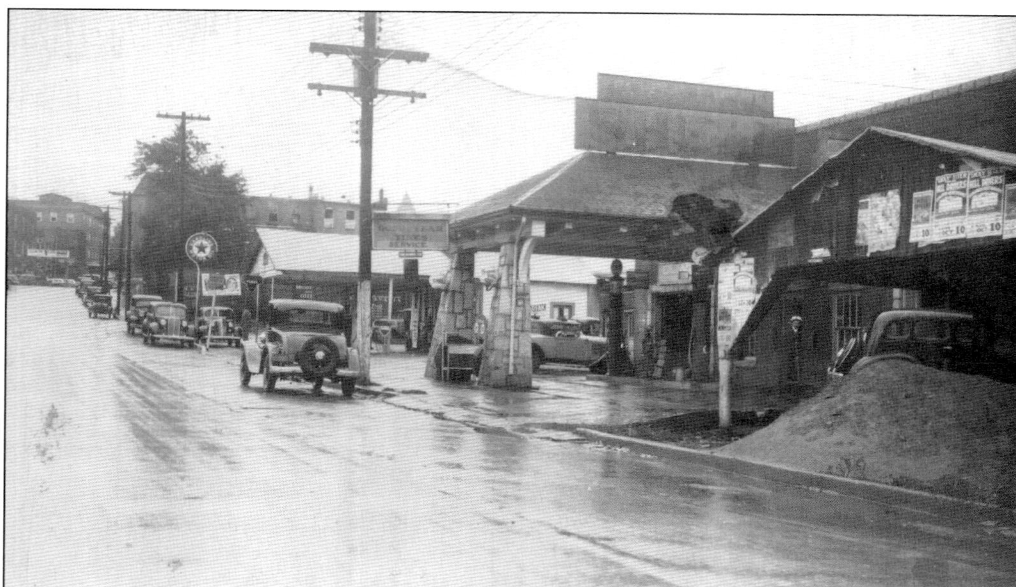

A.O. Bryan's Double Eagle Shell service station, located on the east side of South Bridge Street, opened in 1928. The Hotel Elkin, built in 1925, is up the hill in the left background. The Elkin Ice and Fuel Company is in the center of the picture, behind Bryan's station. The business sold Texas Oil Company products, and the building suffered heavy losses during the 1940 flood. (JWP.)

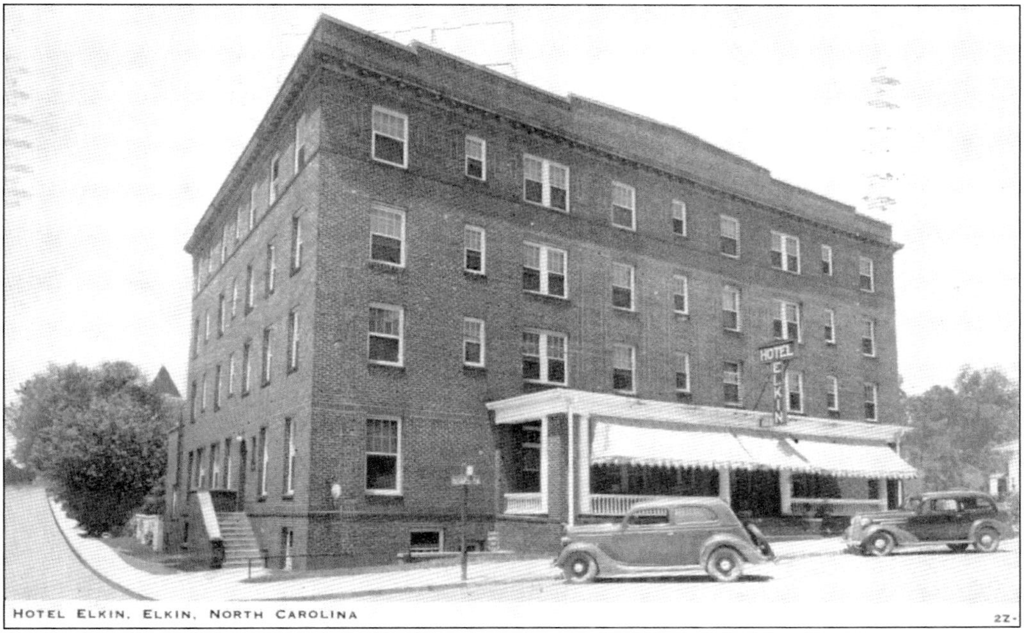

The Hotel Elkin was the result of the Elkin Kiwanis Club's desire to build a hotel on US Highway 21, the "Lakes-to-Florida Highway." Shown here in 1940, the hotel opened for business on May 7, 1925, and was first managed by Ralph Hartman. It originally had 51 guest rooms, an elevator, beauty shop, barbershop, banquet rooms, and a dining room and kitchen. It was located on the northwest corner of Market and Bridge Streets and was razed in 1969 to make way for Yadkin Valley Bank, which occupies the site today. (SJC.)

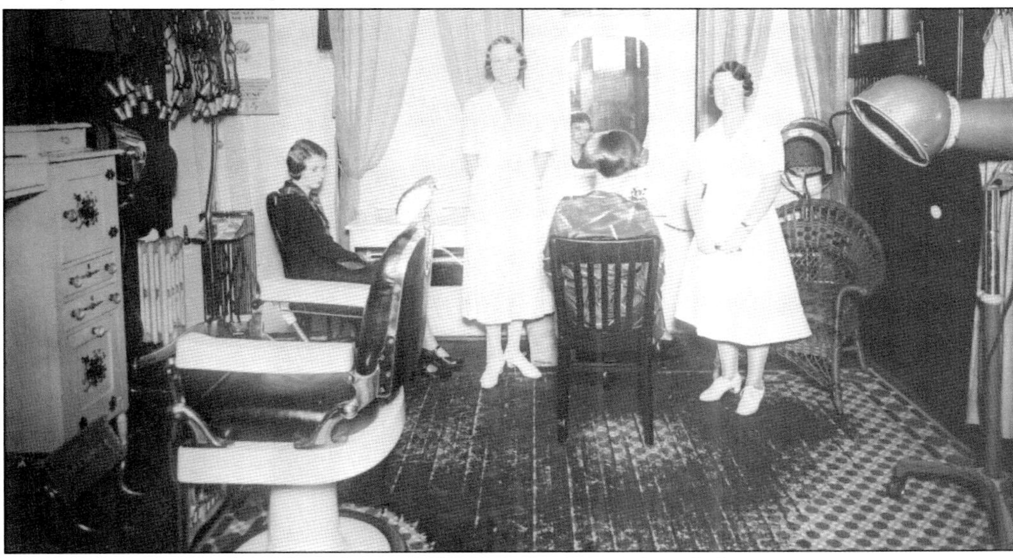

The first beauty shop in Elkin, located above Sydnor-Spainhour's department store, is pictured in the late 1920s. It was operated by Lucy Gray and Mary Cockerham. In 1938, Gray opened her own business in the Hotel Elkin and eventually moved into her own building on Church Street in 1962. The women in this picture are, from left to right, Agnes Gray, Mary Cockerham Barbour, Ohna Bivins, and Lucy Gray. (EHC.)

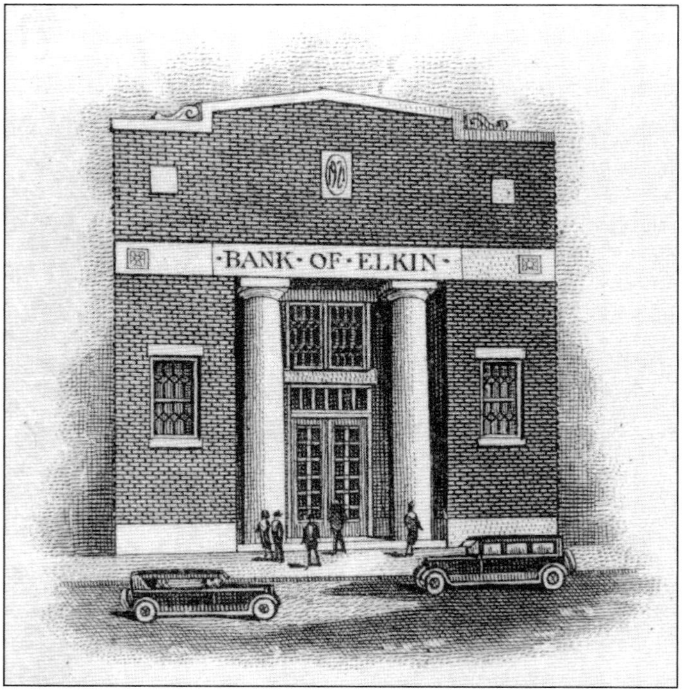

The Bank of Elkin was founded in 1922 and was originally located at 111 East Main Street. It was reorganized in 1933 and moved to the northwest corner of Bridge and Main Streets—the former location of the Elkin National Bank—in 1937. The Bank of Elkin changed its name to Northwestern Bank after a 1961 merger. After extensive remodeling, this building later housed W.M. Wall Jewelers until 1993. (SJC.)

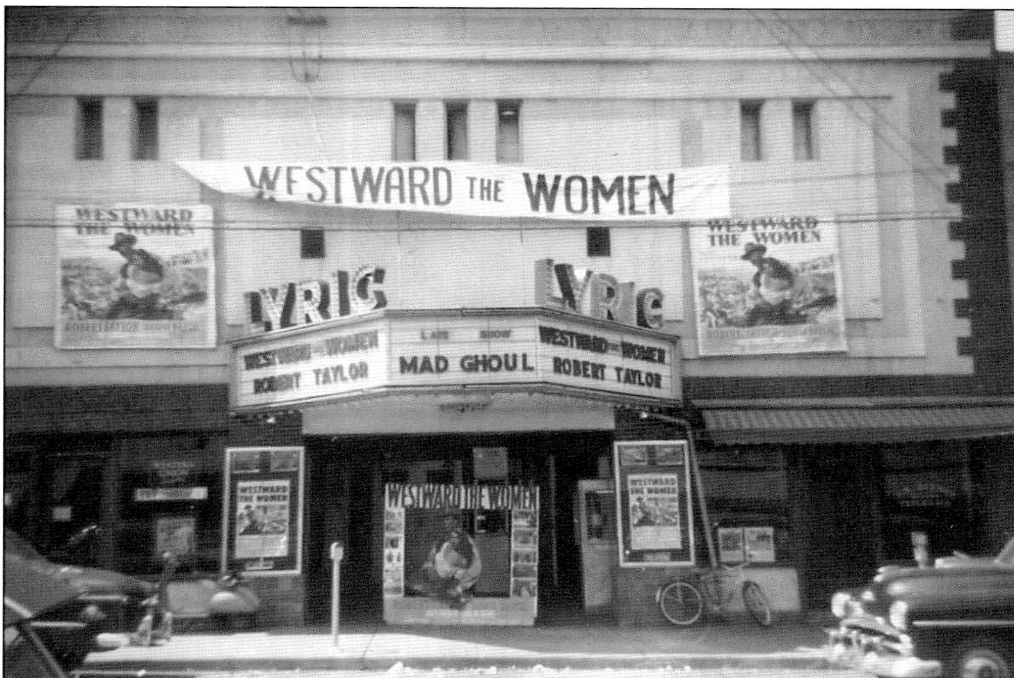

The Lyric Theatre opened on June 14, 1928, and was operated by Louis Mitchell. The building was owned by Rosa M. Roth and was located on the north side of East Main Street, between Speas Home and Auto and W.M. Wall Jewelers. Today, this site is a parking lot. The projectionist was Garland Morrison, who began his career at the Amuzu, Elkin's first movie theater. (BS.)

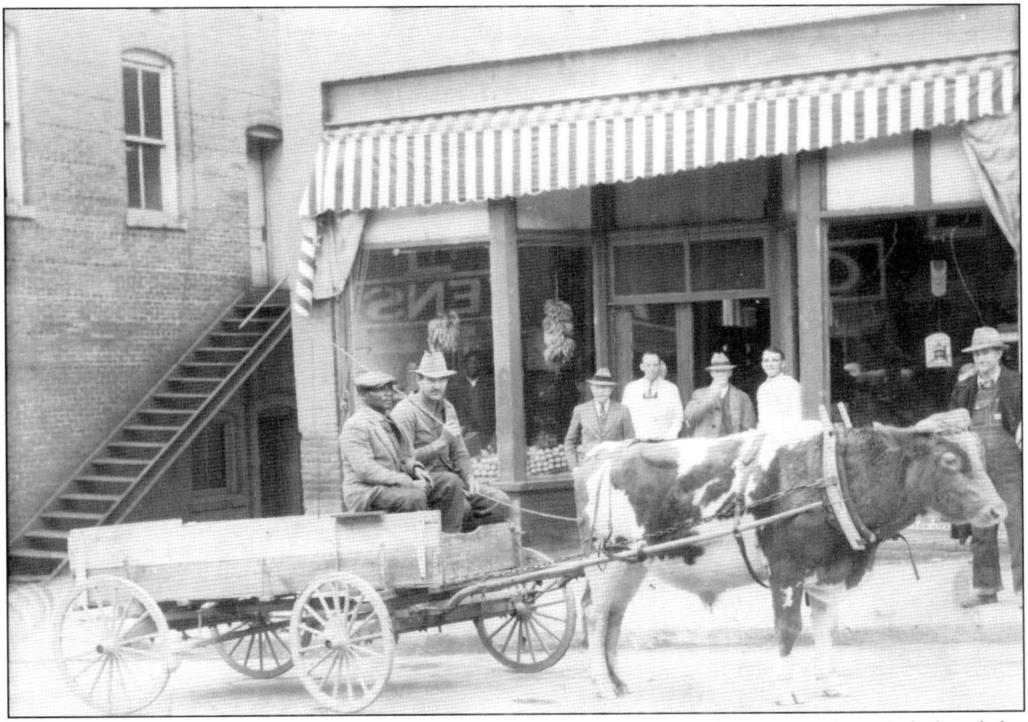

Dick Grier's grocery store was located on the west side of North Bridge Street, directly behind the Elkin National Bank building. The steps at the back of the bank are at left in the picture. The grocery store advertised service anywhere in the city limits, with three-minute delivery—day or night. When Grier opened the store, prompt grocery delivery was a novel idea. His first deliveries were made by a boy on a bicycle and, later, by a delivery truck. In the above photograph, Duke Ward and an unidentified man are seated on the wagon, and standing in the doorway are, from left to right, Grier, unidentified, W.D. Poplin, and Marvin Byrd. The interior of Grier's grocery store in the 1920s is pictured below. The neatness of the displays and the cleanliness of the store are apparent. In 1923, it advertised "staple and fancy groceries and fresh meat." (Both, JWP.)

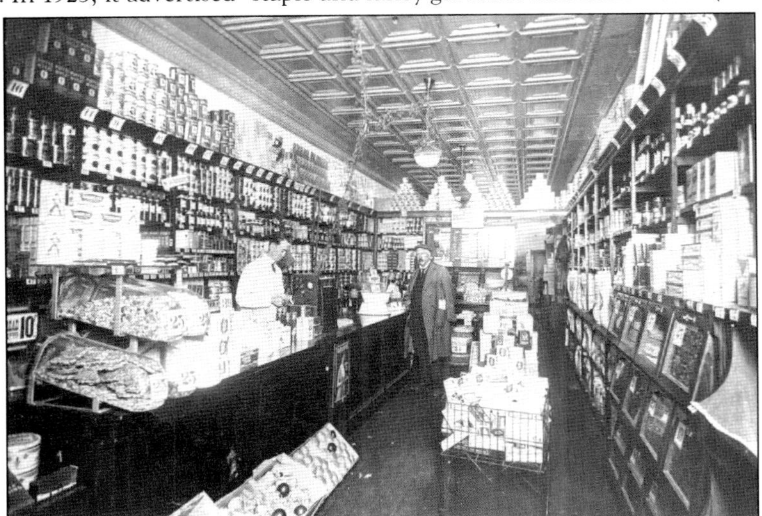

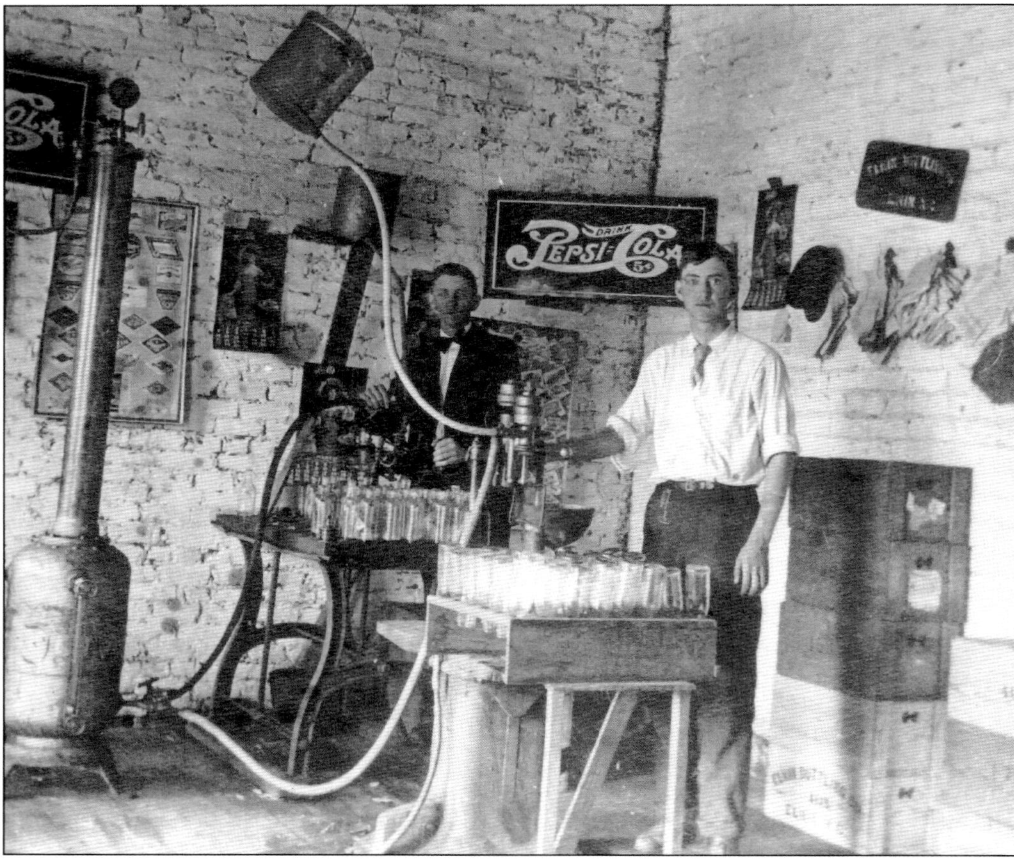

The Elkin Bottling Company was organized in 1904 and bottled both Pepsi-Cola and fruit drinks. In this pre-1913 image, Bob Brendle is on the right; the other man is unidentified. At this time, all the bottles were washed and filled by hand. The carburetor is at left in the picture. J.H. Tharpe bought an interest in the company in 1911, the plant was refurbished with new machinery in 1913, and production increased dramatically. (SJC.)

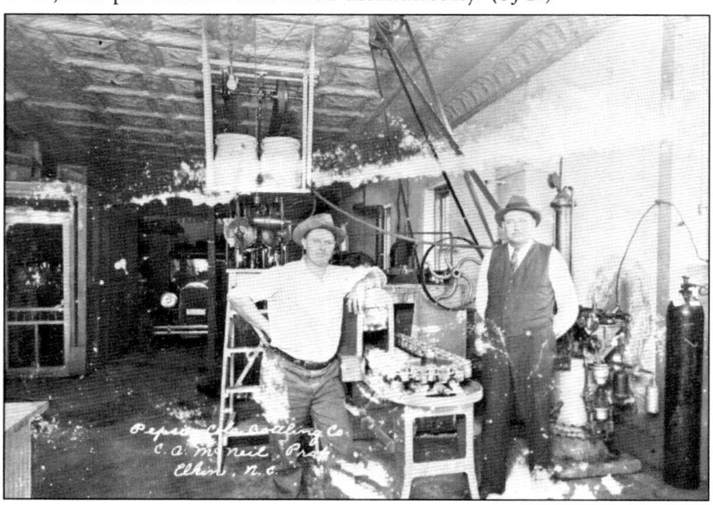

The Elkin Bottling Company, pictured here in the late 1920s, was located south of the railroad tracks, on the west side of Bridge Street, in the large brick building formerly known as the Hotel Myrtle. By 1926, Claude A. McNeill (right) had bought the business. The fruit drinks were marketed under the name McNeill's Beverages and, according to a 1940 advertisement, came in seven flavors. (JWP.)

Two

Elkin from 1930 through the 1950s

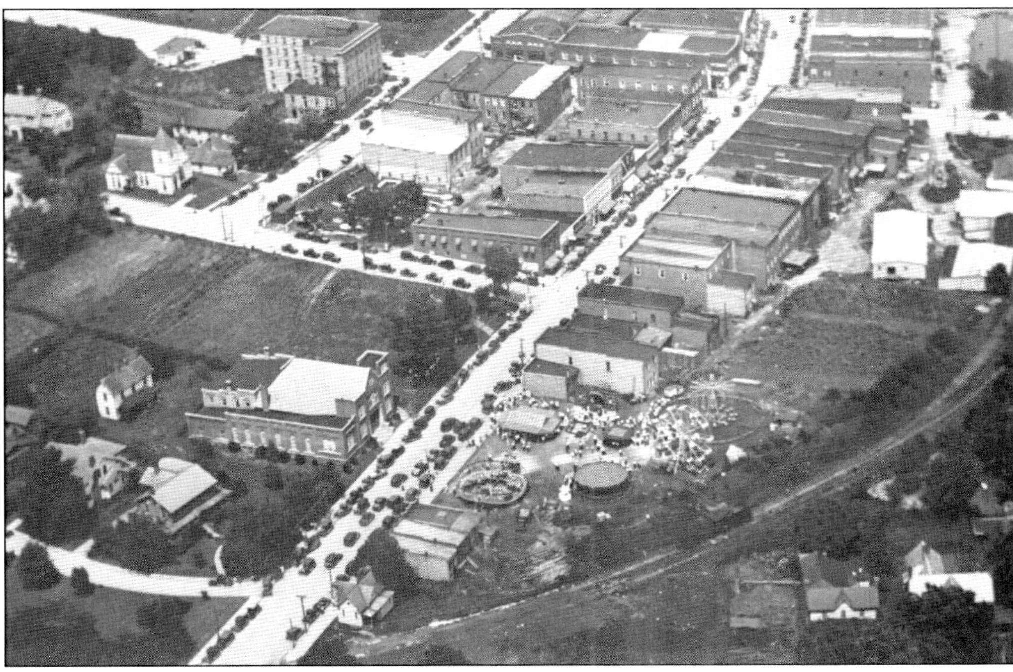

This aerial view of downtown Elkin on July 4, 1931, shows a carnival in the present-day location of the post office. The old tracks of the Elkin & Alleghany Railway can be seen at right. The Presbyterian church is in the upper left, where Market Street ends at Church Street. The First Baptist Church is in the lower left, across from the carnival. (JWP.)

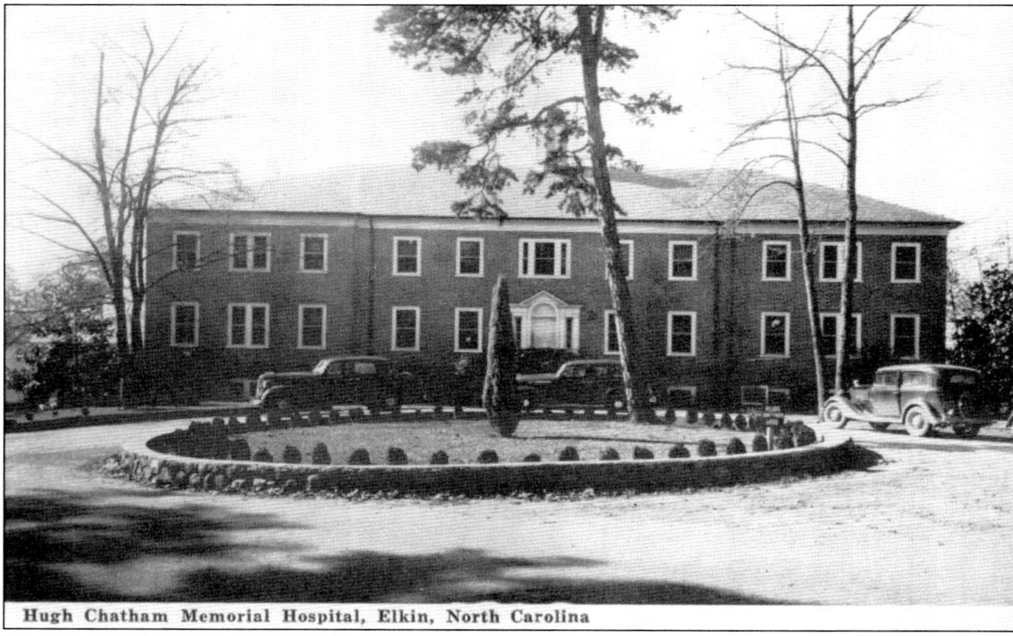

The Hugh Chatham Memorial Hospital, pictured in 1940, began admitting patients on April 20, 1931. The total cost of the building was $85,000, secured with funding from the Chatham family, local citizens, and the Duke Endowment. Chatham Manufacturing donated the 15 acres of land on which it was built. Leadership from the Methodist church played an important role in the early years. Located on Hawthorne Road, it served as a hospital until 1973, when the new hospital opened on Parkwood Drive. (SJC.)

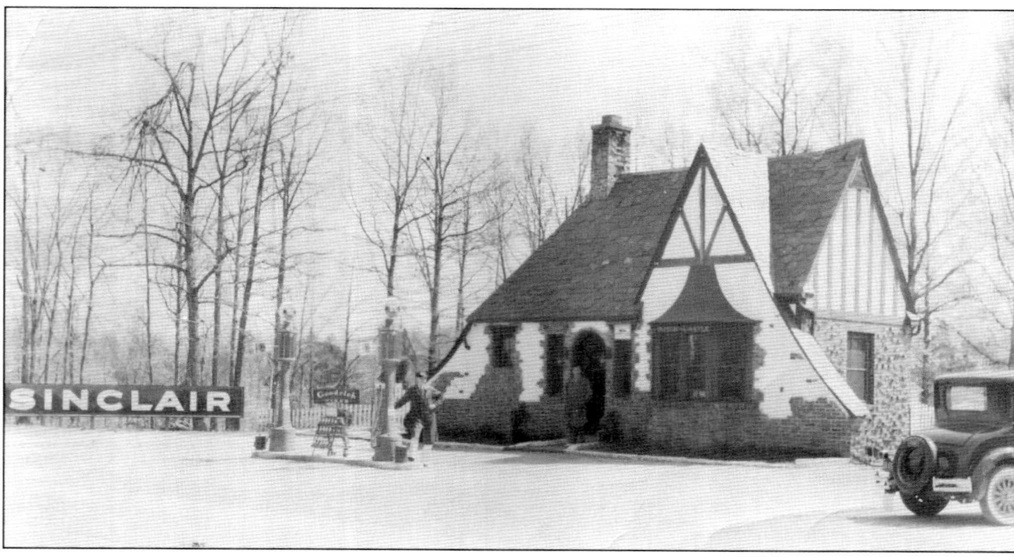

The Dutch Castle, shown in 1935, was built in 1933 by Carl E. Chappell and is located at 656 North Bridge Street. It was originally a Sinclair service station. Chappell built the tower and north addition a few years later, where he maintained his insurance office. In the late 1940s and 1950s, it was the home of the Dutch Castle Sandwich Shop. It has also been used for apartments and offices. (JCB.)

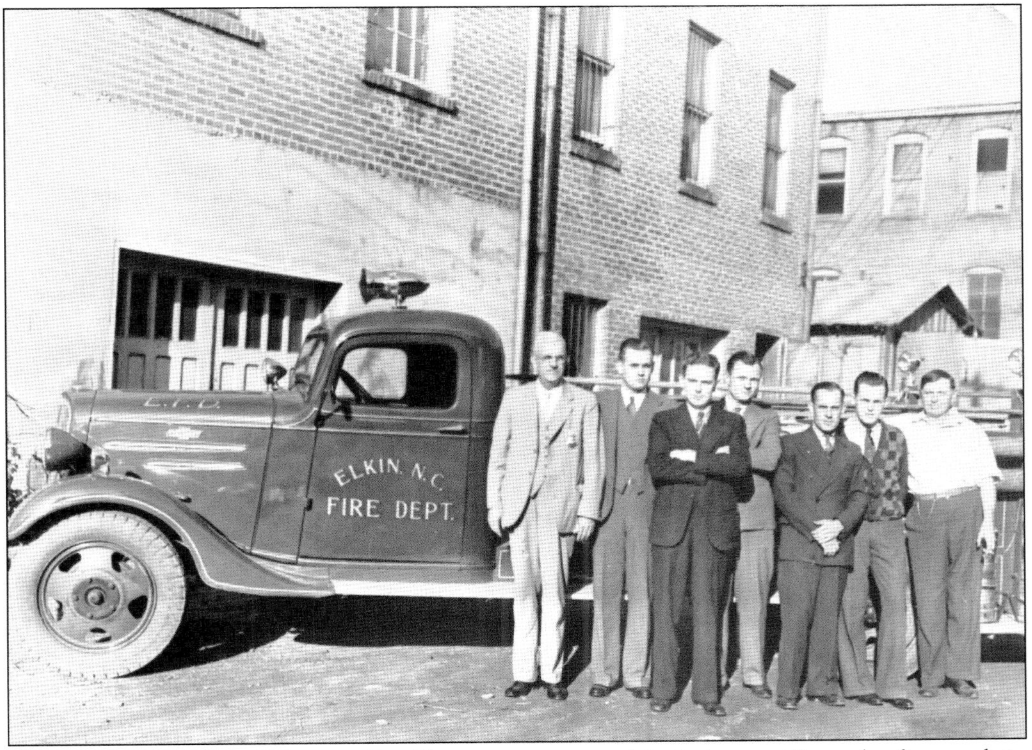

Members of the Elkin Volunteer Fire Department pose with their new Chevrolet fire truck in 1936. They are, from left to right, chief W.W. Whitaker, Ted Brown, E.F. Harris, Clyde Hall, Raymond Felts, J.C. Brown, and Paul Eidson. Members of the fire department not pictured were Carl Young, Clarence Holcomb, Grady Harris, and W.G. Carter. (BHS.)

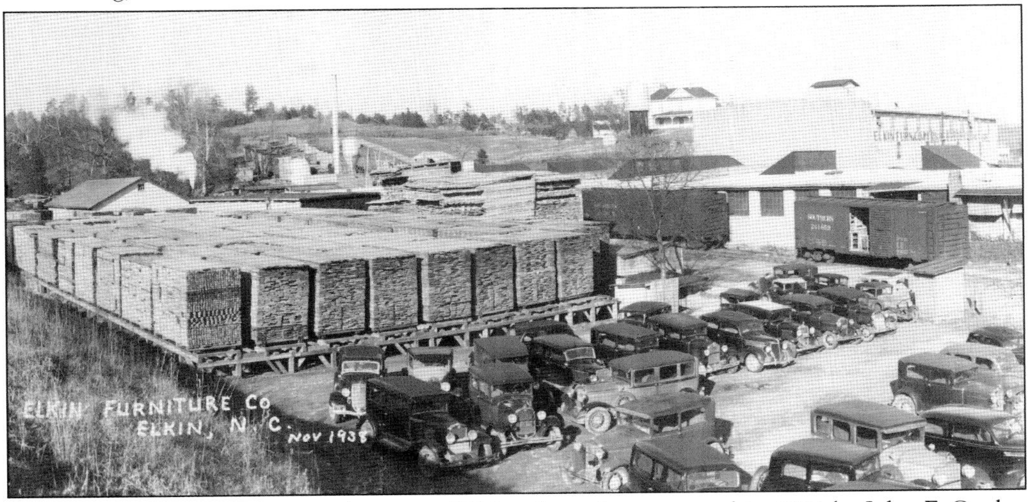

The Elkin Furniture Company began in 1896 and was incorporated in 1904 by John F. Cooke, W.J. Boyles, S.M. Arnold, and J.W. Arnold. It was originally located on the northwest corner of Market and Bridge Streets, where the Hotel Elkin was built in 1925. In 1907, the furniture company moved east of downtown Elkin and is pictured here in November 1938. In 1942, it merged with Vaughan-Bassett of Galax, Virginia. (SP.)

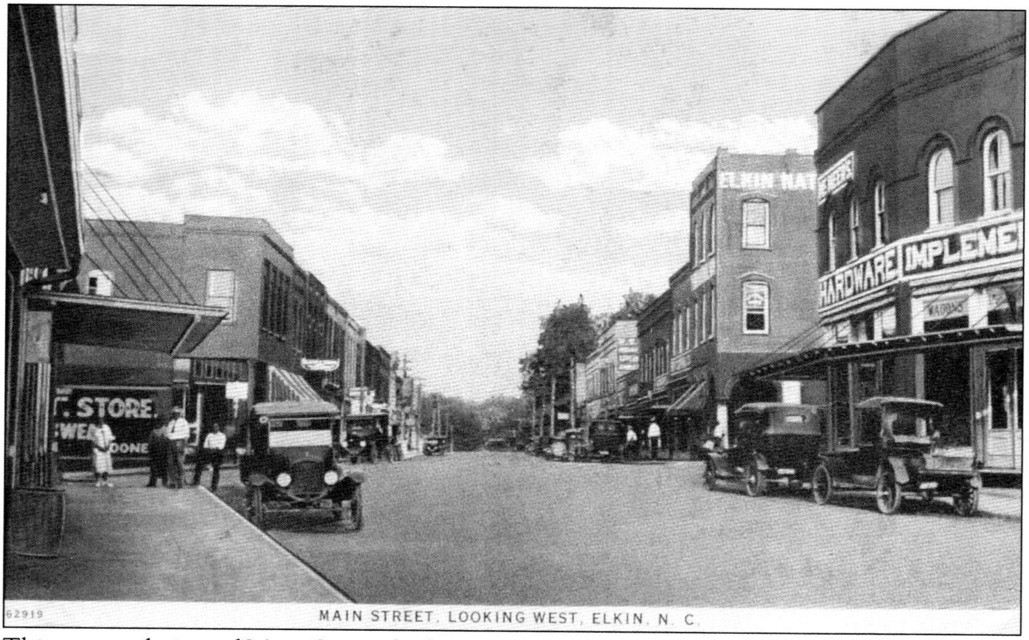

This postcard view of Main Street, looking west, was taken before 1933. The Elkin Hardware Company, shown at right, burned to the ground on December 24, 1935. The Elkin National Bank, which closed in 1932, is on the corner, and behind it is M.Q. Snow's clothing store. Sydnor-Spainhour's department store opened in 1926 in the old Click Building on the left corner, behind it are McDaniel's Department Store and Surry Hardware. (SJC.)

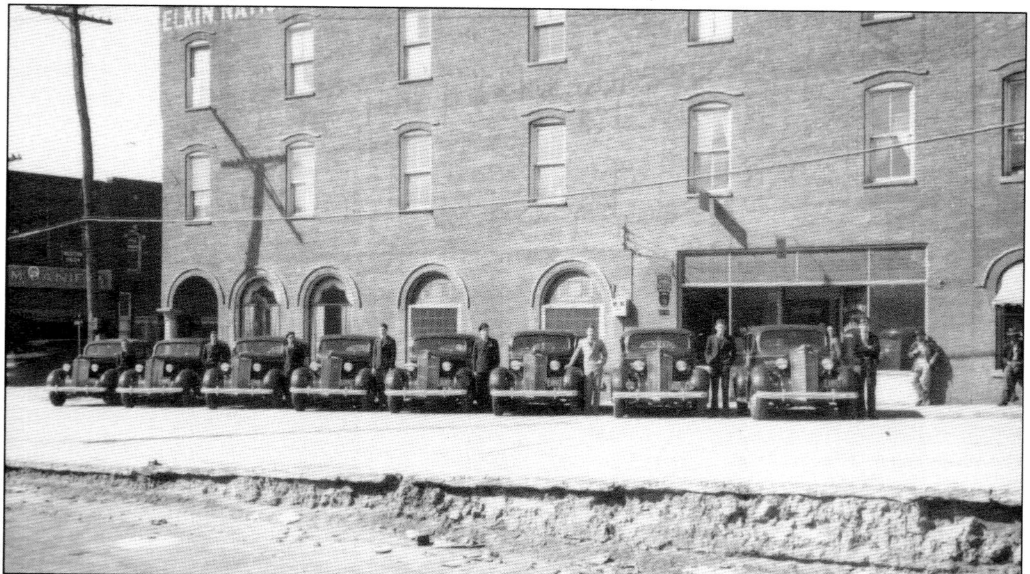

This 1936 photograph shows the City Cab Services fleet of Packard taxis lined up on Bridge Street, next to the Elkin National Bank building. The seats of these cars were covered with some of the first automobile upholstery made by Chatham. McDaniel's Department Store is on the far left. The Elkin Hardware building once stood at the location from which this picture was taken. The Belk-Doughton department store opened at this site in 1937. (SJC.)

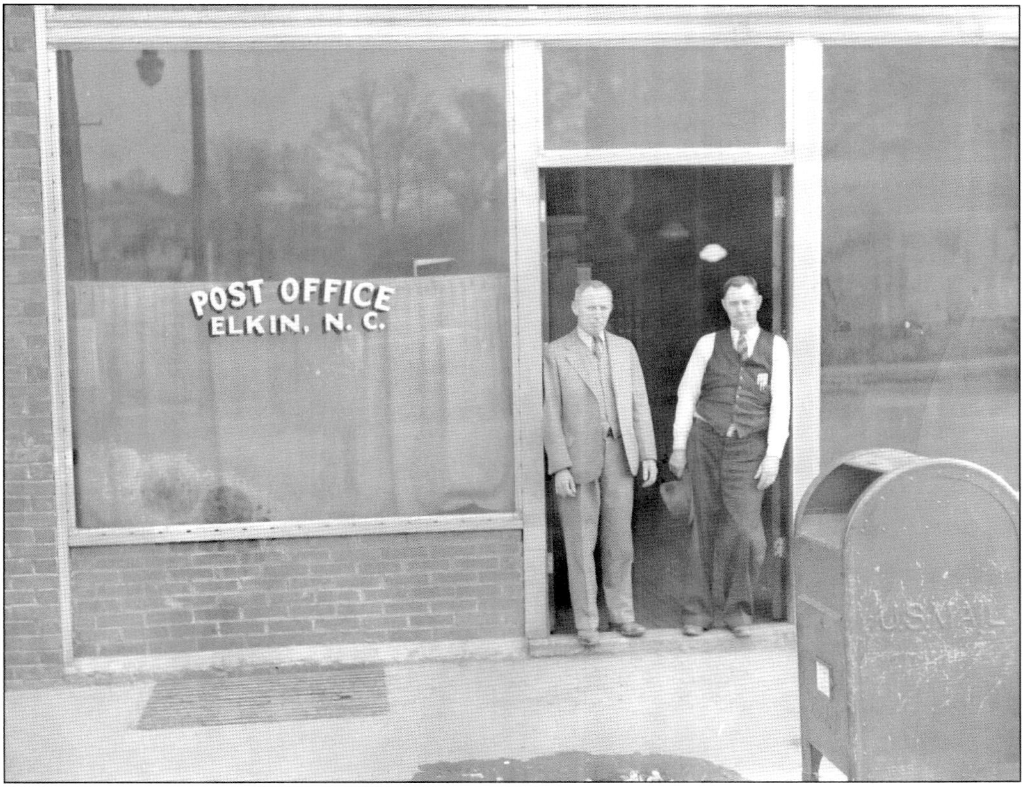

From 1927 until 1938, when the new post office building opened, the Elkin Post Office was located in this two-story building at 111 West Market Street. The upper floor of the structure was occupied by the local telephone exchange. Pictured in the early 1930s, postmaster French W. Graham (left) and postal clerk Cletus Wolf stand in the doorway. (EPO.)

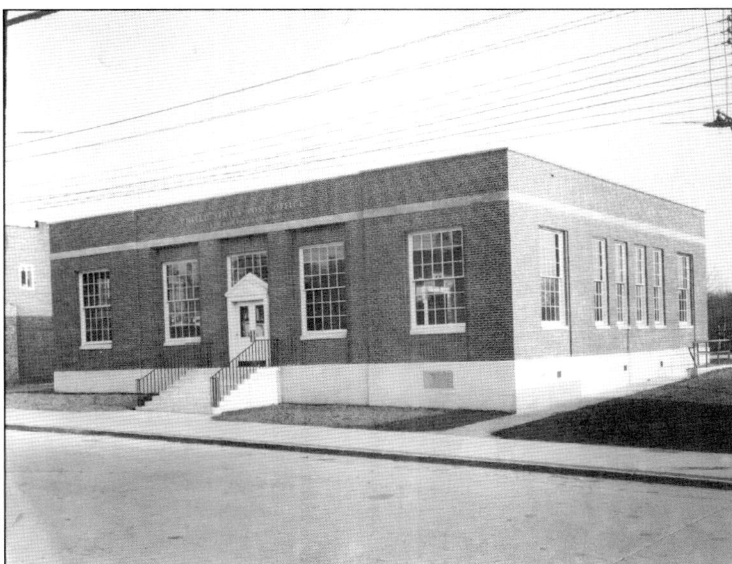

The US post office building, on West Main Street in downtown Elkin, opened on April 7, 1938, and is still in use today. The first post office in Elkin began in 1856, with Richard Gwyn as the first postmaster. Elkin's first home mail delivery was made by Glenn Lewis on March 1, 1942. Most Elkin homes in town received two deliveries per day. (EPO.)

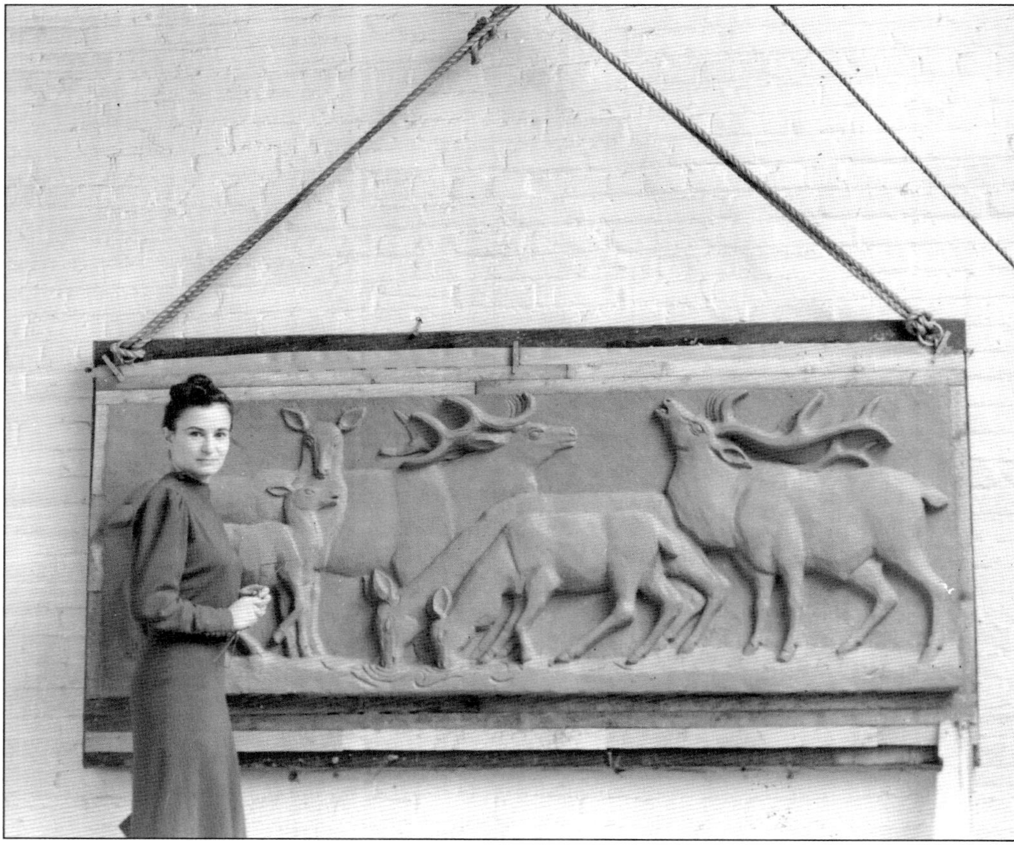

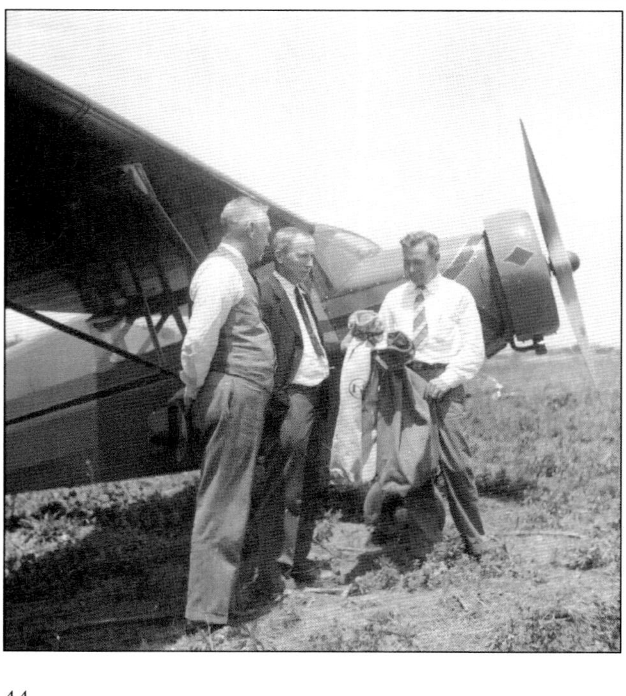

Anita Weschler, a New York City artist, created the plaster sculpture of an elk herd that hangs in the post office lobby. In the 1930s, as part of the Works Progress Administration, she was commissioned by the federal government to create the sculpture; at the time, many artists were commissioned to create art for federal buildings. (EPO.)

In 1938, the first, last, and only airmail flight to Elkin was made when a Winston-Salem pilot delivered a sack of mail to promote "Air Mail Week." The pilot (right) landed on the Austin-Traphill Road, near Pleasant Hill School, and was met by mayor J.R. Poindexter (left) and postmaster French W. Graham (center). (EPO.)

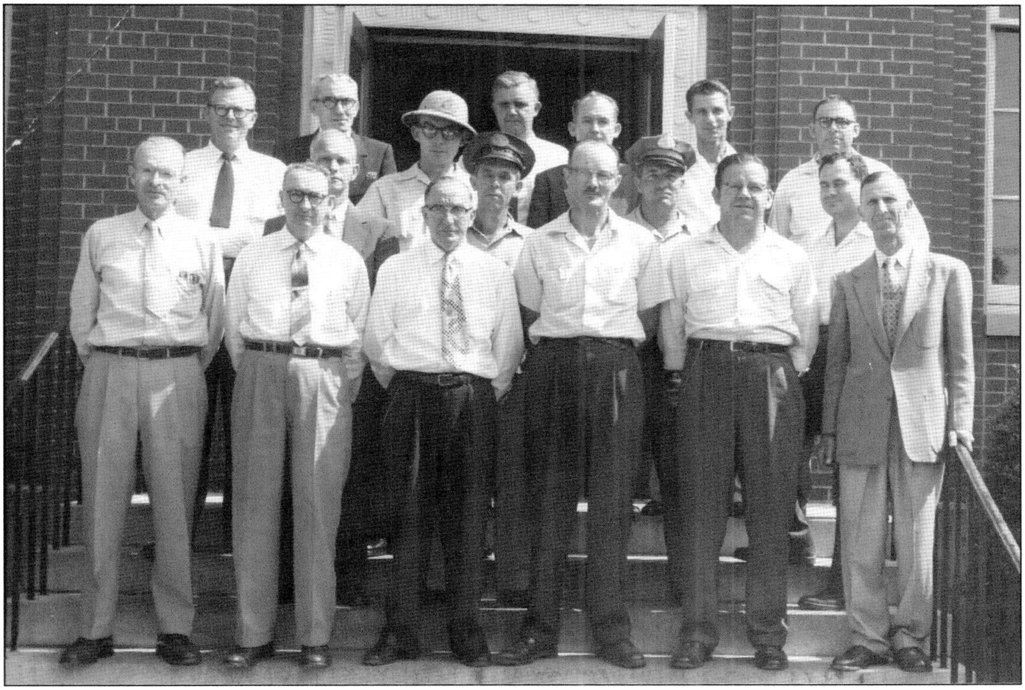

The staff of the Elkin Post Office observed the centennial of the local office on June 4, 1956. Pictured here are, from left to right, (first row) postmaster Linville Hendren, Linville Norman, Worth Graham, Carter Dickson, Alvin Wood, and A.O. Boles; (second row) Joe Transou, Roy Chappell, Raymond Vestal, and Glenn Lewis; (third row) Roscoe Poplin, James Marsh, Kermit Darnell, and Adrian Nixon; (fourth row) Sheffie Graham, Loman C. Richardson, and Frank Tulbert. (EPO.)

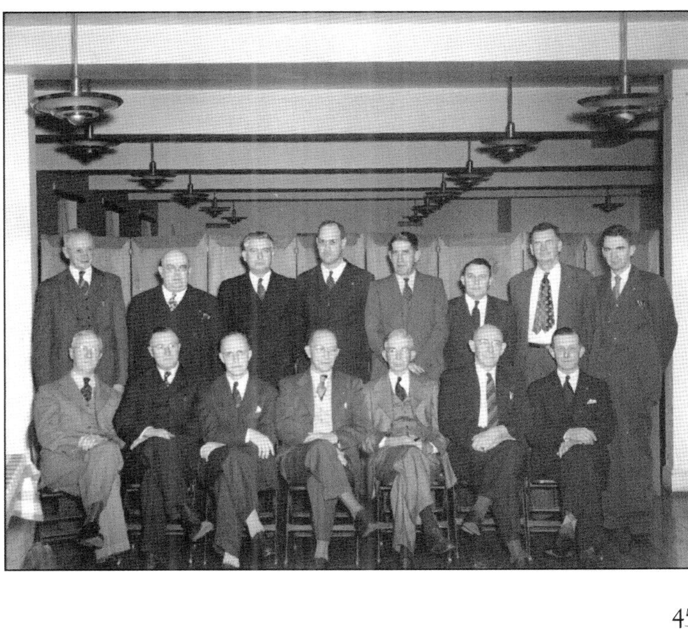

The Elkin Kiwanis Club was organized on March 29, 1923. The past presidents of the club pose for this picture in the mid-1940s. They are, from left to right, (first row) Dr. E.G. Click, George E. Royall, Dr. R.B. Harrell, unidentified, Carl C. Poindexter, J.G. Abernethy, and A.O. Bryan; (second row) H.P. Graham Sr., Harvey F. Laffoon, W. Marion Allen, Dave G. Smith, Raymond W. Harris, Garland Johnson, T.C. McKnight, and Hoke F. Henderson. (GL.)

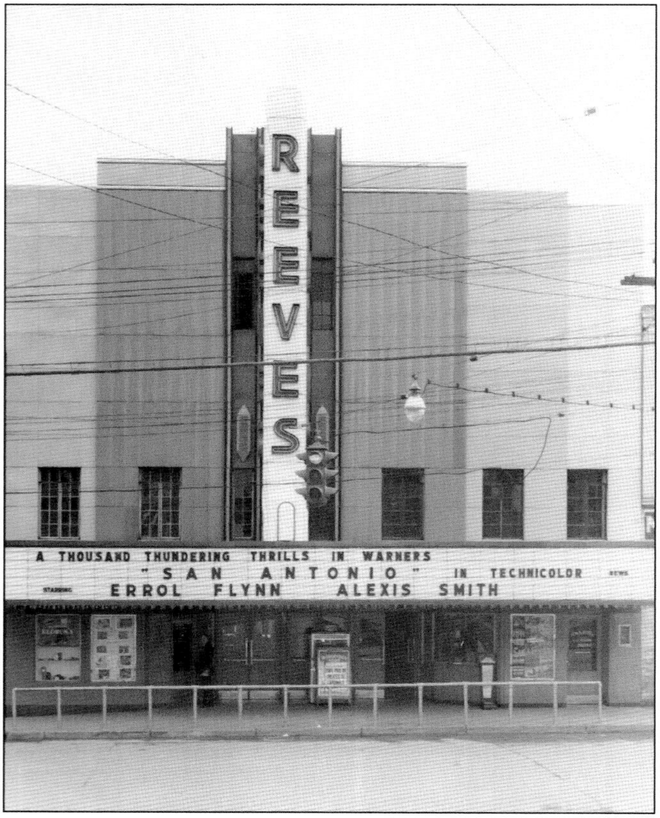

The Reeves Theatre opened on October 30, 1941, and the first movie shown was *Affectionately Yours*. Dr. W.B. Reeves, a local optometrist whose office was upstairs, built the theater. At one time, he also owned the Lyric and State theaters. When the Reeves Theatre was originally built, it had a balcony and seated 700 people. The picture below shows the original interior. It was air-conditioned and had a grand stage for live performances. Many stars came to Elkin and performed here. The main curtain was silver and dusty peach, and the screen curtain was spangled silver. The theater was sold on December 31, 1973, to Piedmont Circle Theatres in Charlotte. In 1978, the balcony was closed off to make two theaters, and it was renamed the Elk Twin Theatre. (Both, TH.)

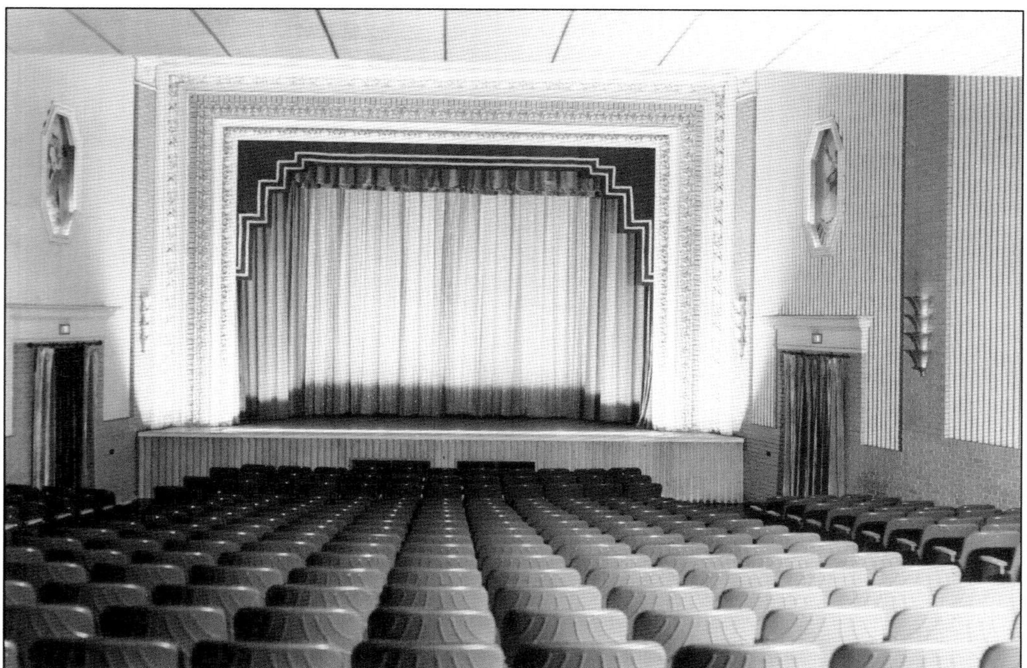

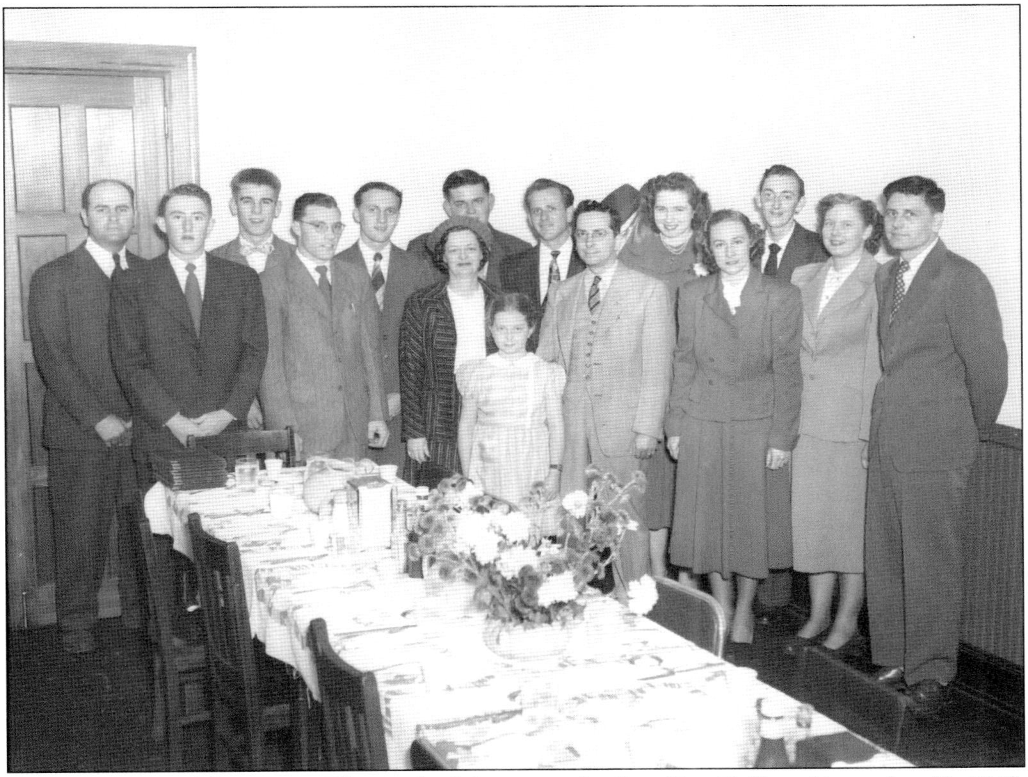

The employees of the Reeves Theatre had dinner at the Bon Ton Grill on November 12, 1948, prior to the theater being leased to the Blue Ridge Theatres Corporation. Pictured here are, from left to right, (first row) Roland Brown, Glenn Burton, Belva Reeves, Gale Page Reeves, Dr. W.B. Reeves, Gloria Milan, Pearl Roseberry, and Leslie Sprinkle; (second row) Grady Sullins, Jack Pardue, Jack Sprinkle, Bob Tulbert, Odell Seymour, Betty Swift, and Bud Durham. (TH.)

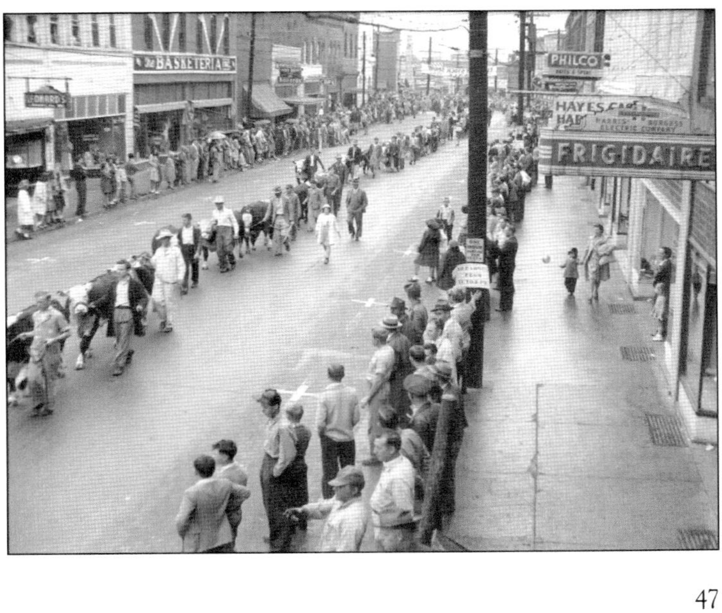

In 1942, the Elkin Jaycees began hosting the annual Fat Stock Show and Sale. It was cosponsored by the Elkin Merchants Association and was the oldest event of its kind in North Carolina, serving Wilkes, Alleghany, Watauga, Yadkin, Iredell, and Surry Counties. This October 1946 photograph shows the fourth annual Fat Stock Show Parade on West Main Street. It was taken from atop the marquee on the Reeves Theatre, looking east. (EJ.)

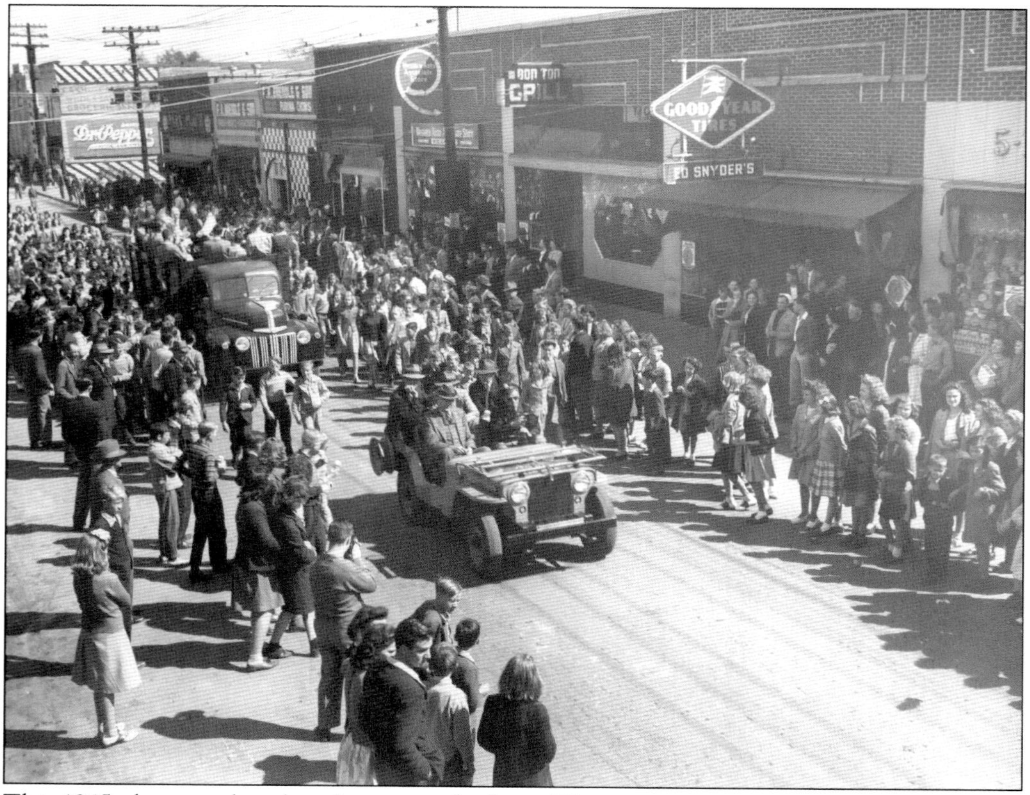

This 1945 photograph, taken from atop the Lyric Theatre marquee, is not of a World War II victory parade, as has been cited on several occasions; it is the third annual Elkin Jaycees Fat Stock Show and Sale parade. Gov. R. Gregg Cherry (in passenger seat), who was the keynote speaker at the banquet that year, rides in an Army jeep with Gene Aldridge (driver) and mayor J.R. Poindexter as the parade heads west on East Main Street. (EJ.)

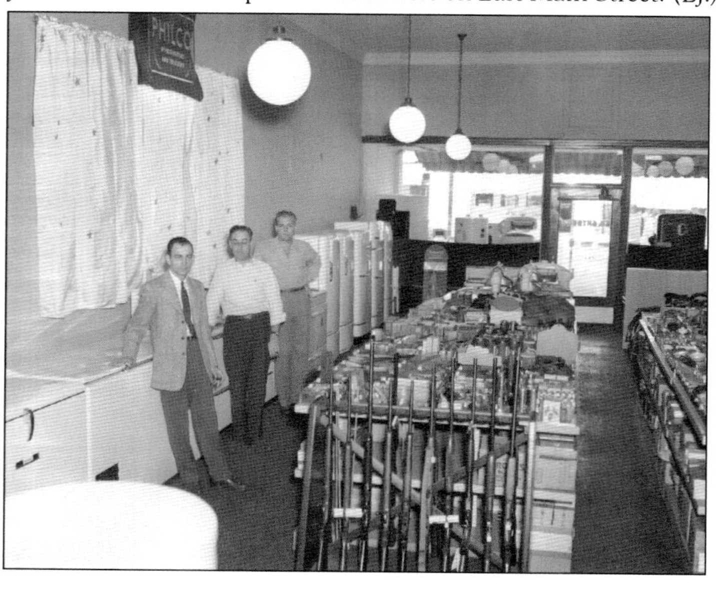

In 1940, Ed Snyder's opened in the old rescue squad building on East Main Street. In the early 1940s, it moved into this structure at 116 East Main Street, where the business remained until December 1972. Employees Graham Shumate (left) and Kelly Rose (center) are pictured with owner Ed Snyder around 1943. It was the first business in downtown Elkin to sell televisions. Elk Pharmacy moved into this building in 1976. (KCS.)

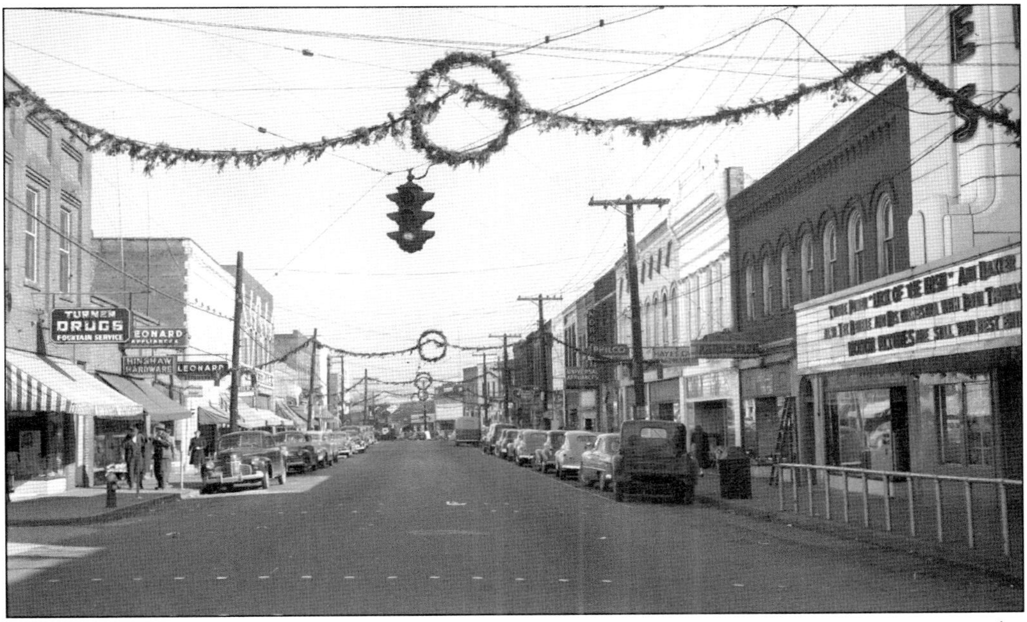

This view of West Main Street, looking east, was taken on November 23, 1949. Businesses on the left include Turner Drug Company, Hinshaw Hardware, Leonards Jewelry, Rogers Shoe Shop, and the Basketeria. On the right are the Reeves Theatre, Harris-Burgess Electric, Hayes Cash Hardware, Hayes and Speas Furniture, and Eagle Furniture. (SJC.)

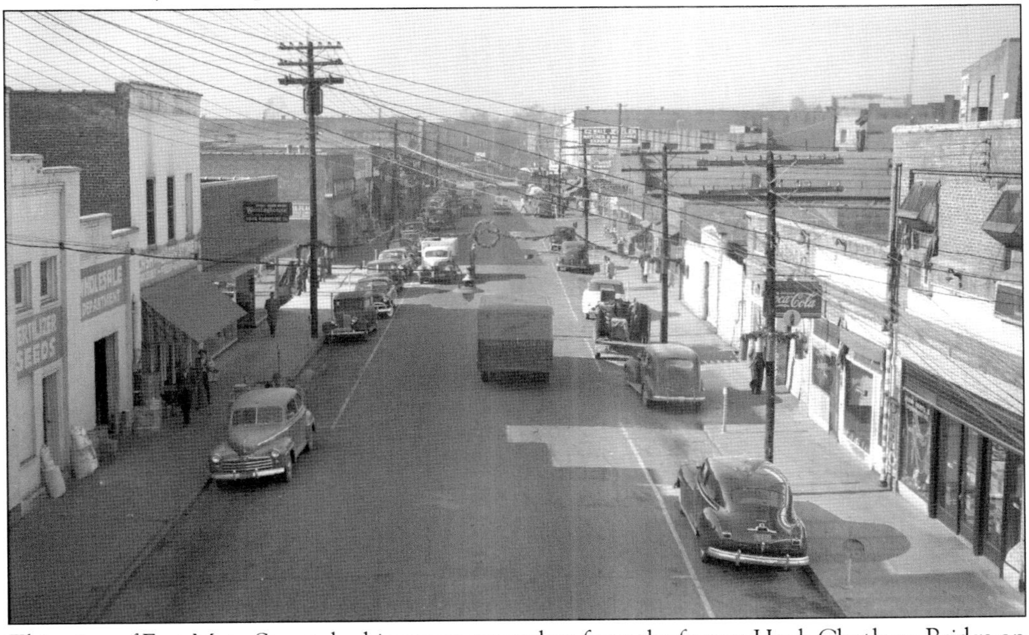

This view of East Main Street, looking west, was taken from the former Hugh Chatham Bridge on November 23, 1949. Businesses on the left include Cash and Carry Wholesale, Home Furniture, and Park Place. Home Furniture, owned by Avery T. Whittington, had just moved to this building from its location on West Main Street, where it opened in 1937. The first business on the right is the Sample Store. (SJC.)

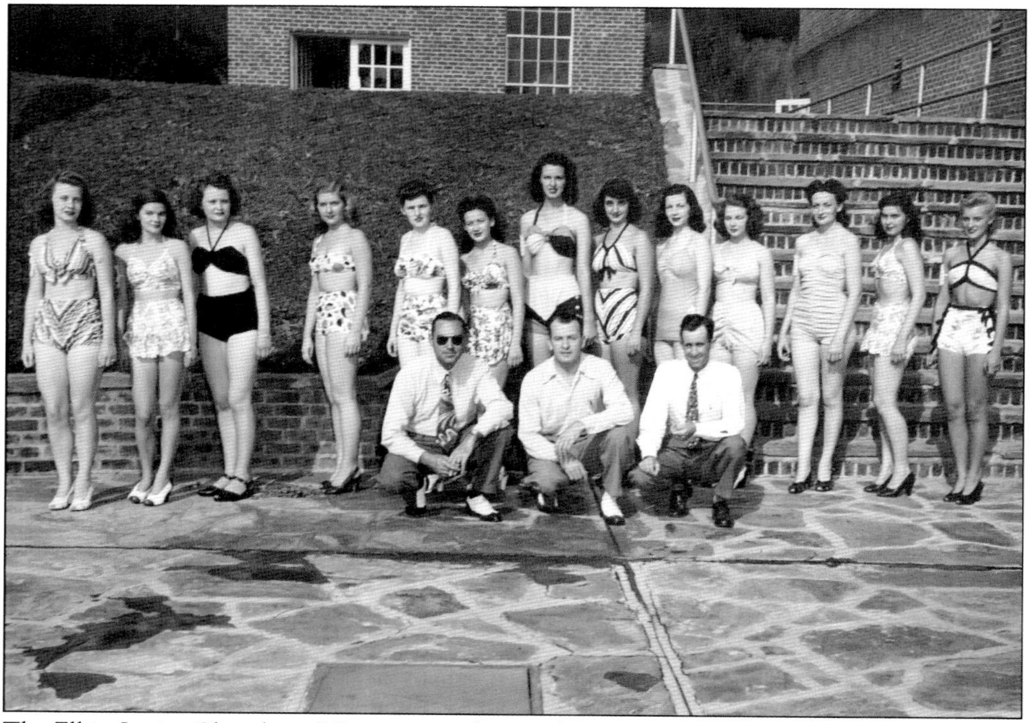

The Elkin Junior Chamber of Commerce, chartered in 1941, held a yearly beauty pageant that served as a local preliminary for the Miss America pageant. Starting in 1961, it was referred to as the Miss Elkin Valley pageant. The contestants in July 1946, pictured here from left to right, are Betty Jo Eidson, Jean Chappell, Eloise Gentry, Kathleen Cochrane, Jewel Warren, Rosemary Jacobs, Opal Holsclaw, Betty Jean Pardue, Mildred Freeman, Peggy Lineberry, Lena Sale, Frances Barnette, and winner Maxine Aldridge. The judges (kneeling in front) are, in no particular order, Lindsay Holcomb, Reid Staton, and Odell Lambert. (KCS.)

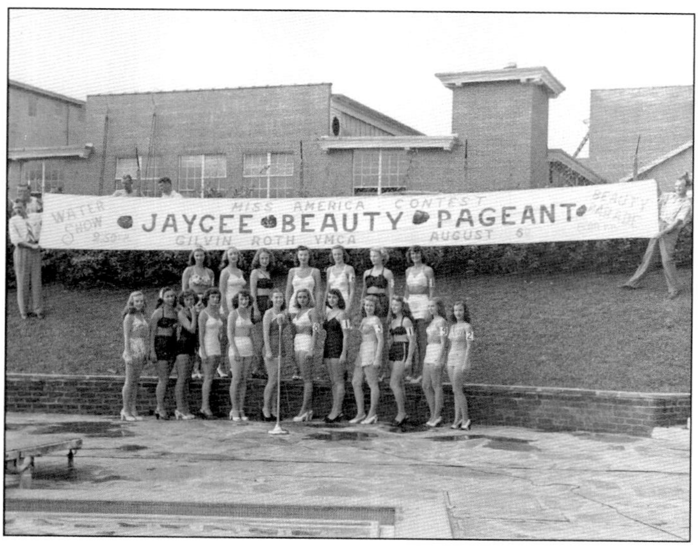

The Elkin Jaycee beauty pageant contestants pictured in 1947 are, in no particular order, Betty Cope, Angie Woodruff, Beulah Yates, Mary Lou Dobbins, Betty Jean Pardue, Doretha Chappell, Lucille Hall, Sara Jones, Ruth Reich, Pauline Waggoner, winner Helen Thompson, Betty Lou Steelman, Lucy Wolfe, Elizabeth Hall, Mary Brown, Jessie Dean Russell, Julia Williams, Christine Ingram, and Margaret Mackie. (DB, photograph by Tom Morrison.)

The Elkin Motorcycle Club is pictured in front of Rose's dime store, which opened in 1939 at 112 East Main Street. Members of the club in this early-1940s image include, in no particular order, Lawrence Wall, Grady Poplin, Charlie Poplin, Paul Luffman, Otto Money, Kenneth Kimmer, Fred Vestal, Claude Hinshaw, Harvey Couch, Hugh Vestal, Winford Stanley, Harvey Finney, Bailey Johnson, and Web Slawter. (DB, photograph by Tom Morrison.)

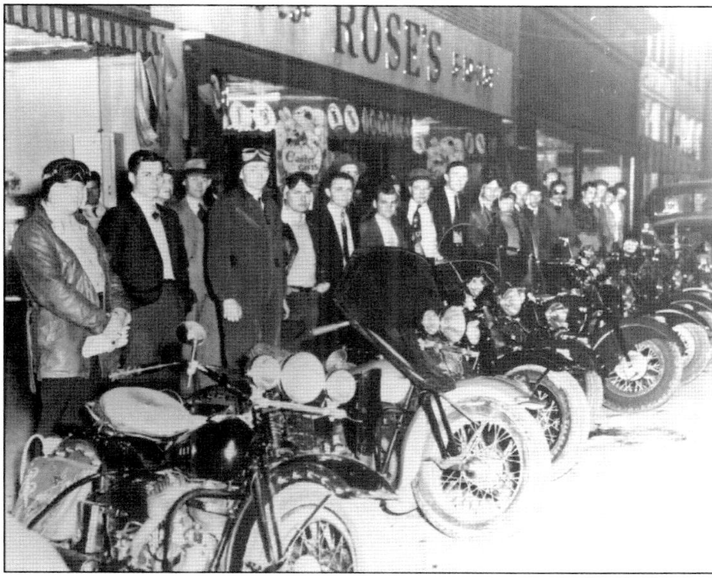

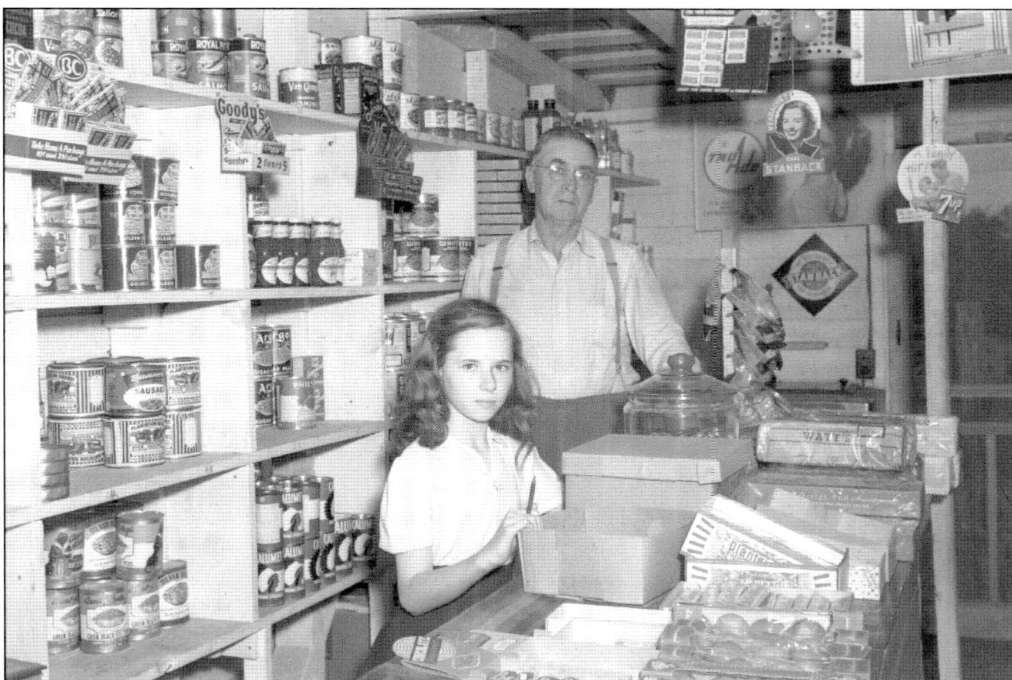

Herschel Tulbert and his granddaughter Wanda Sue Tulbert are pictured in his general store in 1947. After retiring from Chatham Manufacturing, Tulbert ran this little store beside his home on North Bridge Street. It was located a few houses above Claremont Drive, on the right. He sold candy, soft drinks, tobacco, and canned goods, among other items. (SJC.)

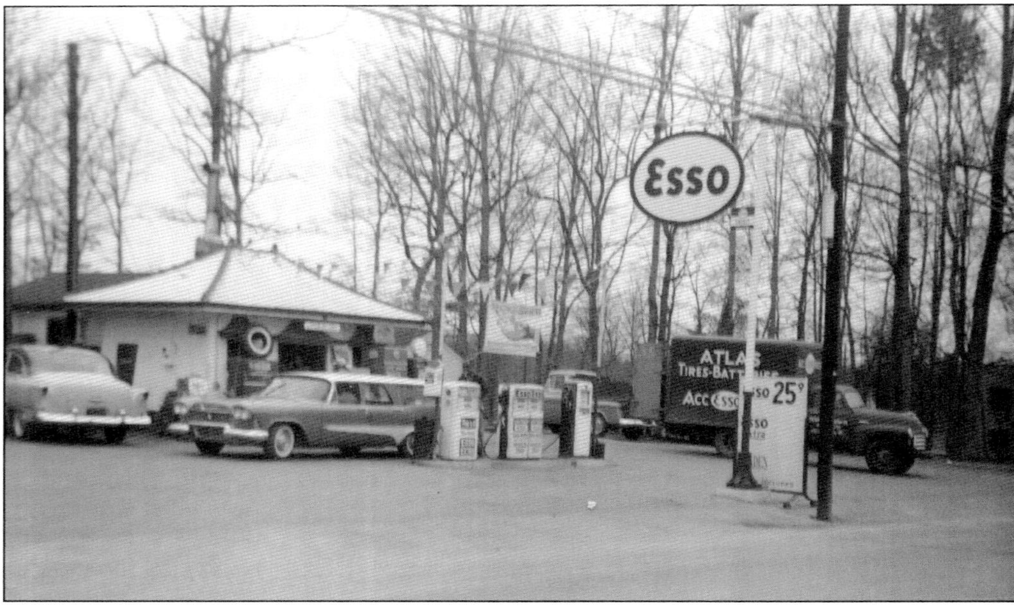

The original G&B Esso service station, located at 667 North Bridge Street, is pictured here in the mid-1950s. In August 1945, Philip A. Greenwood and E. Carl Boyles founded G&B Oil Company. In the mid-1950s, Boyles bought Greenwood's interest in the company. Around 1964, this building was replaced with a newer brick structure, which serves as the current location for G&B Energy. (JWP.)

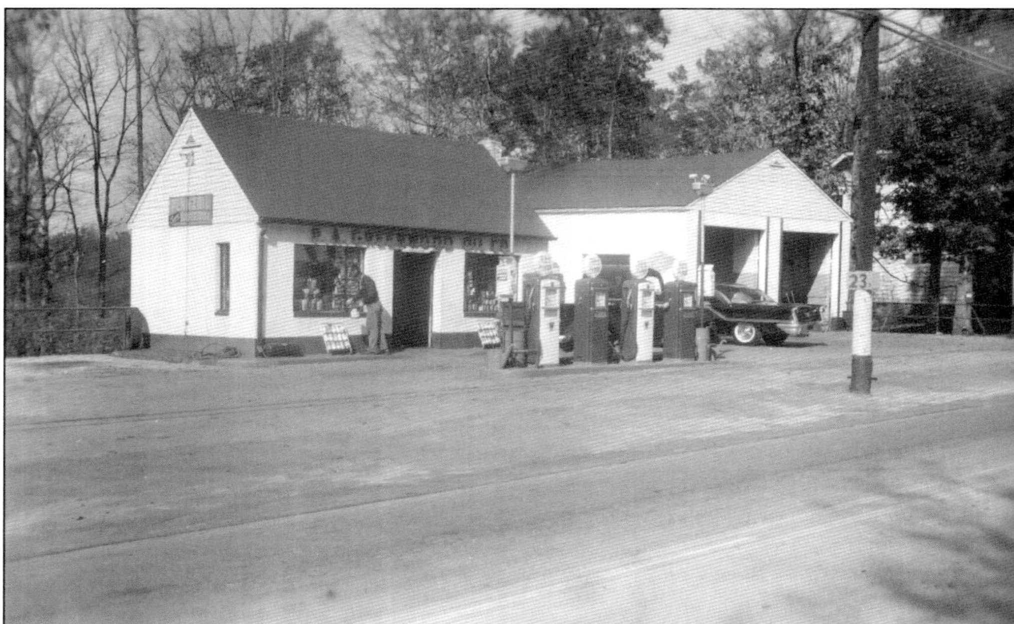

The P.A. Greenwood Oil Company and service station was located on North Bridge Street in the curve in front of the Dr. L.C. Couch house. Shown here in the mid-1950s, the service station was sold to Quality Oil Company in August 1962 and began selling Shell products. Clyde Jennings became manager at that time. (DB.)

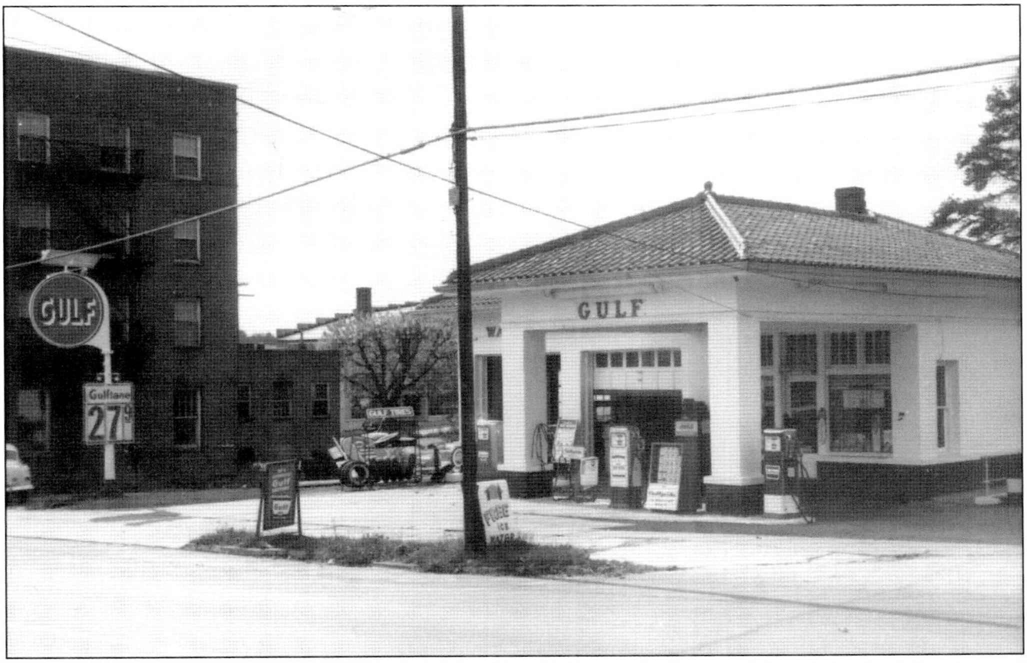

Swaim Brothers Gulf was located north of the Hotel Elkin, which is visible at left. Paul Swaim and his brother Henry bought this Gulf station in 1944. It was previously operated by Bob Church, who relocated the business to this site after the 1940 flood. The building was razed in the mid-1980s and replaced by Yadkin Valley Bank offices. (JWP.)

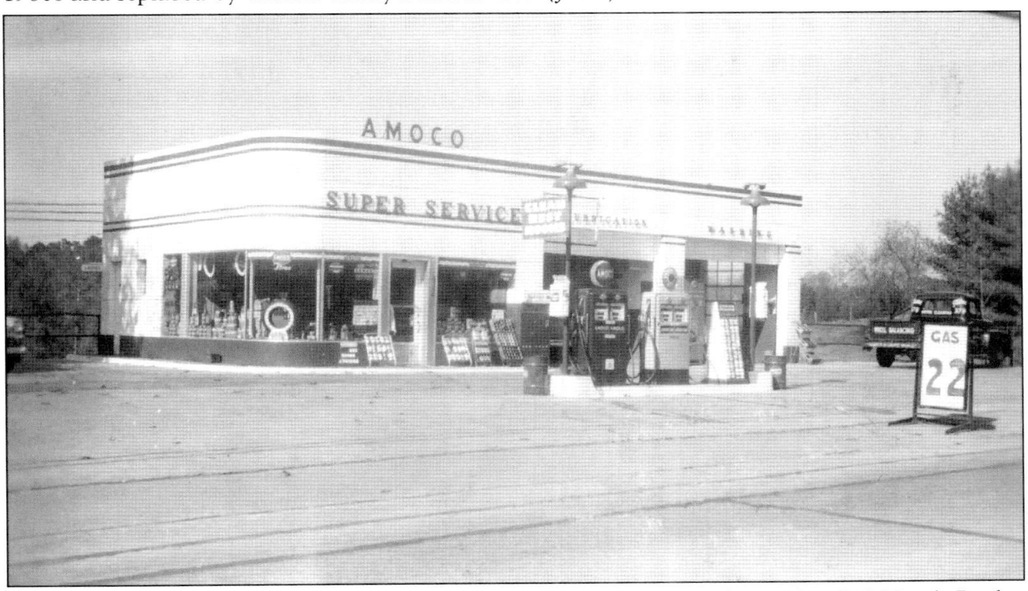

The Amoco Super Service station, pictured in the mid-1950s, was located at 713 North Bridge Street, the present-day site of Watson's Florist. It was started in August 1948 by Dan Hudspeth, who started Super Tire Service next door in 1951. Originally a Shell station, by 1953 it had changed to Amoco and was operated by Tommy Johnson and Howard Hinson. The price of gasoline was 22¢ per gallon. (DB.)

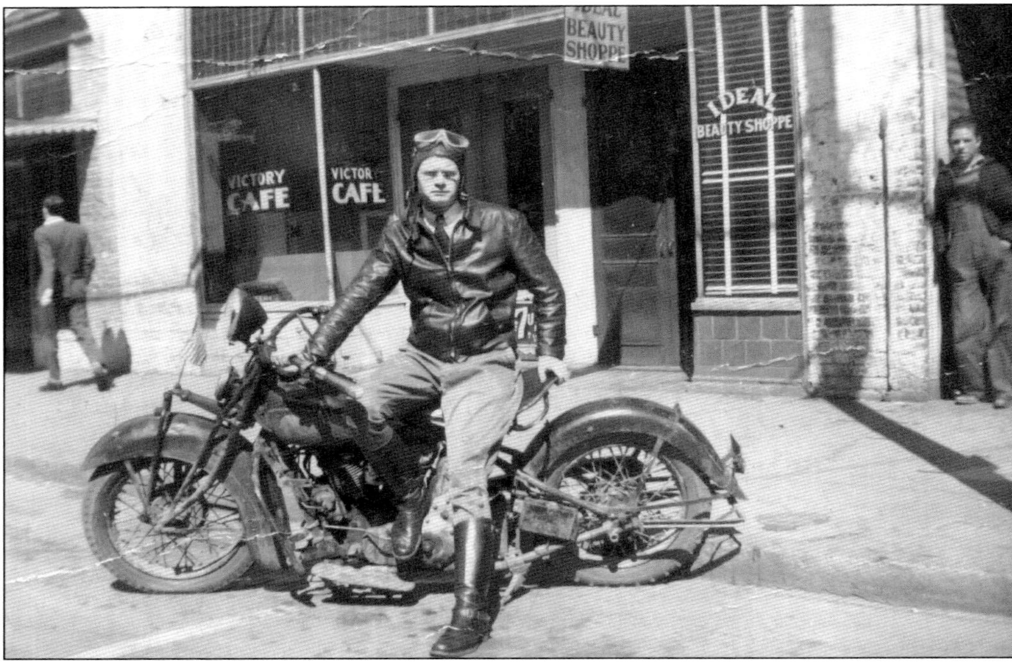

In this c. 1941 image, Evan Vestal is pictured with his Indian motorcycle in front of the Victory Café and Ideal Beauty Shoppe on West Main Street. In 1953, Vestal and Wade Williams bought Kennedy Auto from John Kennedy Sr., who started the business in 1943. It was originally located on the northeast corner of Court and East Main Streets, but by 1953, it had moved to 118 East Main Street. (EV.)

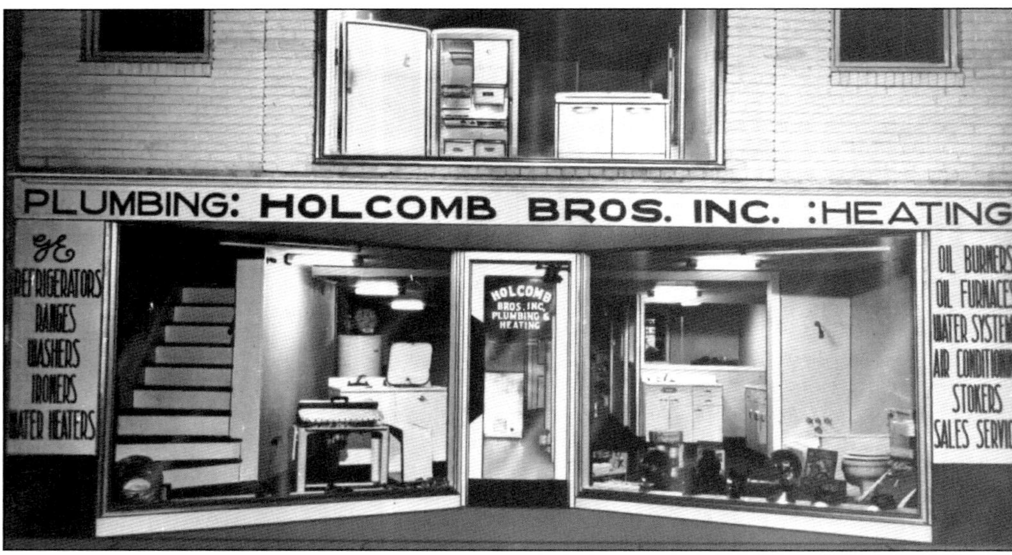

This building was constructed by Dr. W.B. Reeves in 1937 and operated as the Elk Theatre until 1941. At that time, Holcomb Bros. Inc. moved into the building, which was located to the right of Moseley and Reece Wholesale. Jones Holcomb, R.E. Smith, and J.D. Smith started Holcomb Brothers in 1927. Brothers Sig and Jack Holcomb later joined the business. The structure was razed in 1976 by Mutual Savings and Loan. (JWP.)

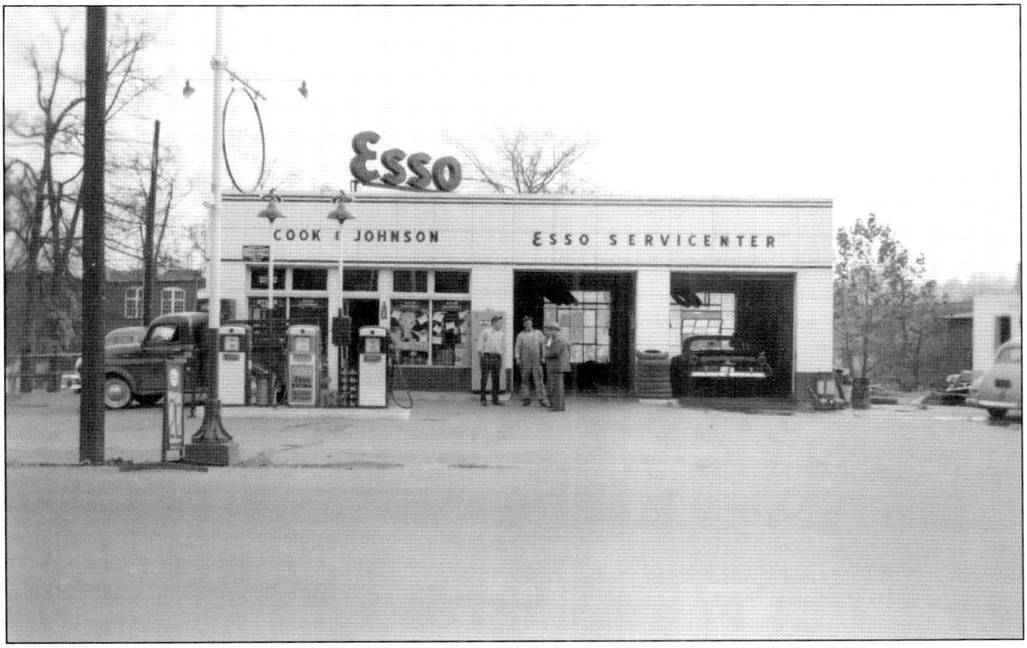

The Cook & Johnson Esso station was located at 262 East Main Street, next to Smithey's Department Store and adjacent to the railroad crossing. Around 1949, it was bought by Evan Vestal and was managed by his brother Homer. In 1954, he sold it to Jasper Cook and a Mr. Johnson. This mid-1950s picture shows the old Chatham Mill in the left background, behind the station. (DB.)

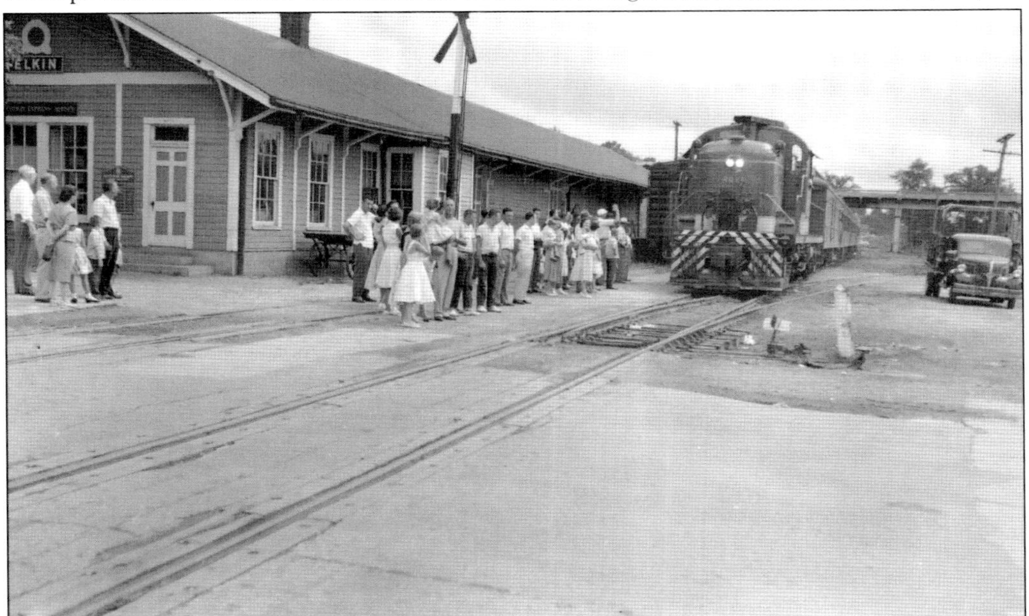

Passenger service to Elkin was discontinued by the Southern Railway System in August 1955. This photograph shows the last passenger train leaving Elkin headed to North Wilkesboro. A crowd of more than 400 people braved the rain that day to witness the end of an era that began in 1890. (JS.)

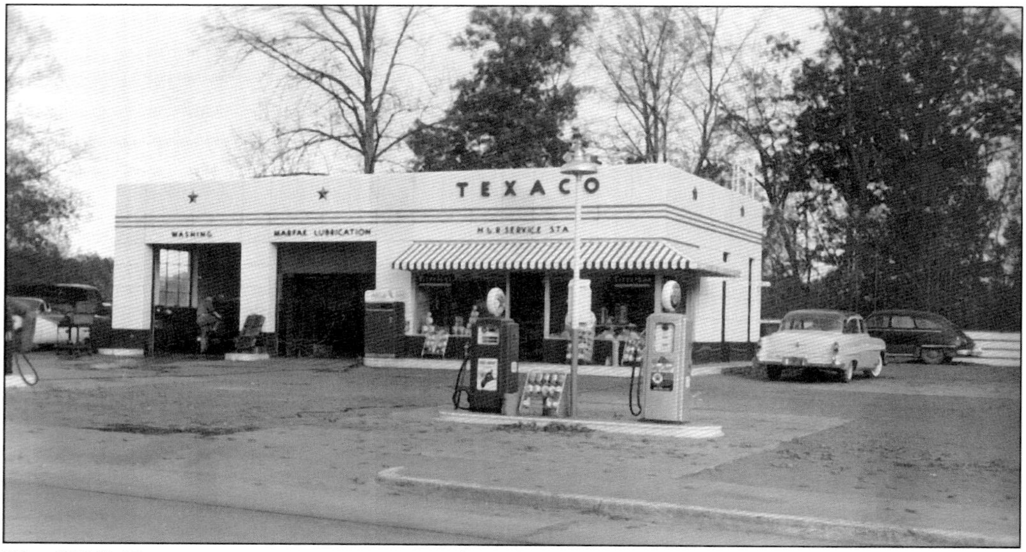

The H&R Texaco service station, pictured in the late 1950s, was located at 620 North Bridge Street, beside the Dr. L.C. Couch house. It was opened in November 1953 by Reece Cockerham and Granville Cheek and was first called Cockerham and Cheek Texaco Service. In 1961, it was named North Bridge Street Texaco and was managed by Cecil Crouse. In the early 1970s, it became a Sunoco station owned by Reece and Greg Cockerham. (DB.)

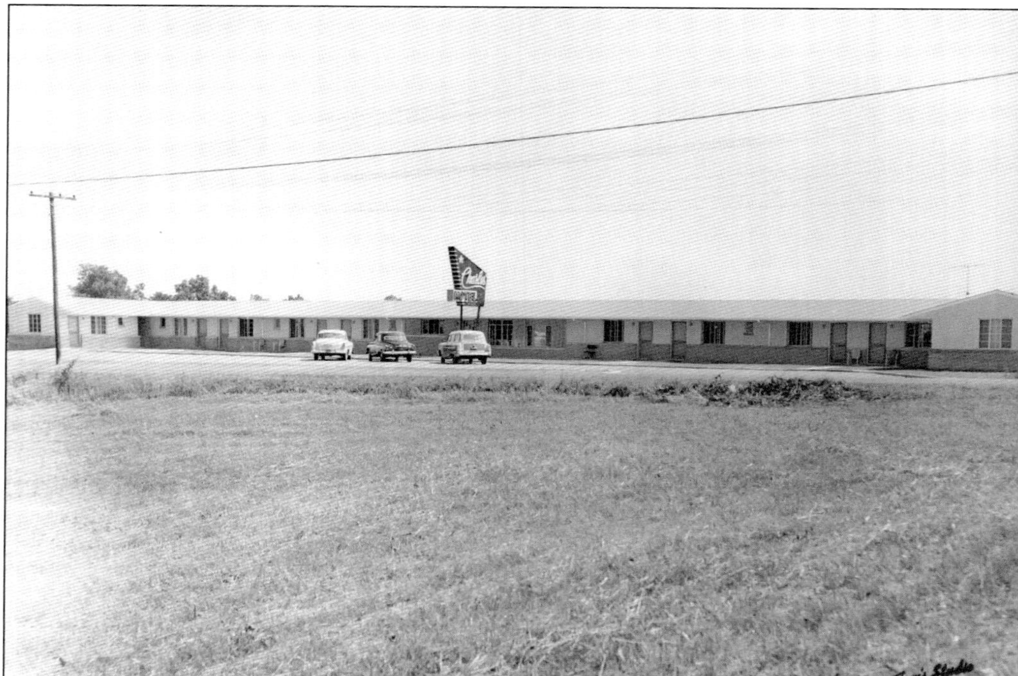

Charles' Motel was located on US Highway 21 in North Elkin and was originally owned by Charles Casstevens. It was bought by Faye and Ronald Sturgill in 1960 and had 12 rooms with televisions, phones, and air-conditioning. Room rates—$5 per night—were the same until the hotel closed in 2005. (DB, photograph by Tom Morrison.)

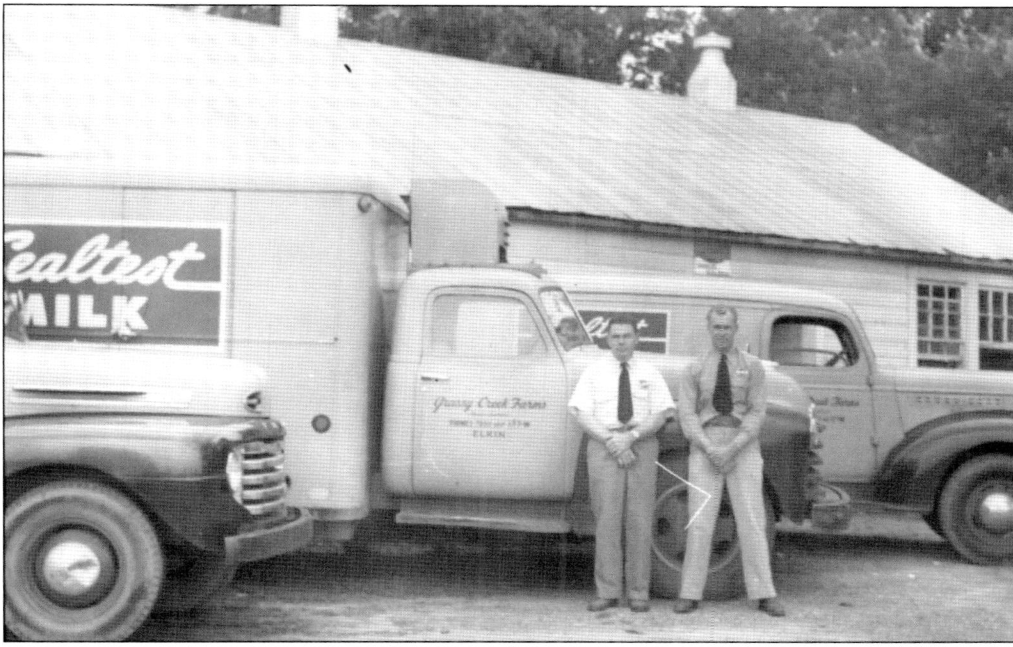

Franklin Miller (left) and Graham Greene owned and operated Grassy Creek Farms Sealtest milk distributorship in the Elkin area for many years, beginning in 1950. Its predecessor was the Grassy Creek Dairy, operated by Franklin's father, J.F. Miller, from the early 1920s until 1949. It was located on Klondike Road north of Elkin. Miller and Greene, pictured here around 1960, developed the Grassy Creek Drive community on part of the old dairy farm. (GG.)

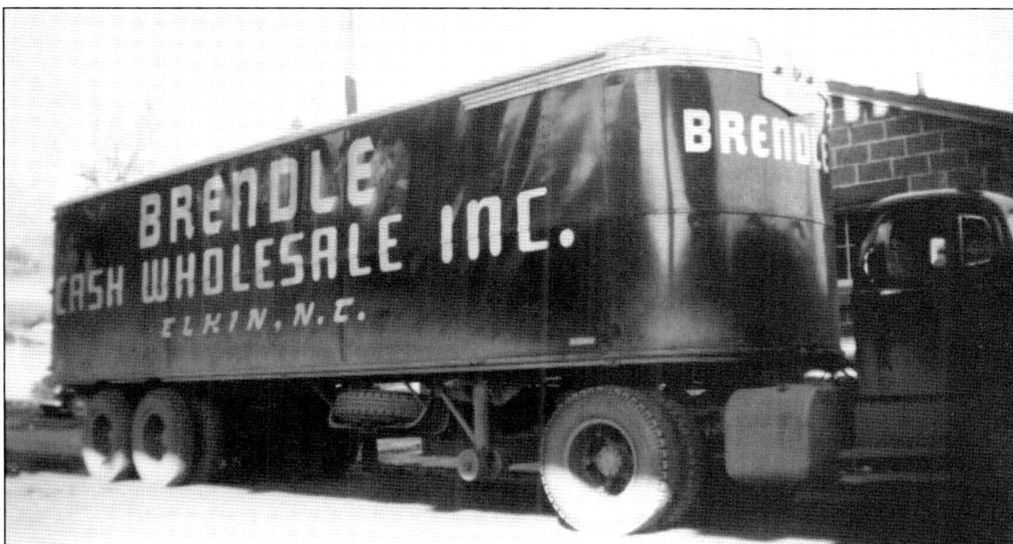

Floyd Arthur Brendle bought the S.W.Y. Supply Company in 1919 and changed the name to F.A. Brendle and Son. In the early 1930s, the company expanded into the grocery business, which was later sold to Cash and Carry in 1961. In 1953, Brendle Cash Wholesale was founded when the first nonfood items were sold; it grew into the Brendle's department store chain, which had over 50 stores in five states at the company's peak in the late 1980s. (JWP.)

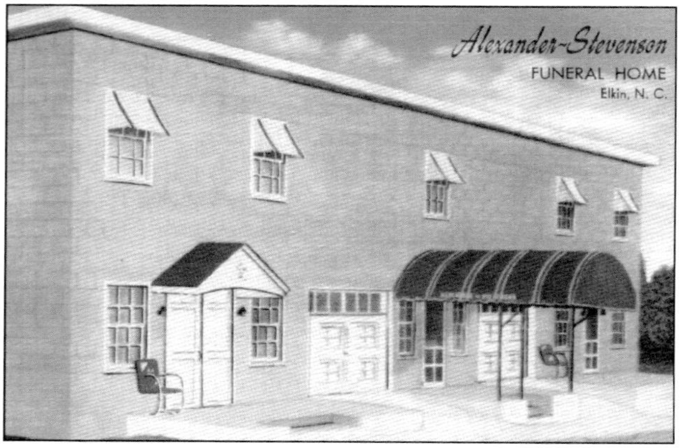

The Alexander-Stevenson funeral home was formally opened on March 6, 1954. It was located on Vine Street, across from Galloway Memorial Episcopal Church. Owners Charlie R. Alexander and Bill N. Stevenson had operated the Hayes & Speas funeral home for six years before opening a business of their own. They also had three ambulances that offered prompt and safe service anytime, day or night. The ambulance service was discontinued in 1968. (SJC.)

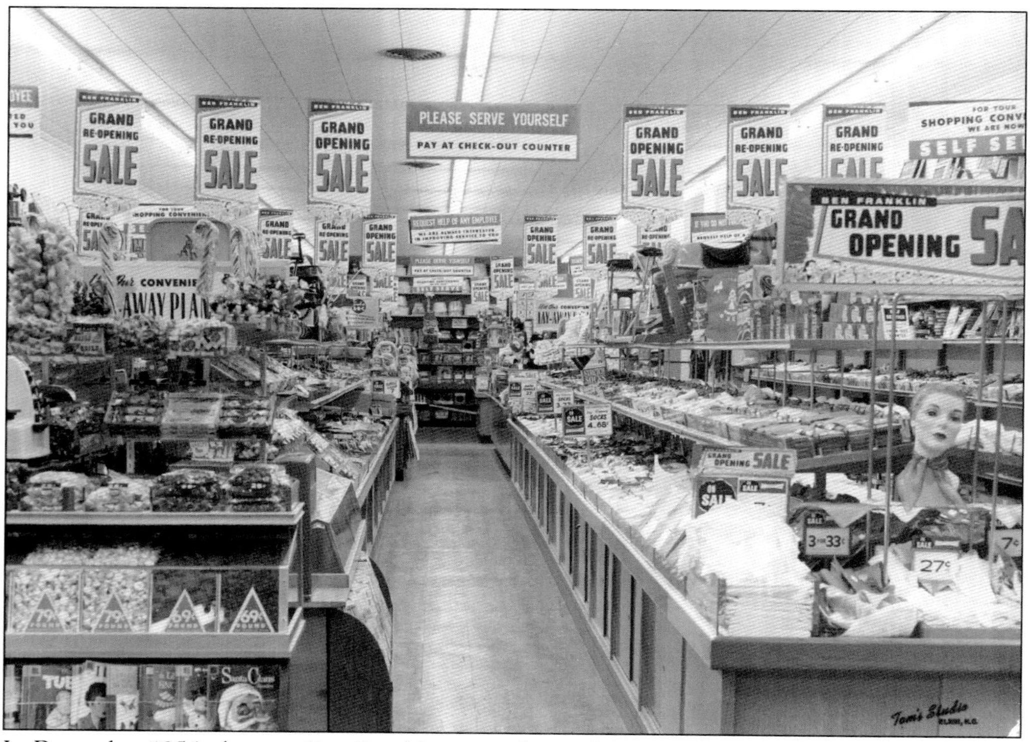

In December 1956, the new Ben Franklin store, located at 107 West Main Street, had its grand opening. It was formally known as the Graham and Click Company, which had served Elkin since 1922. The new owners, Harold C. Kennedy and Charles Ridge, purchased the business from Claude Farrell. The store sold a bit of everything, including candy, toys, clothing, stationery, toiletries, home furnishings, notions, and art supplies. (DB, photograph by Tom Morrison.)

W.S. Reich organized the Elkin-Jonesville Building and Loan Association on February 11, 1908. In October 1956, the association moved into a new building (pictured) on West Main Street, between the Reeves Theatre and Holcomb Brothers Plumbing. This was the former location of Moseley and Reece Wholesale. (BB.)

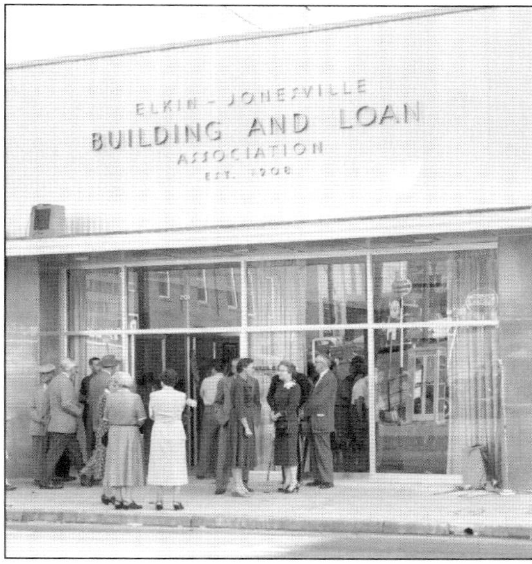

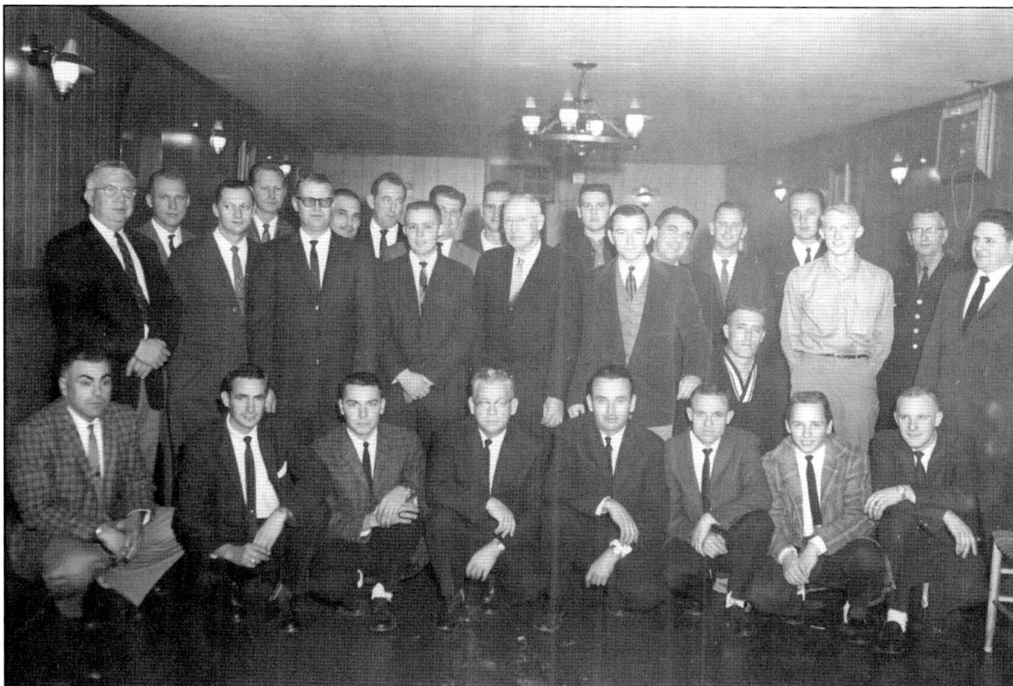

The Elkin Rescue Squad was organized in 1941 and is the second oldest squad in North Carolina. In this picture from the 1959 Christmas banquet, rescue squad members and guests are, from left to right, (kneeling) Arthur Hutchins, Bill Rhyne, Jay Holder, Ray Church, Blan Cockerham, Peanut Blackburn, unidentified, Mickey Cockerham, and Kenneth Blackburn; (standing) Buck Jarvis, Graham Greene, McNeer Everidge, Bill Boles, Hayden Moxley, Roy Kane, Mack Overcash, Bobby Garner, Tommy Johnson, unidentified, town manager Dixie Graham, Bill Blackburn, unidentified, Carl Plaster, Graham Johnson, Franklin "Sonny" Mackie, Jerry Blackburn, Dallas Coe, and Mickey Wagoner. (LHV.)

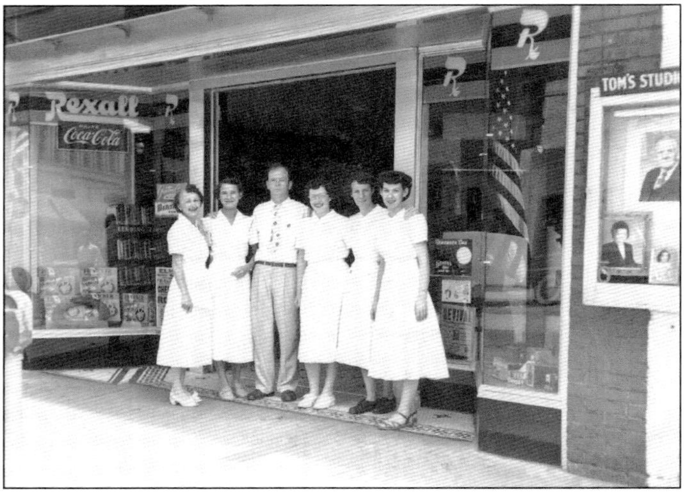

On March 23, 1918, J. Graham Abernethy opened Abernethy's Pharmacy in the former location of the Elkin Drug Company at 109 West Main Street. Les Reinhardt began working at Abernethy's in 1927 and eventually became part owner. Pictured around 1951, the employees are, from left to right, Vena Darnell, Chlorine Transou, Reinhardt, Geneva Stewart, Lucille Pardue, and Virginia Couch. (RCP.)

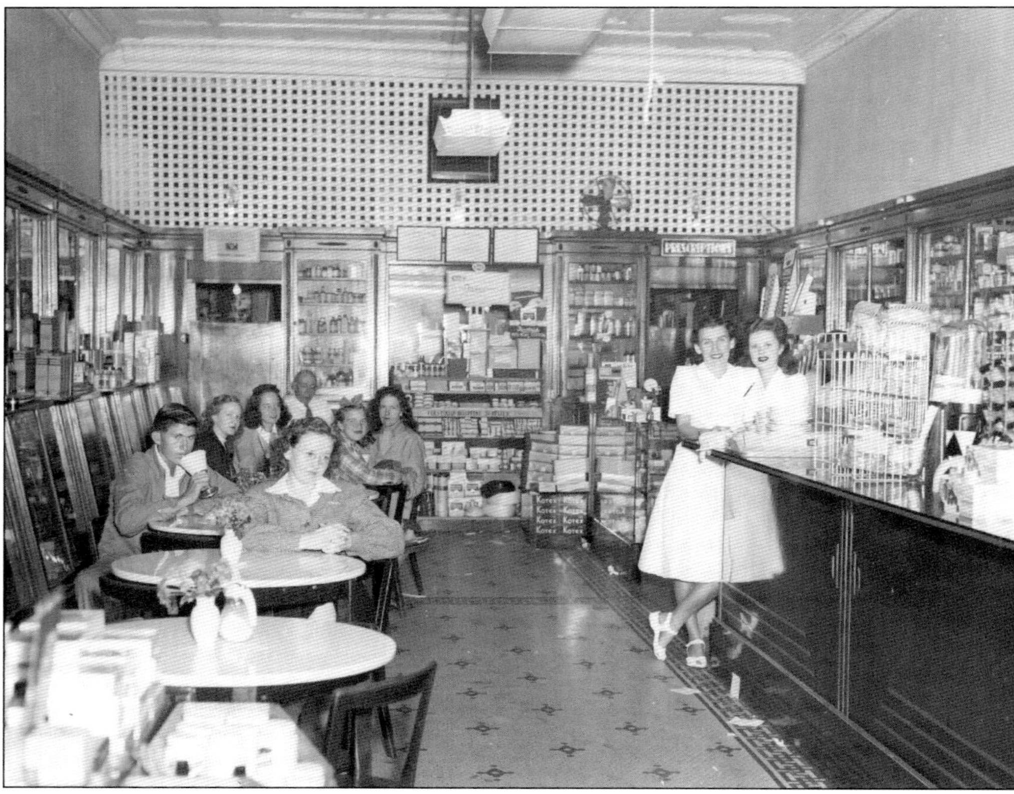

This photograph by Tom Morrison shows the interior of Abernethy's Pharmacy in the early 1950s. Pharmacist J.G. Abernethy (sitting at the table in the back left) died in 1955. Paul Fisher began working as a pharmacist at Abernethy's in 1951; he became sole owner in 1961 and changed the name of the business to Fisher's Pharmacy. The pharmacy went out of business in 1975. (DB.)

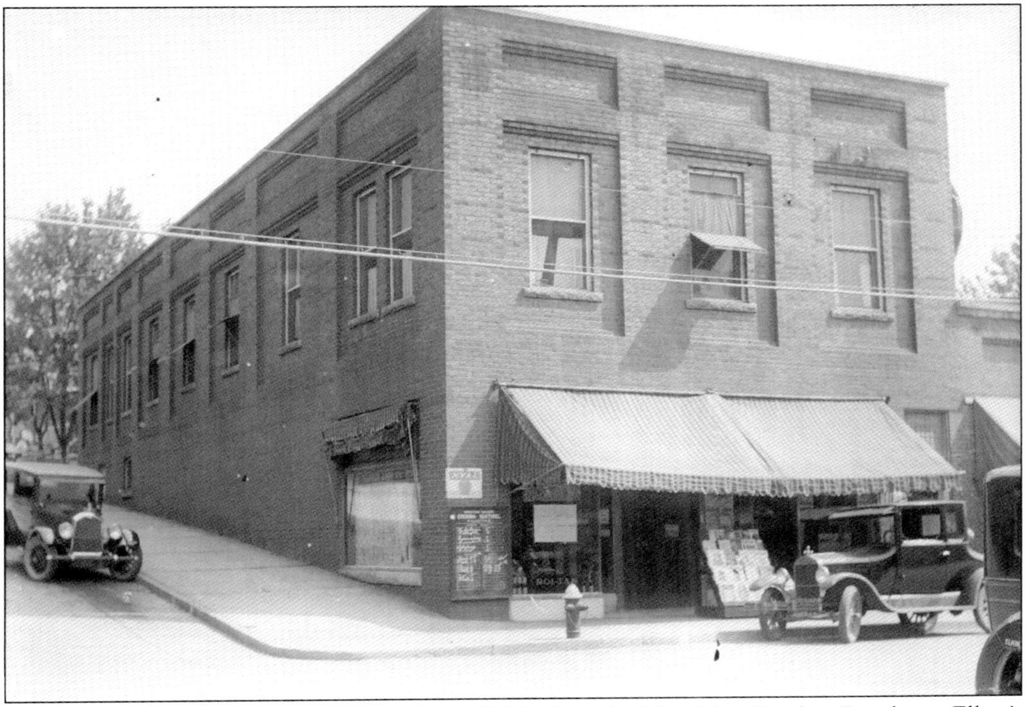

The Salmons Building was constructed in 1923 by local builder John Bartlett Burcham. Elkin's first hospital was operated by Dr. H. Clay Salmons and Dr. Robert Garvey on the second floor from 1924 to 1928. Turner Drug Company, founded in 1916 by Walter Delbert Turner, was on the ground floor. George E. Royall purchased an interest in the drugstore in 1923 and became sole owner after the death of W.D. Turner in 1937. (JP.)

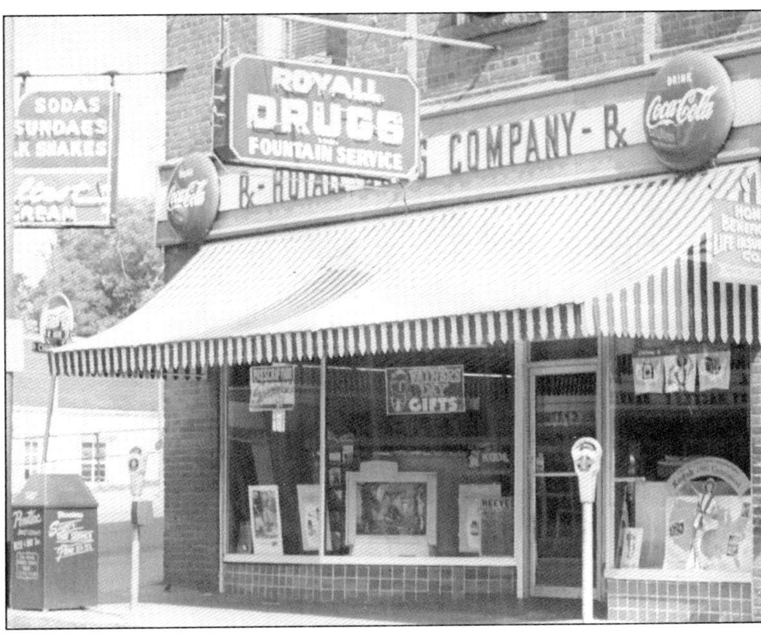

Turner Drug changed its name to Royall Drug Company on January 1, 1953. When George Royall, a three-term mayor of Elkin, retired in 1969, he turned the store over to his son Edwin Royall and his partner Henry Dillon. The pharmacy department closed in 1990, but the soda fountain remains a fixture in downtown Elkin, still serving hot dogs daily. (JP.)

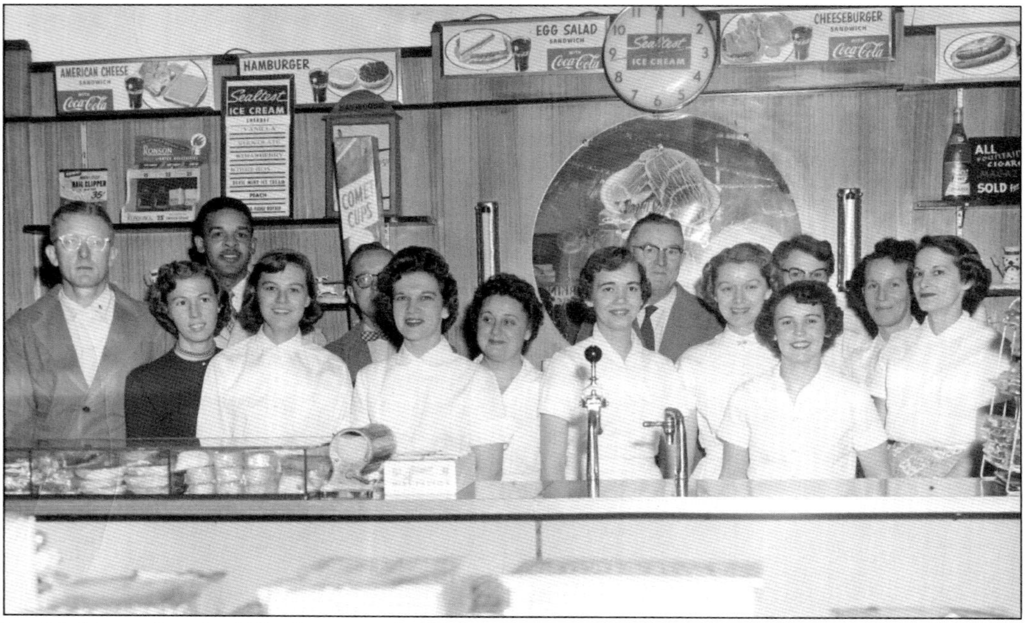

In this December 2, 1955, photograph, the employees of Royall Drug Company pose behind the soda fountain. They are, from left to right, pharmacist Edwin Royall, Betty Roberts, Raymond Hurt, Betty Jane McBride, pharmacist Henry Dillon, Aleine Day, Bea Vestal, Nancy Byrd, George E. Royall, Betty Marion, Pat Parsons, Edna Waddell, Lucille Pardue, and Dot Welborn. (RCP.)

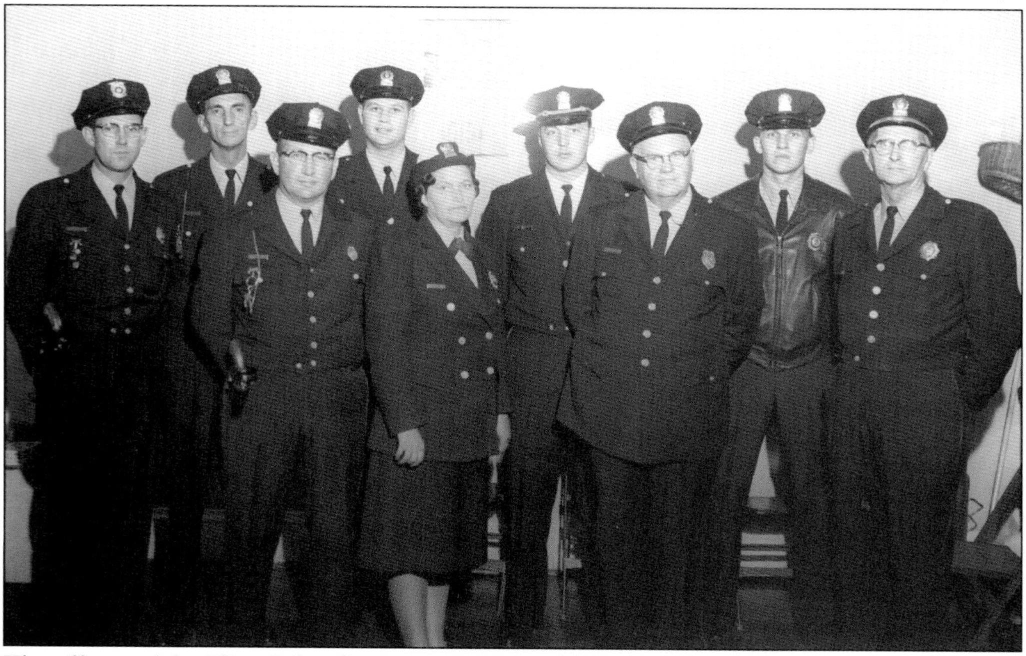

The officers of the Elkin Police Department pictured here in 1964 are, from left to right, Johnny Corder, Clyde Goins, Marshall Bullins, Bob Trivette, Ailene Newman, Chief Franklin "Sonny" Mackie, Goldie Payne, James Nixon, and Dallas Coe. Jim White was also a member of the force at this time, but is not pictured. (JC.)

Three

A HERITAGE OF CHRISTIAN FAITH

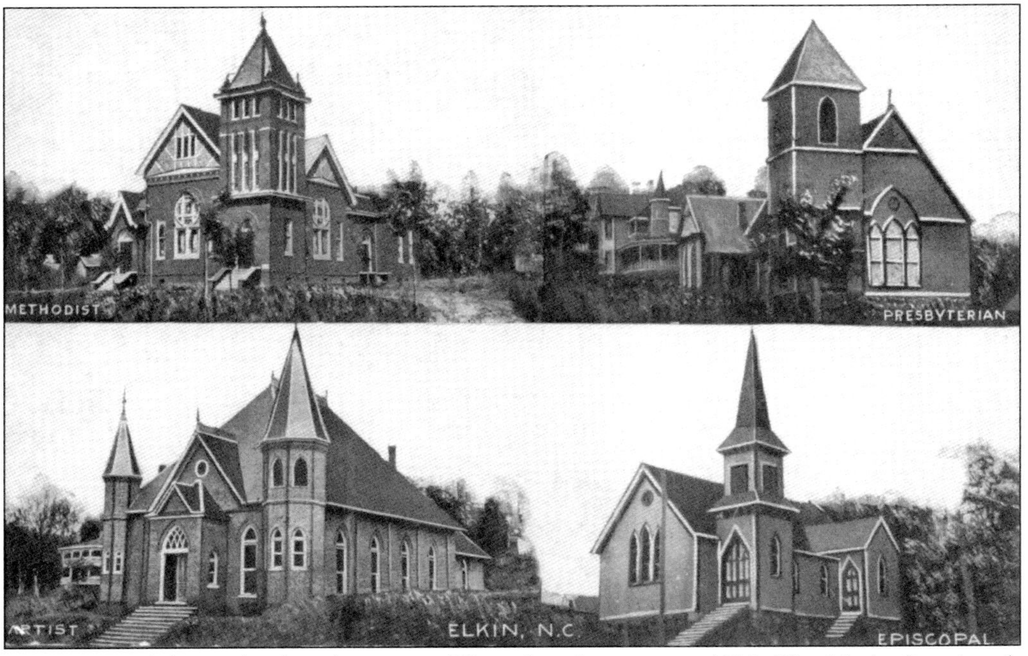

This postcard shows the four downtown Elkin churches prior to 1922. The Methodist church at top left was built in 1905. The Baptist church at lower left was constructed in 1903, and the Presbyterian church at top right was erected in 1895. The Galloway Memorial Episcopal Church, at lower right, was built in 1898 and is the only one of the four that still stands today. (SJC.)

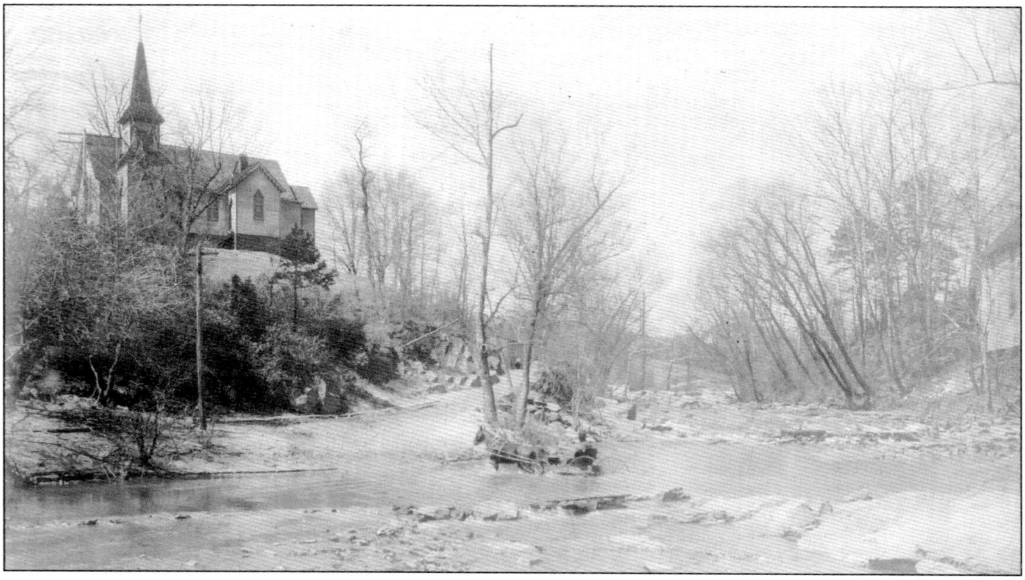

Galloway Memorial Episcopal Church is pictured around 1900 on the west bank of the Elkin Creek. It was built in 1898 by Laura Foard Galloway in memory of her husband, Col. Alexander Broadnax Galloway. It is the oldest church building used for regular worship services in Elkin. The Elkin Manufacturing Company is on the far right. An unidentified man fords the creek with his horse and buggy. (RRB.)

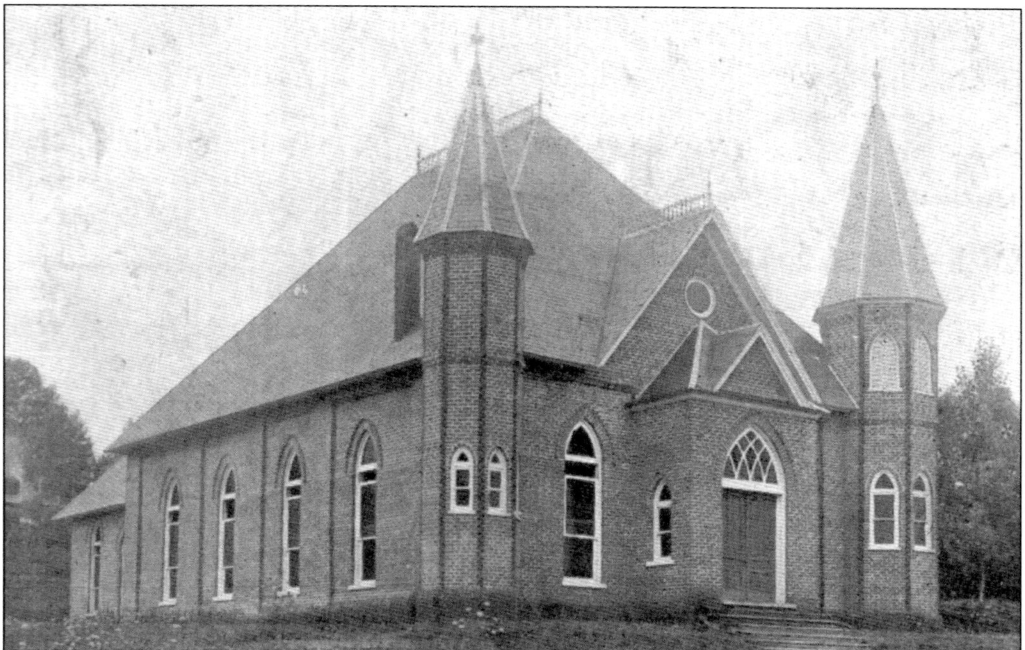

The First Baptist Church was organized in Elkin on May 18, 1889, and first met in a small structure located on Elk Spur Street. The second meetinghouse of the First Baptist Church, as seen in this postcard from 1909, was completed and used for services in early 1903. Around 1922, it was extensively remodeled by local builder John B. Burcham. (SJC.)

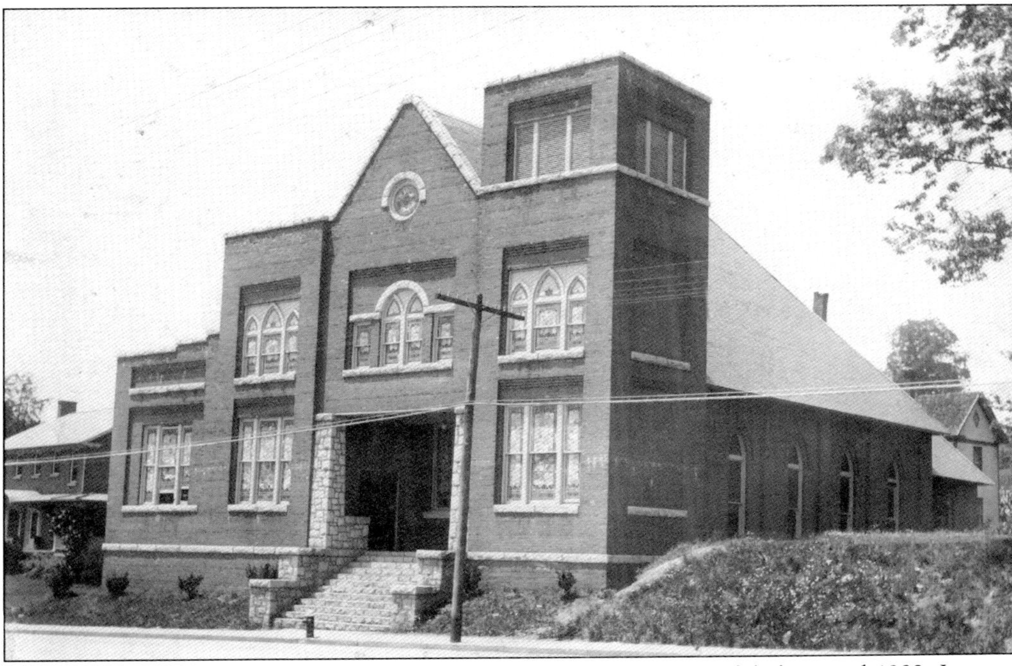

The picture above shows the First Baptist Church after being remodeled around 1922. It stood directly across from the Elkin Post Office on West Main Street. It was torn down in 1956 after the church was moved to its new location on Gwyn Avenue in June 1955. The front steps and trim around the windows and top of the church were made of granite. The bell was salvaged and placed in the steeple of the new building. Below, the size of the building is put in perspective by a group of more than 100 children and teachers assembled on the steps for Vacation Bible School around 1950. The law offices of James W. Partin are currently located at this site. (Above, CB; below, HMS.)

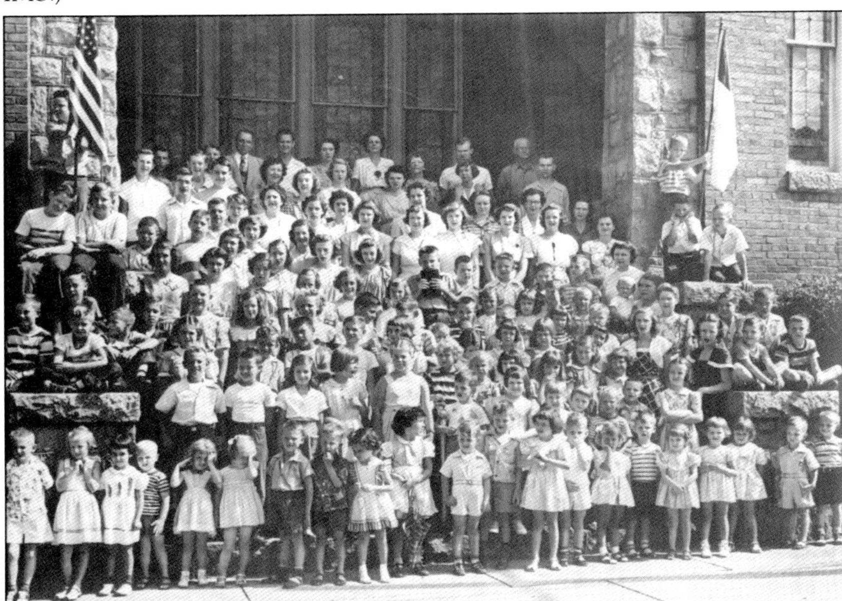

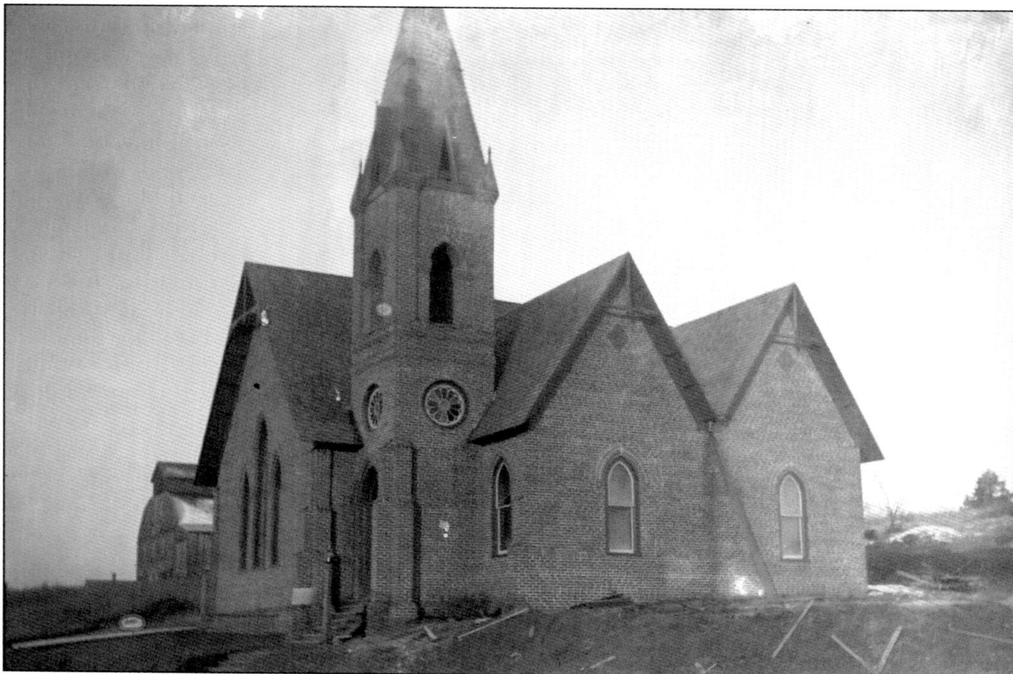

The third Methodist church building, constructed in 1895 and pictured above, was located on the north side of East Main Street and east of Court Street. It was used for services until 1905 and was torn down by 1914 to make way for a proposed hotel to be built by W.S. Gough. The hotel would have extended from Main Street to Market Street, but never materialized. In the picture below, the congregation leaves church services on Easter Sunday in 1902. The cornerstones from this building, as well as the 1905 church, were laid in the floor of the narthex of the current church, constructed in 1959 on Hawthorne Road. The Hugh Gwyn Chatham house is at right, on the site where the First Baptist Church would be built in 1955. (Both, BCR.)

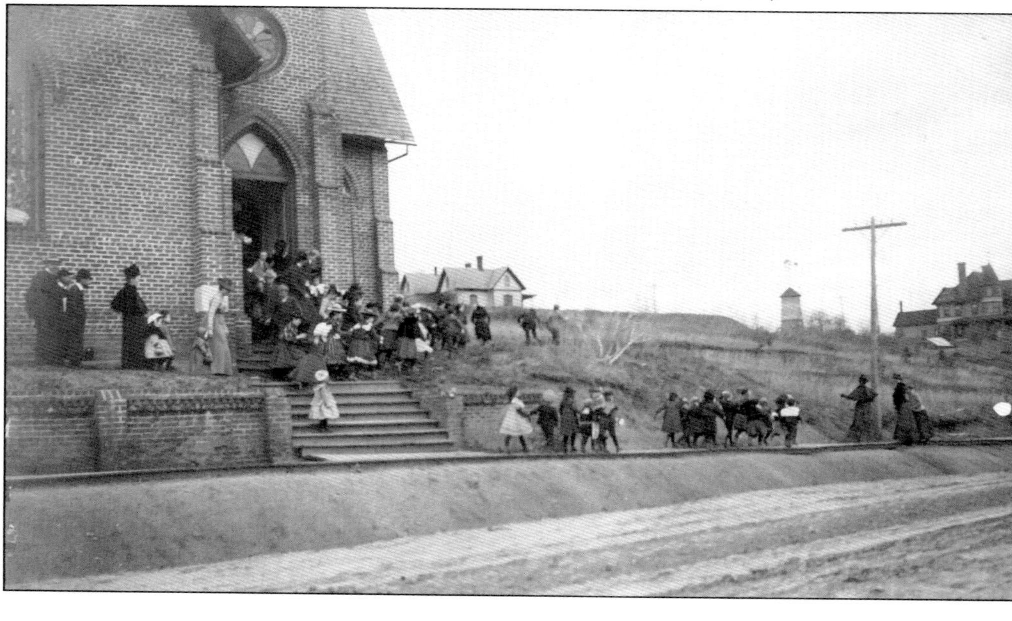

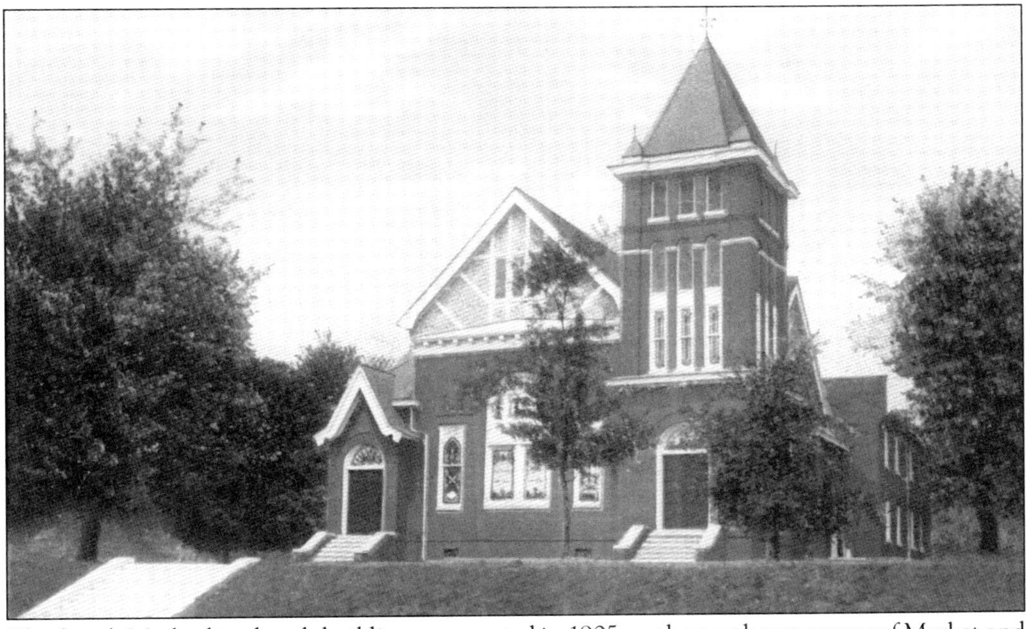

The fourth Methodist church building was erected in 1905 on the northeast corner of Market and Bridge Streets. The church remained there until 1959, when it was moved to its current building on Hawthorne Road. The interior of the church is visible in the image below, from December 18, 1949, when a combined choir from the Baptist and Methodist churches performed a Christmas program. The choir members are, from left to right, (first row) director Nellie Ruth Irwin, Phyllis Johnson, Edna Bumgarner, Mable Sale, Sterling Browning, Jean Royall, Frances Fletcher, Bonnie Hall, and Bonnie Jean Moore; (second row) Maude McNeer, Louise Johnson, Frances Lovelace, Macie Leinbach, Carolyn Dillon, Lillian Browning, Addie Kane, Mary Crowe, and Bettie Alice Bowers; (third row) Joe Wood, Van Dillon, Alan Browning, Calvin Wright, Sam Boose, John Sagar, George Littman, Jim Freeman, unidentified, and Jack Walker. (Both, SJC.)

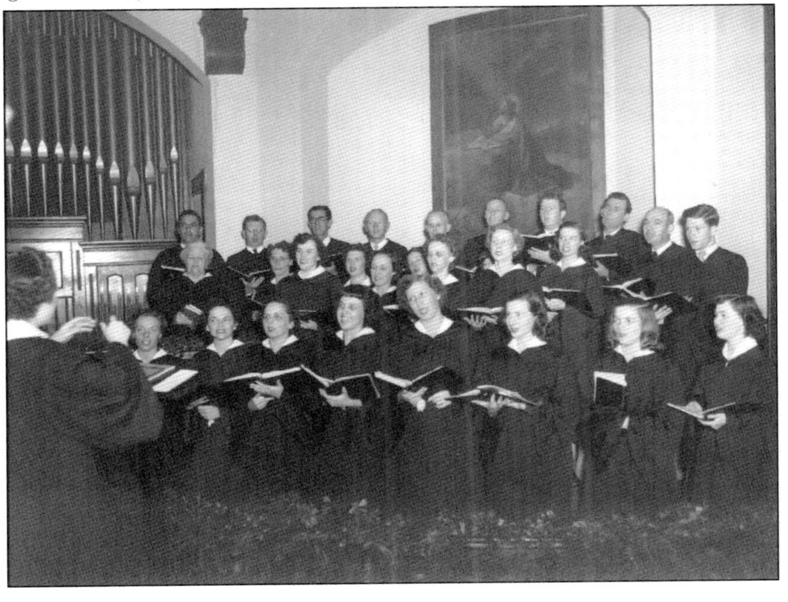

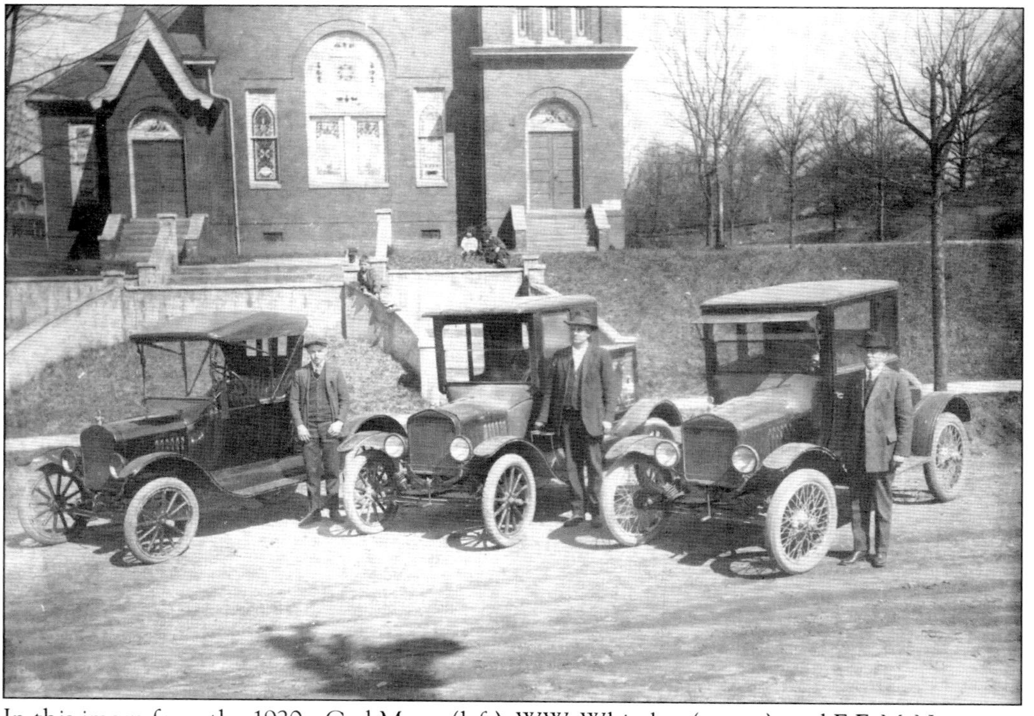

In this image from the 1920s, Carl Myers (left), W.W. Whitaker (center), and E.F. McNeer pose with their cars on Market Street, in front of the fourth location of the Methodist church. This building was razed in 1962 to make way for a parking lot. The Hotel Elkin was across the street to the left of the church. (EHC.)

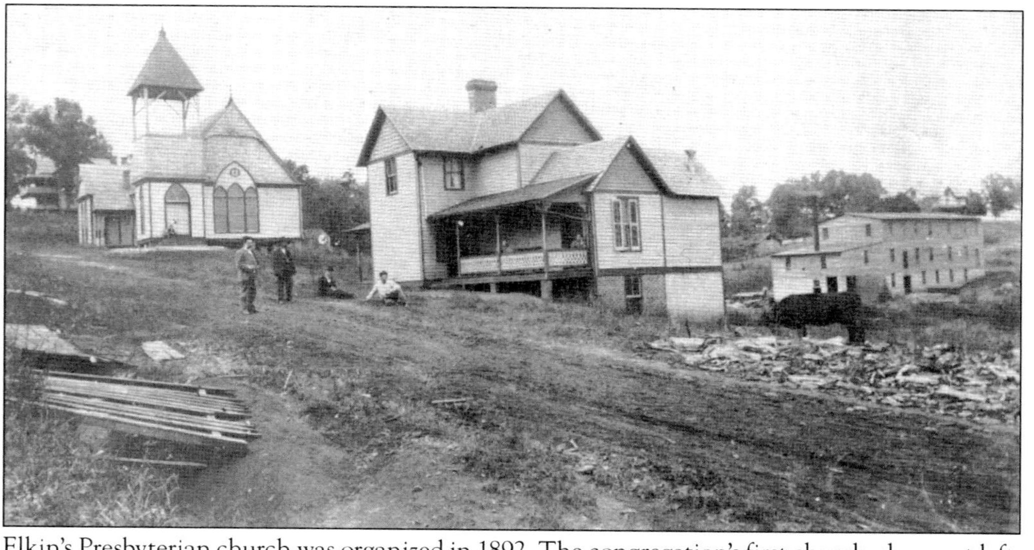

Elkin's Presbyterian church was organized in 1892. The congregation's first church, shown at left, was built between 1895 and 1897 and was located on the northeast corner of Church and Market Streets. It remained there until 1937, when the new building was completed on the corner of Spring and Bridge Streets. This c. 1906 image also shows the first location of the Elkin Furniture Company at right, the same site on which the Hotel Elkin was built in 1925. (SJC.)

Pleasant Hill Baptist Church was organized in 1897 and is located on Pleasant Hill Drive, just west of Elkin. The new church building was completed in 1940 and was fully paid for by 1943. The dedication service was postponed until July 20, 1947, when all the World War II veterans had returned home; approximately 2,000 people attended. (SJC.)

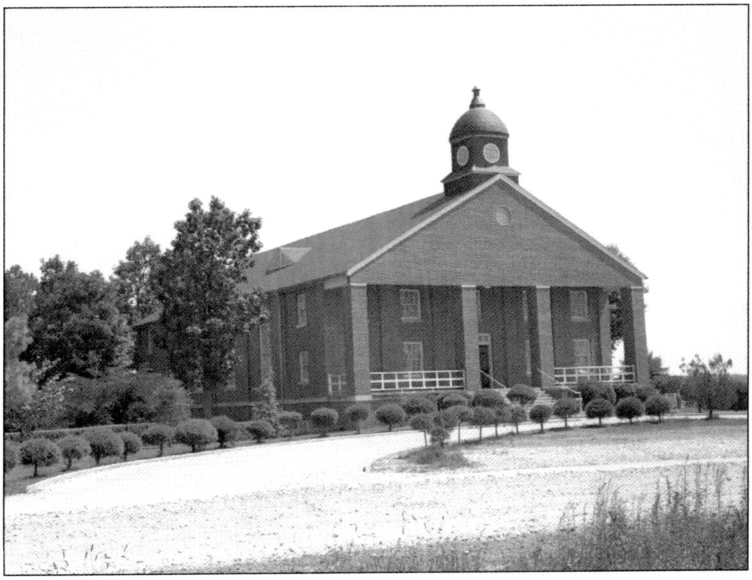

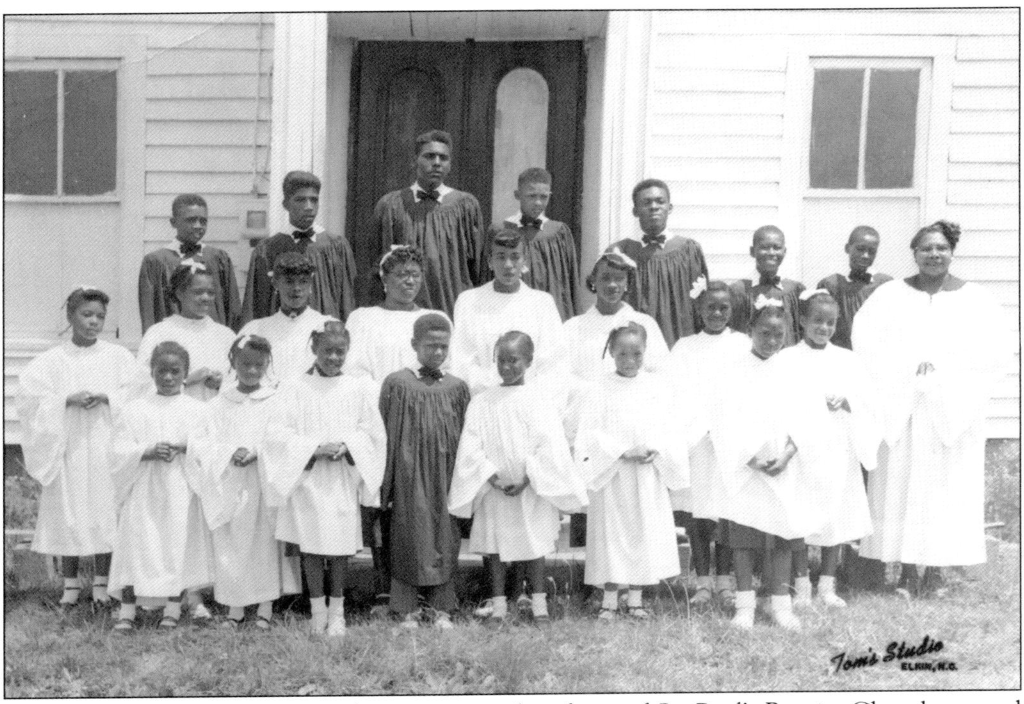

The Oak Grove Community Choir is pictured in front of St. Paul's Baptist Church around 1952. Pictured here are, from left to right, (first row) Paulette Kyle, Kathleen Hurt, Etta Hoosier, unidentified, Helen Vaneaton, Emma Lou Vaneaton, and Carolyn March; (second row) Mary Hurt, Dixie Hurt, Nancy Hurt, Louise Gwyn, Margaret Ann March, Dorothy Green, Francis Hoosier, Mary Nell Kyle, and director Rossie Williams; (third row) Ralph Hurt Jr., Zeb Hurt Jr., Winfred March, Johnny Hurt, Richard Lytton, James Lomax, and Vernon Hoosier. (PKG, photograph by Tom Morrison.)

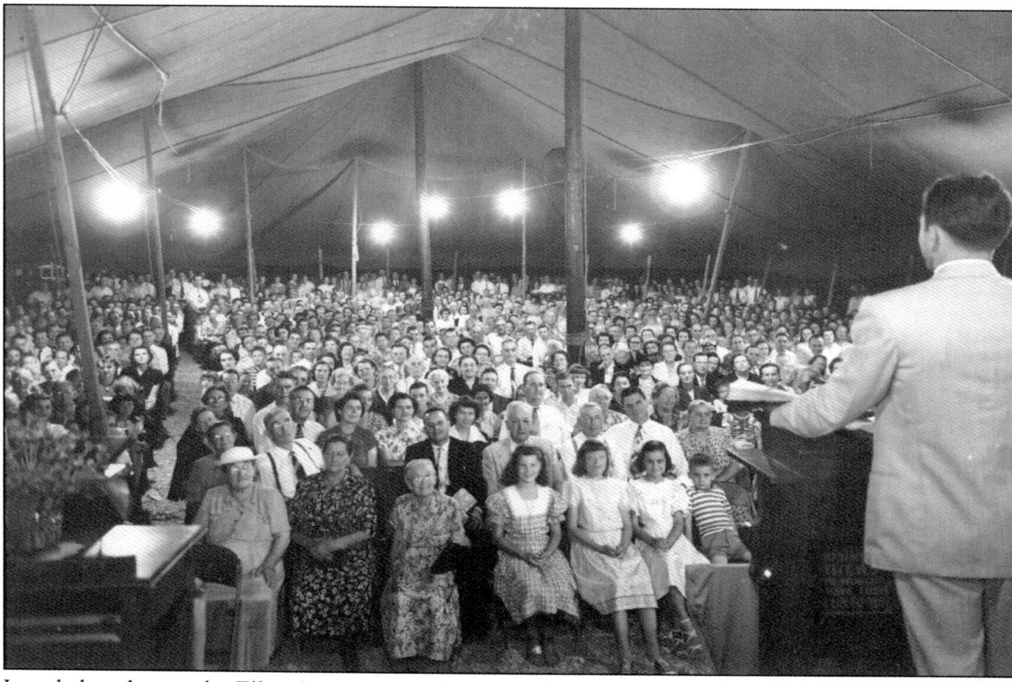

Local churches in the Elkin Baptist Association held this tent revival meeting in the late 1940s in Jonesville, North Carolina. Rev. J. Clarence Gwaltney, the pastor of Elkin Valley Baptist Church, is at the podium. Events such as these brought area congregations together to worship and share the gospel of Jesus Christ with surrounding communities. (SJC.)

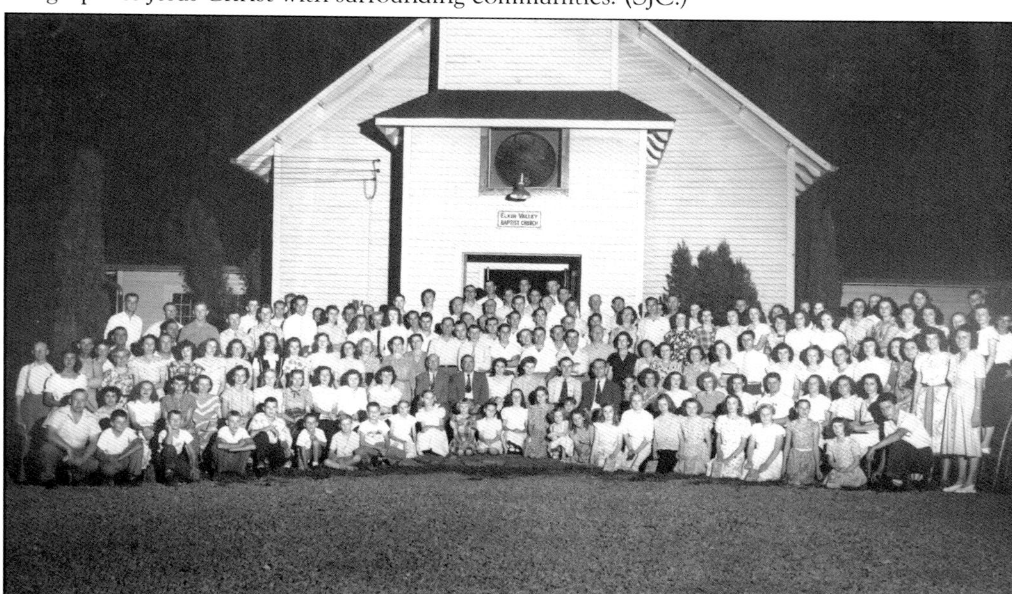

On August 1, 1948, a singing school was held at Elkin Valley Baptist Church in North Elkin. People from several local churches attended the event and are pictured outside the old church, built in 1912. This structure was replaced with a larger brick building in 1953. Elkin Valley Baptist Church was organized in 1884 and was originally located near the Elkin Valley Woolen Mill. (LJ.)

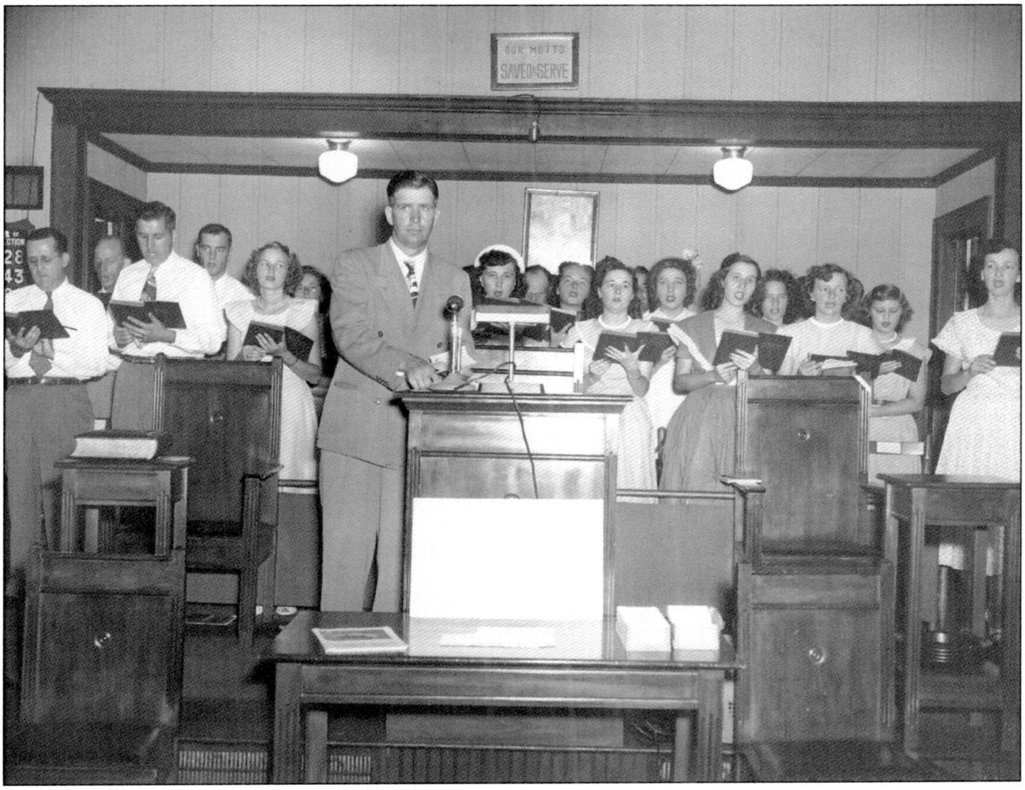

In September 1949, the Elkin Valley Baptist Church choir members are, from left to right, Vaughn Higgins, Brady Settle, Earl Konkle, Herbert Adams, Roberta Groce, Pauline Cass, Rev. J. Clarence Gwaltney, Mattie Johnson, unidentified, Opal Collins, Lula Johnson, unidentified, Kathleen Chambers, Eva Johnson, unidentified, Ruth Martin Gambill, Betty Mitchell, and director Alice Johnson. This picture was taken inside the old church at North Elkin, built in 1912. (SJC.)

A World War II veterans' lunch was held at Elkin Valley Baptist Church in the fall of 1946. Included in this picture are, from left to right, Rev. Clarence Gwaltney, Tom Deborde, Tyre Royall, I.V. Couch, Vaughn Higgins, Garvey Chambers, Dewey Simmons, Riley Mickle, Joel Johnson, Ralph Lawrence, Wilson Lawrence, Fred Reece, Jack DeBorde, Sidney Fletcher, Lytle Tulbert, Junior Joyce, Garvey Tulbert, Ralph Collins, Frank Farley, Mason Osborne, Tommy Collins, Arvil Lawrence, and Fred Hemric. (SJC.)

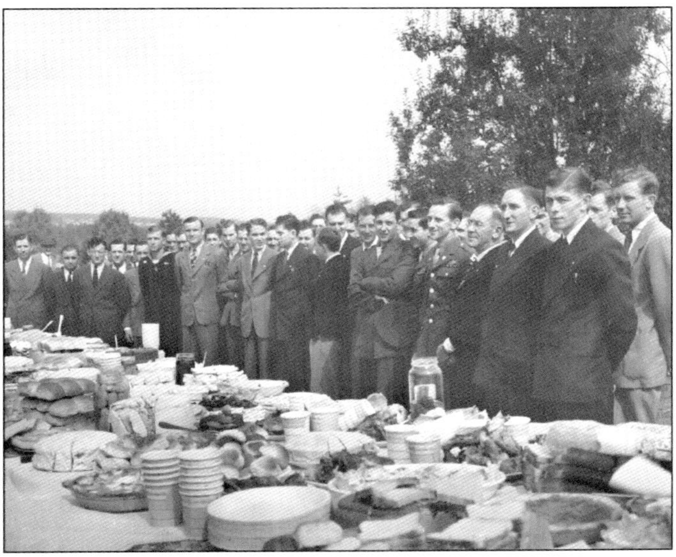

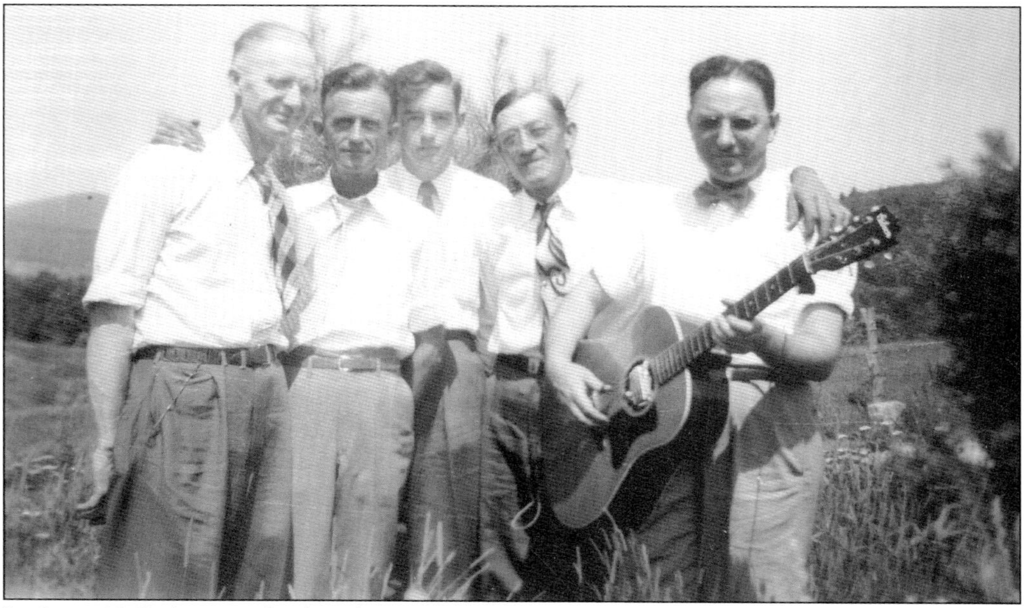

In this c. 1947 photograph, the Liberty Quartet poses at a stop while traveling to a gospel quartet convention in Lawrenceburg, Tennessee. Pictured here are, from left to right, Odell Harpe, Walter Couch, James DeBorde, Robert Collins, and Floyd Carter (holding guitar). The group sang on weekly radio programs in the 1940s on WKBC in Wilkesboro, North Carolina.; WPAQ in Mount Airy, North Carolina; and, later on, WIFM in Elkin. (SJC.)

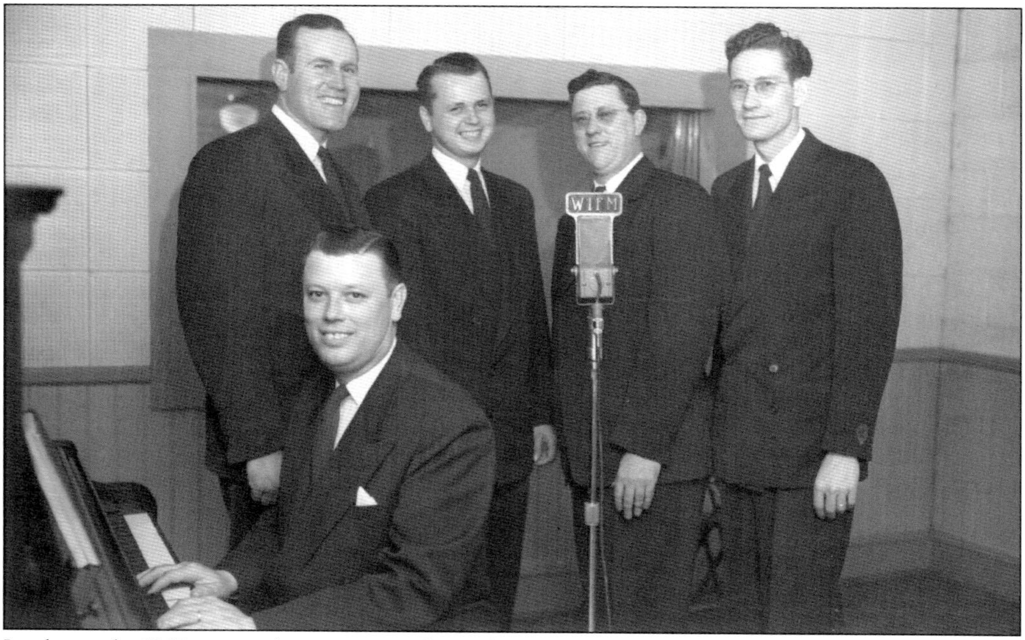

In the early 1950s, gospel quartets, such as the Rhythmaires, had weekly programs on Elkin's local radio station, WIFM. Members are, from left to right, Charles Jones (playing the piano), Harold W. Hurt, Tom Stanley, Claude Reece Pardue, and Howard Frasier. WIFM first went on the air on August 11, 1949. (KCH.)

Four

Excellence in Education

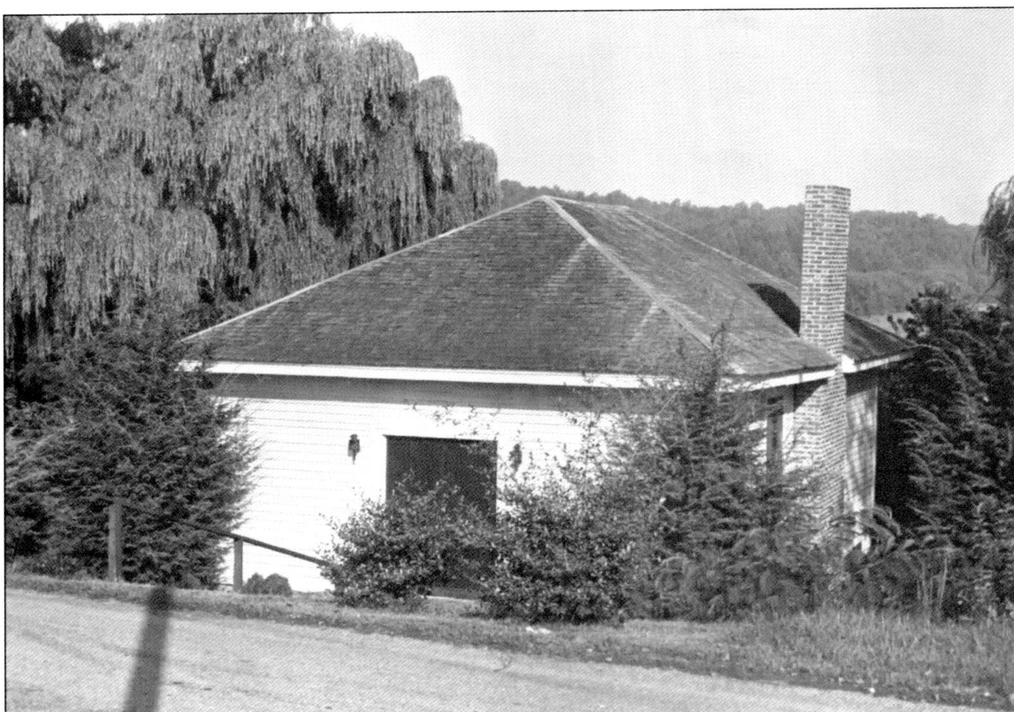

The Richard Gwyn Museum was built around 1850 by Elkin's founding father Richard Gwyn. It served both as Elkin's first school and its first Methodist church. It remained at its original site behind the current elementary school for over 100 years before being moved to its present location on Church Street. In 1952, the Jonathan Hunt Chapter of the Daughters of the American Revolution began restoring it to its original condition and developing it into a local history museum. (JWP.)

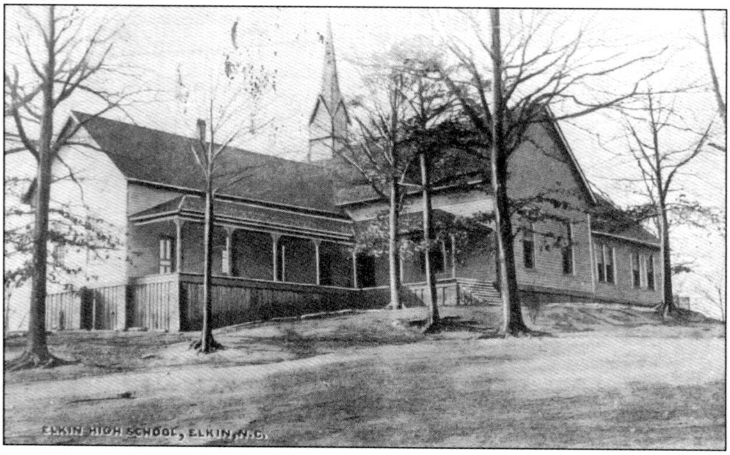

This postcard from 1909 shows Elkin High School, located on the west side of Church Street at the top of the hill. Originally built in 1870, it served as the second location of the Methodist church in Elkin until 1895, hence the name "Church Street." The new Elkin Graded School was built on this site in 1915. (SJC.)

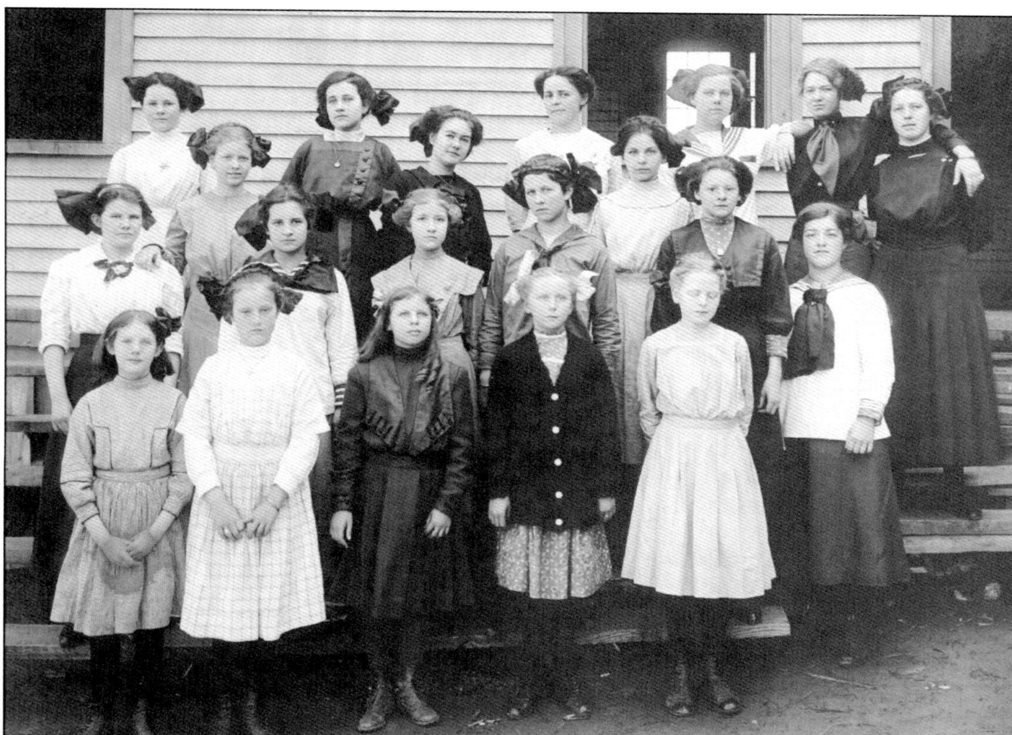

Students in Nell Rouseau's Elkin High School music class are pictured in 1911. They are, from left to right, (first row) Louise Harris, Nina Whitaker, Sadie Greenwood, Mary Reeves, and Willie Paul Hunter; (second row) Lucille Rangeley, Gladys Reich, Maude Snow, Marjorie Chatham, Ohna Harris, and Sallie Blackwood; (third row) Mattie Paul Armfield, Maude Gentry, and Mary Reece; (fourth row) Vista Harris, Boyd Haynes, teacher Nell Rouseau, Inez Billings, Mary Paul Crews, and Catherine Hubbard. (EHC.)

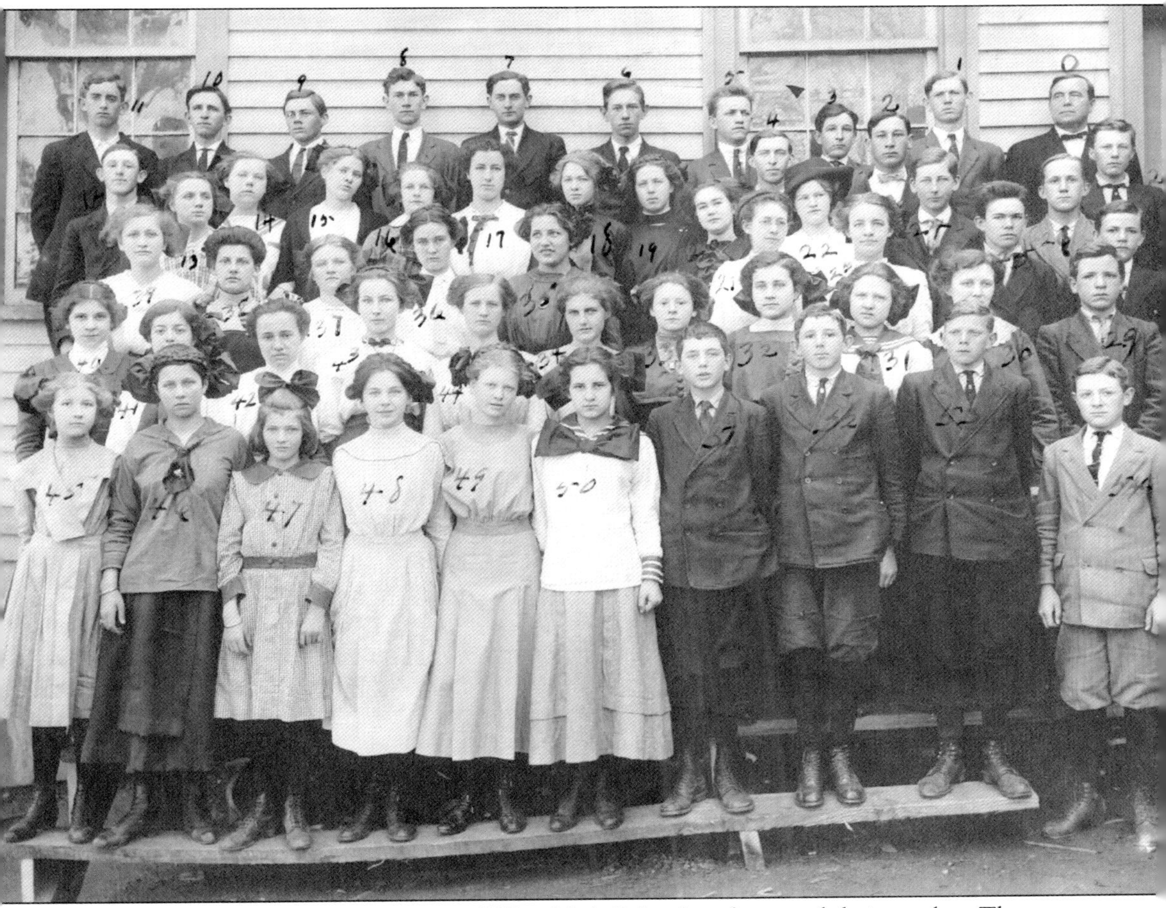

This 1912 photograph depicts a group of Elkin High School students and their teacher. They are, from left to right, (first row) Maude Snow, Marjorie Chatham, Evelyn Bell, Mary Reece, Mattie Paul, Gladys Reich, Marion Allen, Green Casstevens, Wade Ball, and David Holcomb; (second row) Ruth Hubbel, Sallie Blackwood, Jennie Hamby, Mollie Phillips, Ruby Blackwood, Esther Snow, Ohna Harris, Boyd Haynes, Flossie Martin, Bertie Davis, and Paul Reich; (third row) Rena Llewellyn, Nora Russell, Edith Cockerham, Nell Chatham, Annie Russell, Bessie Hamby, Mamie Combs, Carl Gentry, and Harold Click; (fourth row) Noah Casstevens, Fay Alexander, Inez Billings, Mary Franklin, Janie Bell, Effie Crater, Mary Paul, Catherine Hubbard, Maude Gentry, Ruby Cockerham, DeWitt Phillips, Hosea Arnold, and Worth Lyons; (fifth row) Clyde Woodruff, Clyde Beamer, Joe Gentry, Joe Bivins, Carl Gentry, Albert Bivins, Rom Llewellyn, Rufus Felts, Charley Crater, George Gray, Austin Ball, and Prof. J.H. Allen. (EHC.)

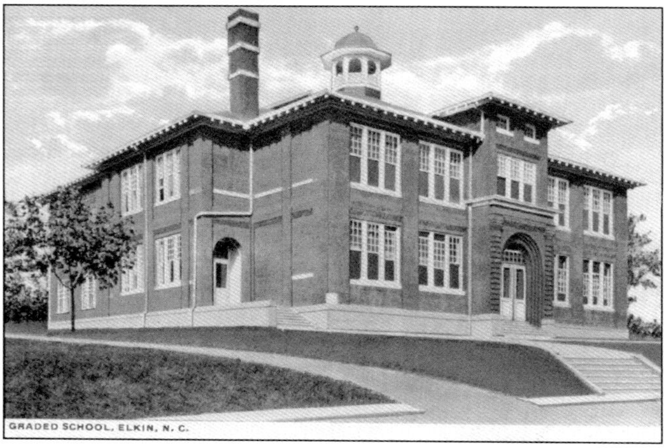

The Elkin Graded School was located on Church Street, at the present-day location of the elementary school playground. The school was designed by local architect John Bartlett Burcham and was built in 1915 at a cost of $25,000. It served the elementary through high school grades until 1936. Prof. Zeno Hadley Dixon was the principal from 1913 until 1925. The building was razed in 1975, but the cupola and bell were preserved. (SJC.)

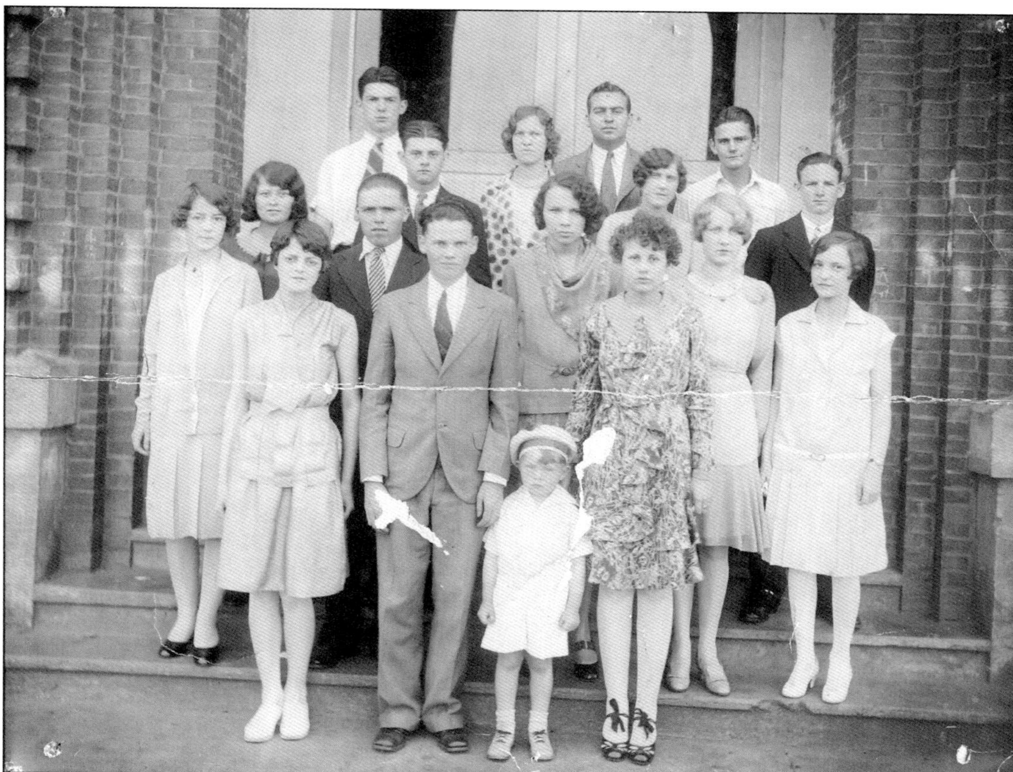

Members of the Elkin High School class of 1929 (some of whom are pictured) include, in no particular order, Mano Brown, Angie Smith, Sue Byrd, Caroline Lillard, Irene Brown, Betty Mae Mastin, Catherine Church, Mae Johnson, Mary Gladys Carter, John Reich, Ben Kirkman, John Triplett, Lawrence Walker, Glenn Darnell, Conrad Gentry, Harold Sale, Berlie Combs, Harvey Gentry, and Dick Evans. Joe Harris is the mascot in the first row. (BHS.)

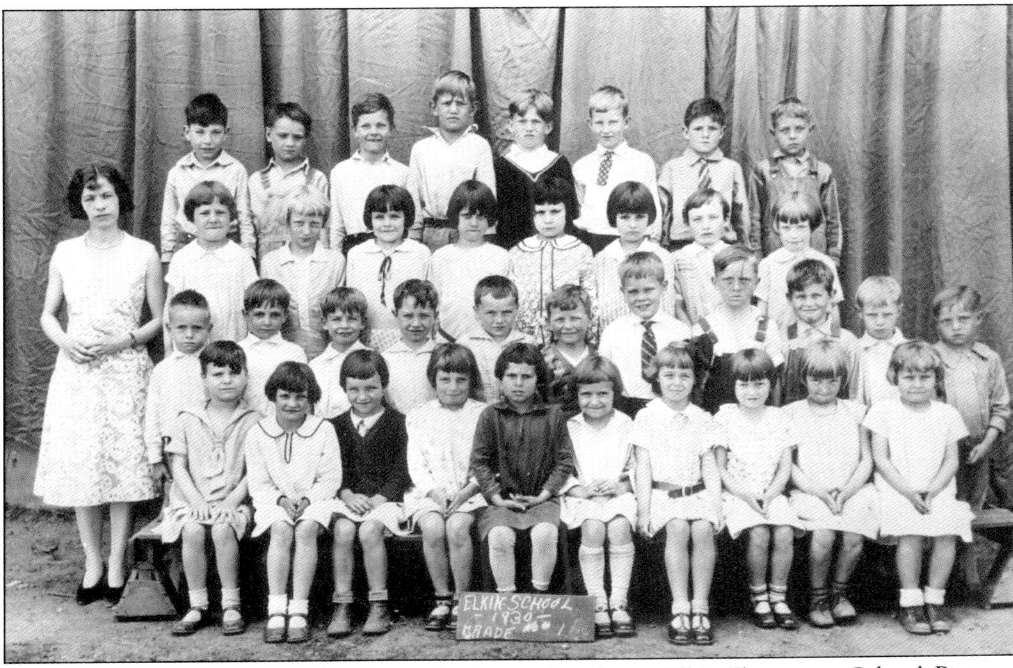

This 1930 photograph depicts the first-grade class and teacher at Elkin Elementary School. Pictured here are, from left to right, (first row) Nancy Moseley, Dilva Burcham, Louise Vestal, Iva Lee Hinson, Annie Collins, Lucille Alexander, Clyde Myers, Mary Teague, Ruth Martin, and Mae Hayes; (second row) Bobby Brandon, Fred Baker, Fred Norman, Bob Chatham, Billy Graham, Phillip Yarborough, James Harrell Sr., Monroe Haynes, Greenville Gambill, Junior Evans, and James Bates; (third row) teacher Mary Hendren, Arlena Arnold, Mary Holcomb, Hazel Billings, Nell Martin, Pansy Burcham, Mary Crater, Lena Sale, and Margaret Day; (fourth row) Tom Whatley, Walt Jenkins, Hugh Laffoon, Buck Lyons, Red Powers, Donnie Harris, Mayhew Swaim, and Bill Eldridge. (JRS.)

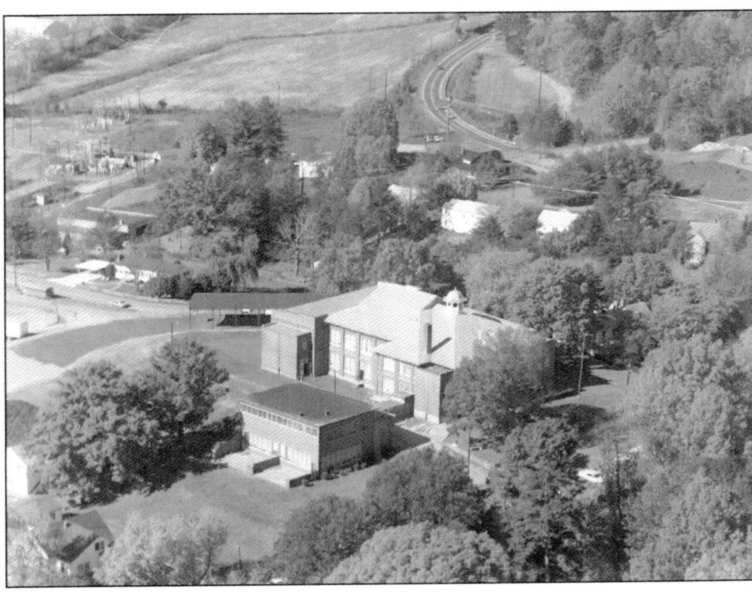

Elkin Elementary School, built in 1915, is shown in this early-1970s photograph by Henry DeWolf Aerial Surveys. The Neaves' bottomland along Highway 268 is at the top of the picture, where the Elkin Municipal Park would be built in 1979. The smaller square building in the foreground is the cafeteria. (EHC.)

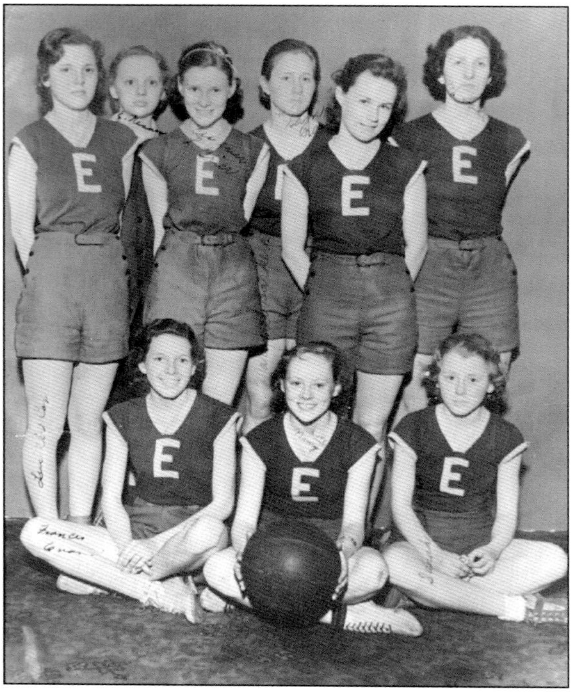

Members of the 1932–1933 Elkin High School girls' basketball team are, from left to right, (first row) Frances Evans, Nancy Click, and Sarah Atkinson; (second row) Lucille Cox, Emalene Neaves, Louise Grier, Margaret Barker, Margaret Greenwood, and Margaret Sale. (EHC.)

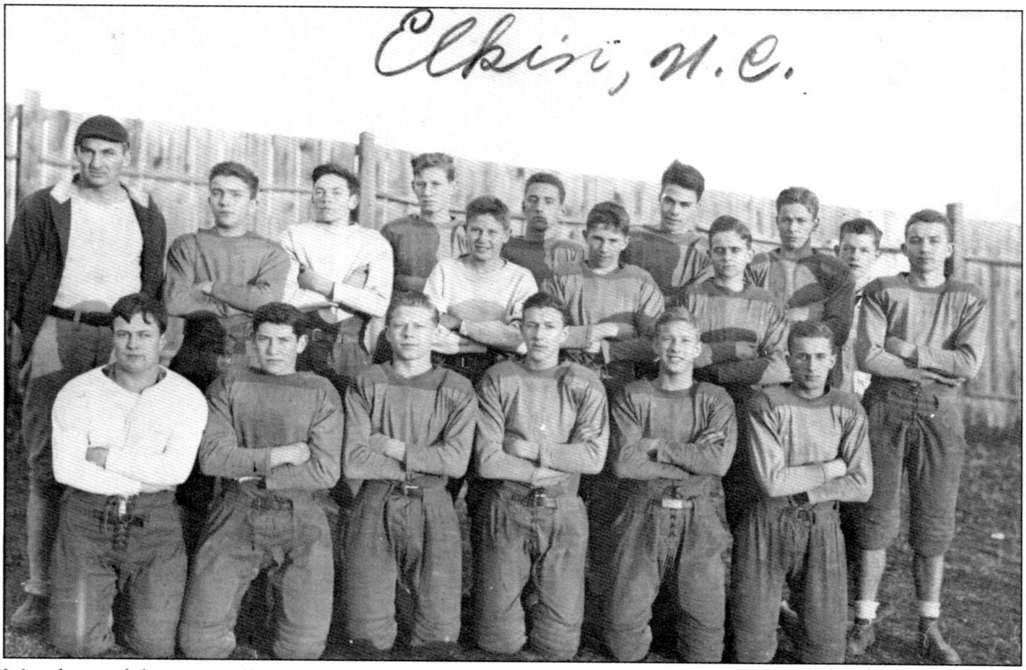

Members of the 1933 Elkin High School football team and their coach are, from left to right, (first row) Gene Hall, Claude McNeill, Lon Dillon, Rufus Crater, Joe Transou, and Clyde Cothren; (second row) coach Brody Hood, John Mastin, Herbert Graham Jr., Charles Harris, Bud Ratledge, Russell Burcham, James Powers, Irving Wade, Bill Welborn, Moir Hall, Rich Chatham, and Alex Chatham. (EHC.)

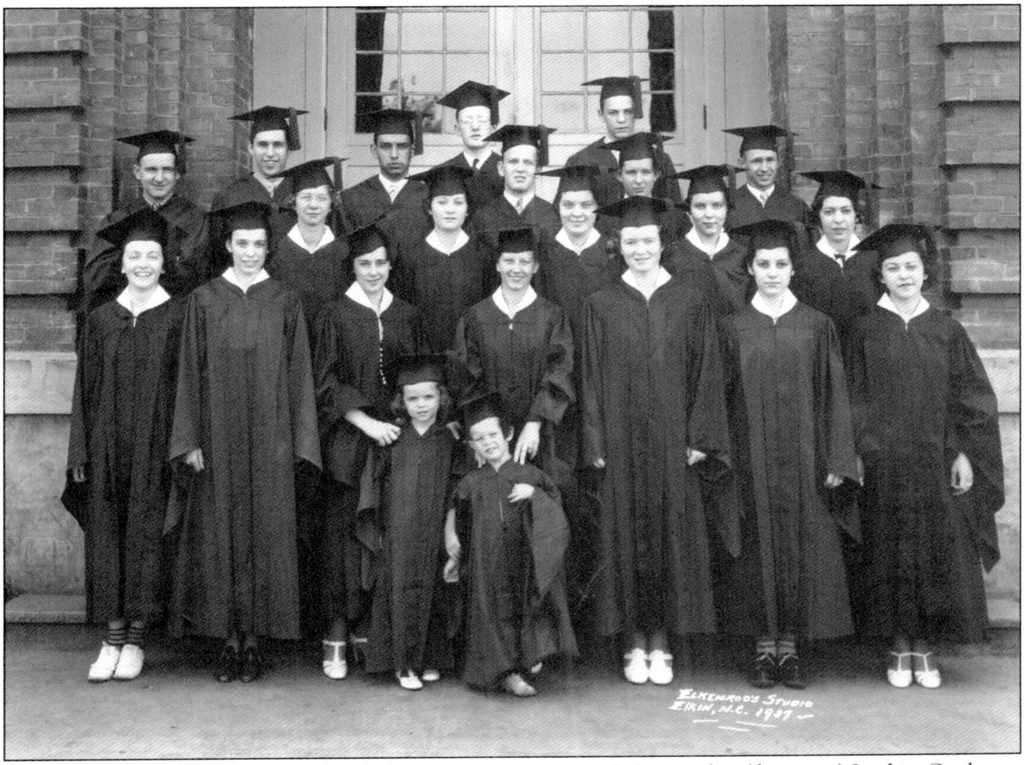

Members of the Elkin High School class of 1937 are, from left to right, (first row) Lesbia Graham, Oleen Norman, Lorine Fulp Carter, Mattie Lee Eidson, Mary Foster, Virginia Lawrence, and Ruth Shumate; (second row) Iris Collins, Lubeth Cochrane, Louise Tulbert, Frances Davis, and Ruth Bell; (third row) Richard Collins, McNeer Fields, Fidell Sale, Herman Sale, Raymond Harris, and Lytle Osborne; (fourth row) Edwin Royall and Cletus C. Wolfe Jr. The mascots in the front are Anna Katherine Dobson (left) and Tommy Roth Jr. (ER.)

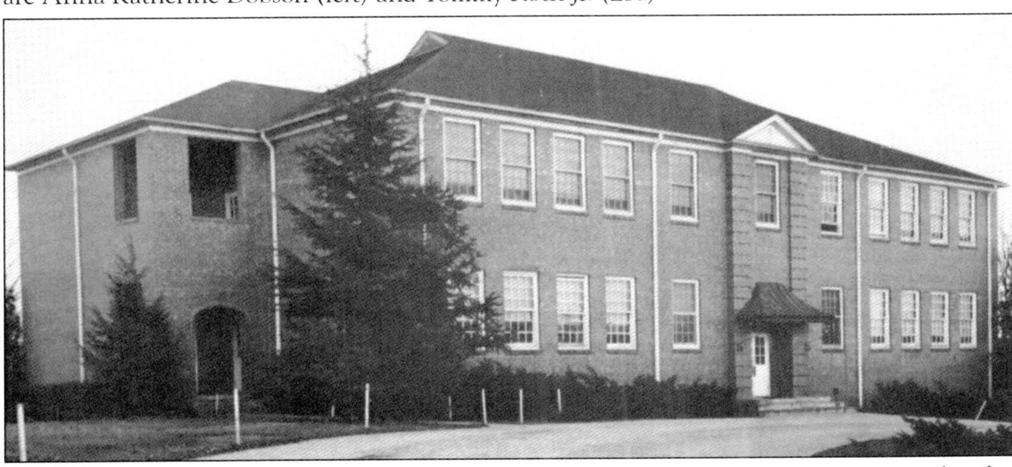

Shown here in 1949, the new Elkin High School building on Elk Spur Street was completed in 1936. Until 1946, North Carolina schools only had 11 grades. Elkin graduated its first twelfth-grade class in 1947, and there was no graduating class in 1946. This building was demolished in 2009 and replaced with a more modern structure. (SJC.)

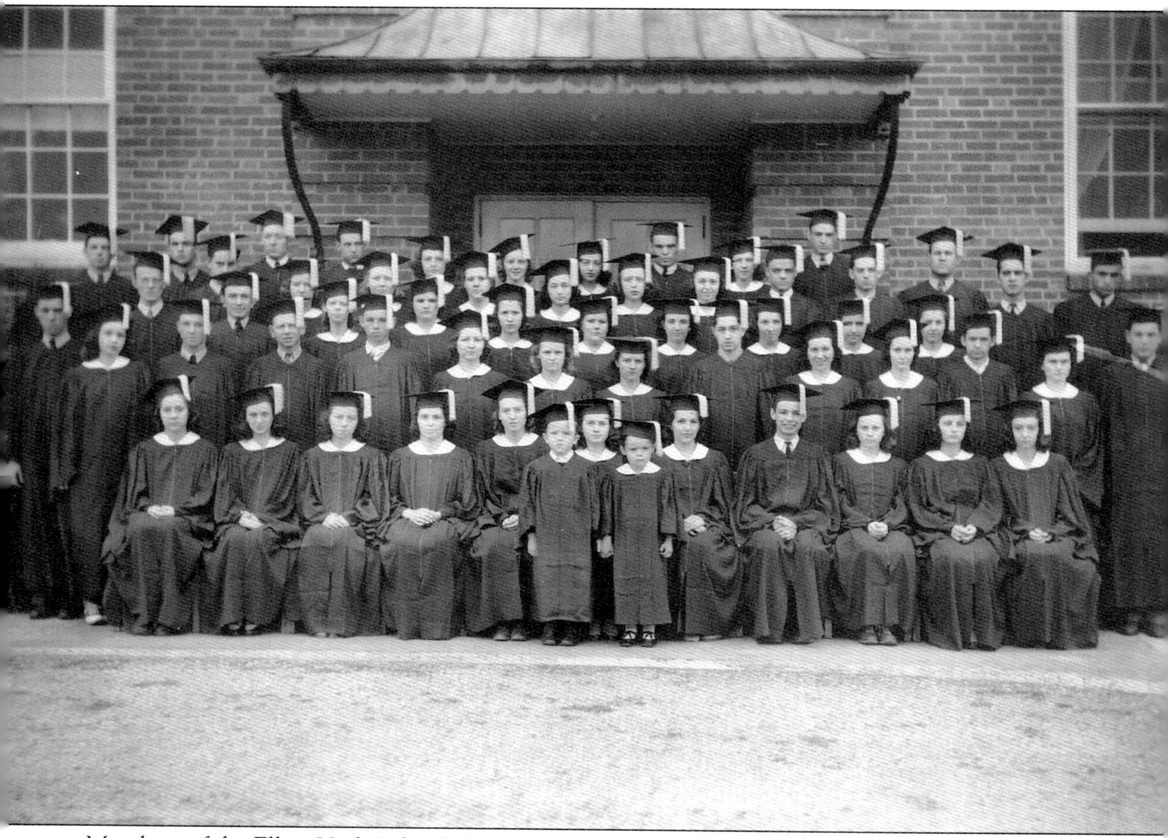

Members of the Elkin High School Class of 1941 are pictured on the front steps of the 1936 school. They are, from left to right, (first row) Josephine Barker, Ann Newman, Connie Hinson, Juanita Gentry, Gladys Blalock, mascot Ray Ferrell, Joy Kingsley, mascot Janice Butner, Mary Crater, Fred Norman, Nan Johnson, Ruby Beulin, and Bessie Absher; (second row) Faye Atkins, Leighton Brown Jr., Sam Collins, Roger Gentry, Grace Cochrane, Margaret Carter, Virginia Holcomb, Robert Chatham, Edna Fulp, Eloise Sparks, Wade Greenwood, Marjorie Kingsley, and Tom Whatley; (third row) J.R. Gentry, Bill Donovan, George Felts, Lillian Mickle, Dilva Burcham, Eva Johnson, Violet Childress, Mary Felts, Evelyn Brown, Lucille Alexander, and Louise Eidson; (fourth row) Hugh Greenwood, Henry Tulbert, Ruth Ray, Susie Grace Hemric, Arlene Arnold, Mabel Davis, Peggy Royall, Clyde Myers, Eugene Aldridge, Jack DeBorde, Harold Hurt, David Jordan, and Walt Burgiss; (fifth row) John Gambill, John Young, Monroe Freeman, Madeline Myers, Geraldine Barker, Helen Gibbs, Hugh Holcomb Jr., Nues Bray, and Clifton Davis. (KCH.)

Nevette Hefner "Skinny" Carpenter was born in Pocahontas, Virginia, in 1911 and died in 1993. Pictured in the 1947 Elkin High School yearbook, he came to Elkin in 1945 and became the principal of the high school and the first superintendent of Elkin City Schools, retiring in 1974. The gymnasium at Elkin High School was named in his honor. (SJC.)

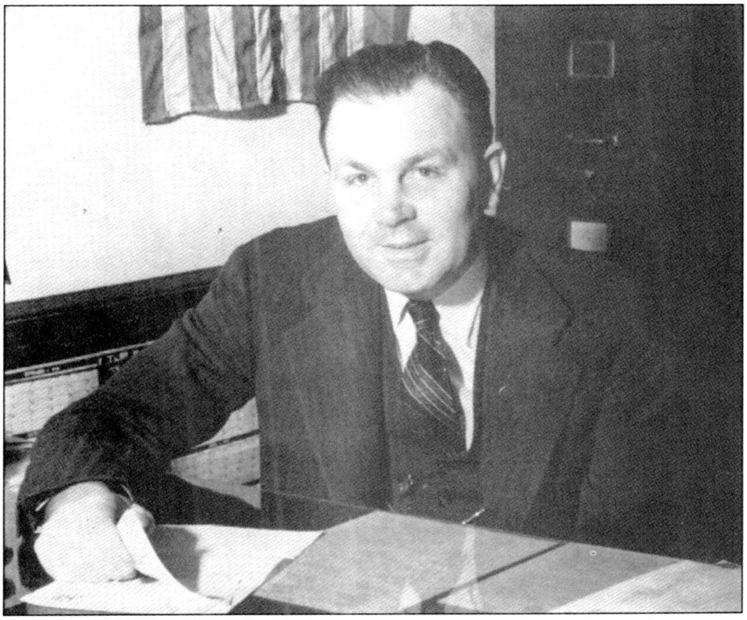

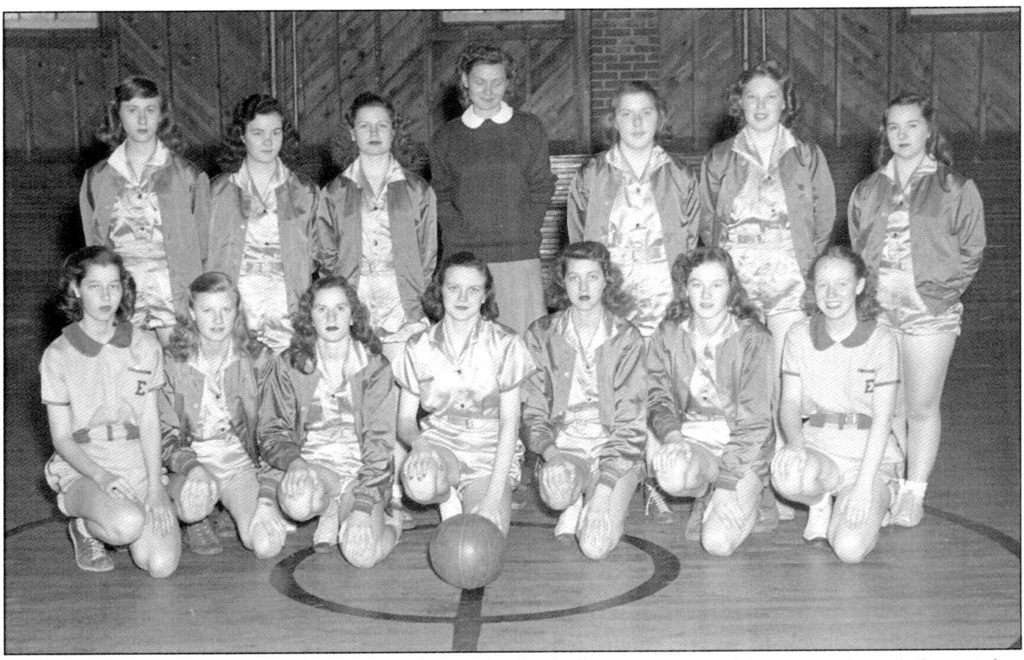

Members of the 1946 Elkin High School girls' basketball team pictured here are, from left to right, (first row) Martha Harris, Libby Royall, Oma Haynes, Betty Lou Steelman, Opal Holcomb, June Miller, and Ruth Masten; (second row) Gene Gwyn Click, Margaret Ann Click, Peggy Kennedy, Geneva Atkinson, Sue Shugart, Louise Smith, and Patty Rue Young. (BHS.)

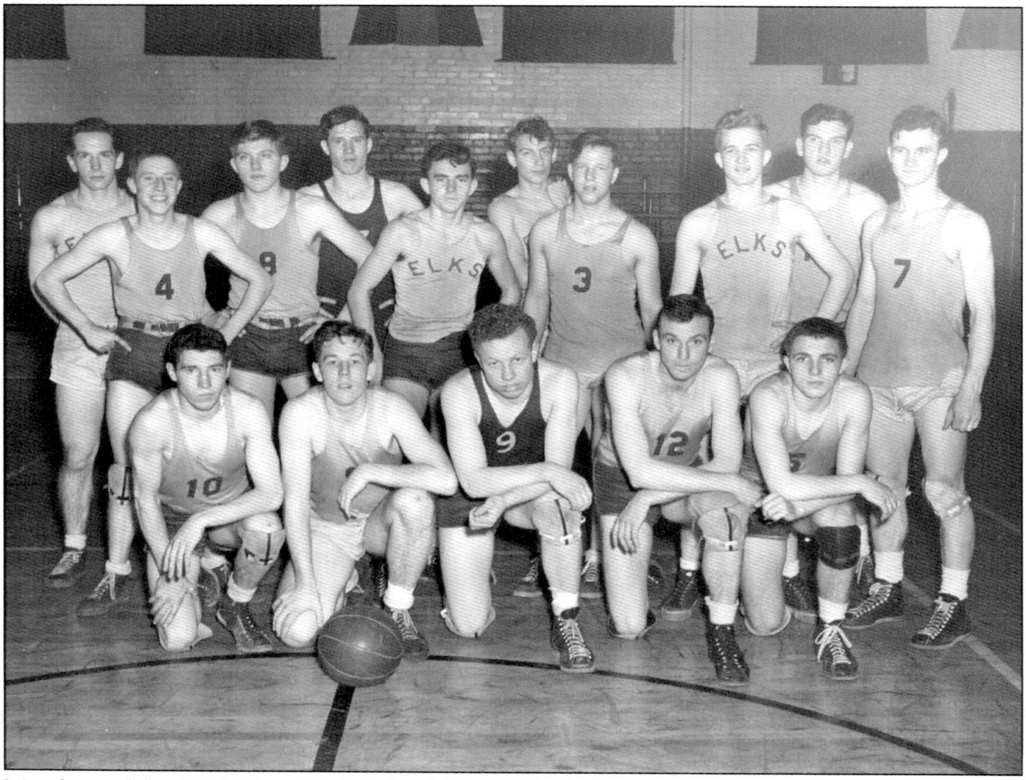

Members of the 1947 Elkin High School boys basketball team are, from left to right, (kneeling) Bob Ratledge, Bradie Osborne, Bob "Cotton" Harris, Robert McCann, and Ketchel Adams; (standing) Coney Couch, Fred Ratledge, Sam Shugart, T.M. Eldridge, Jack Park, Jimmie Crowe, Paul Blackburn, Alvin Eldridge, Bob Lawrence, and Claude Eldridge. (HMS.)

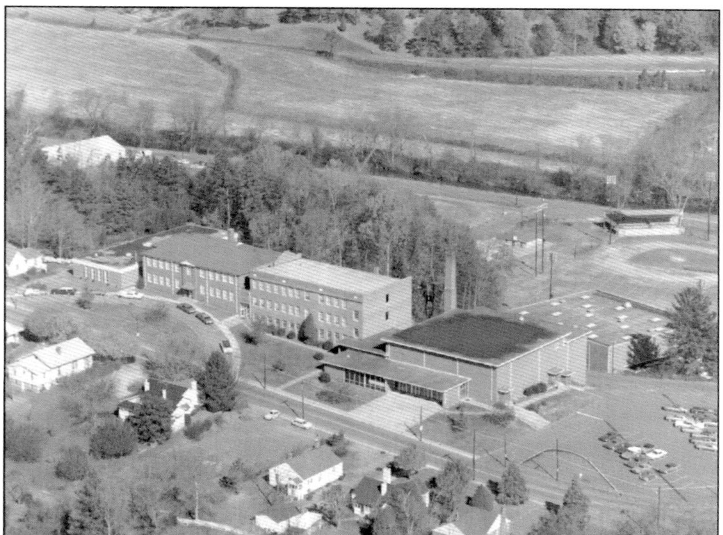

This aerial photograph by Henry DeWolf shows Elkin High School in the early 1970s. The vocational wing on the north end was completed in 1969. The center cafeteria addition was built in 1949, and Dixon Auditorium, named for former principal Zeno Dixon, was completed in 1961. The N.H. Carpenter Gymnasium, located behind the auditorium, was finished in 1965. (EHC.)

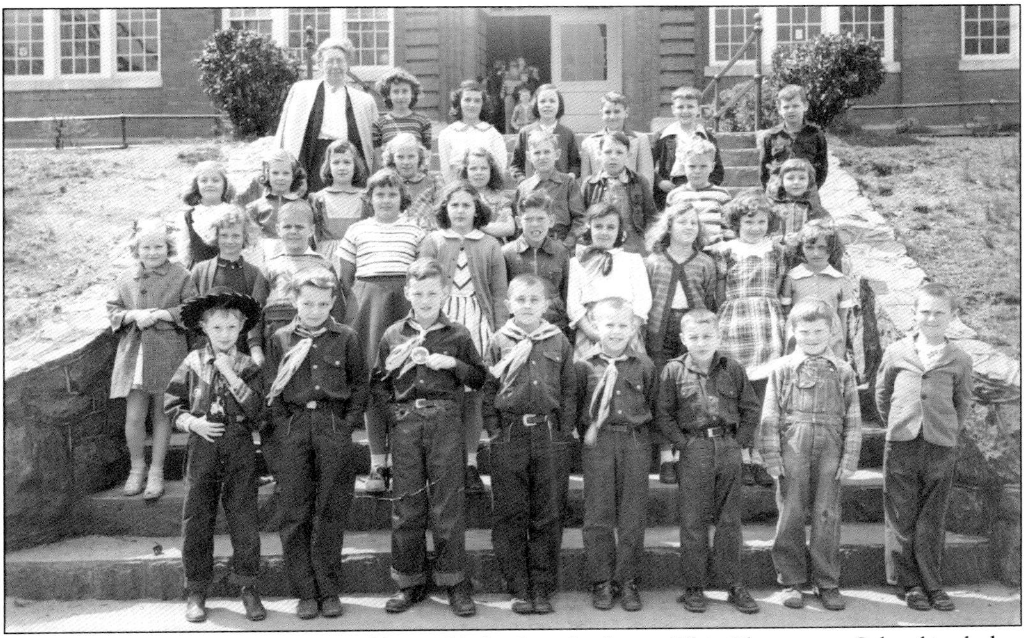

This photograph of Mrs. Spence and her 1950 third-grade class at Elkin Elementary School includes, from left to right, (first row) Tom Dillon, Norman Graham, Larry Darnell, Larry Sprinkle, Ronnie Transou, Johnny Welborn, Charles Harris, and Sam Sloop; (second row) Anne Harpe, Wanda Settle, Donald Couch, Linda Eidson, Patsy Hemric, Gayle Money, Mary Lou Meed, Anne Hayes, Kay Francis, and unidentified; (third row) unidentified, Mary Lee Benge, Sarah Redmon, Alice Cranford, unidentified, Jerry Hemric, Larry Garris, David Helton, and Nancy Adams; (fourth row) Mrs. Spence, Maxine Hemric, Savanna Carrico, Mary Ann Johnson, Frank Gentry, Benny Caudle, and Tommy Lawrence. (SJC.)

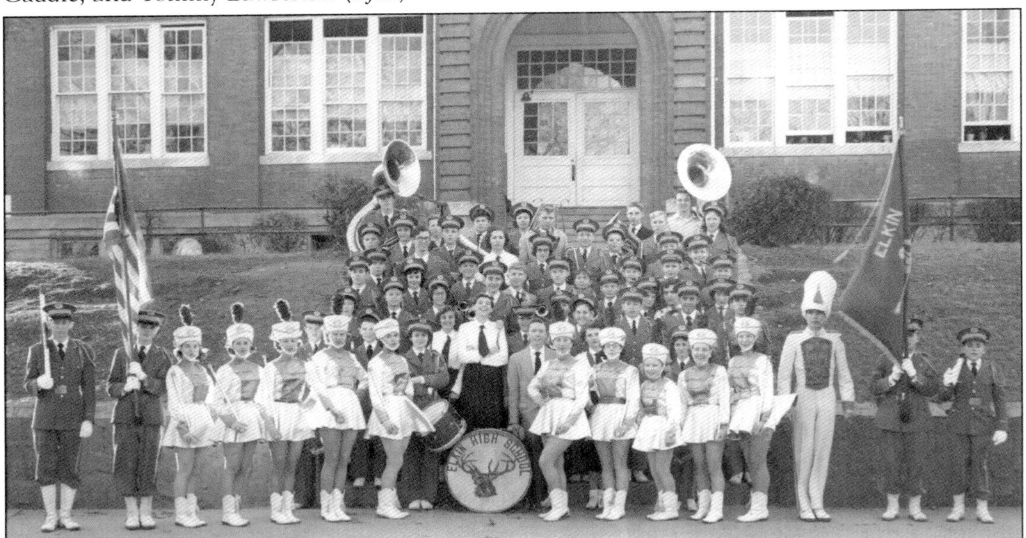

The Elkin High School band, majorettes, and color guard are pictured on the steps of the Elkin Elementary School in 1954. T.A. Orr was the band director, and Jimmy Darnell was the drum major. Many class pictures were taken on these steps throughout the years. (SJC.)

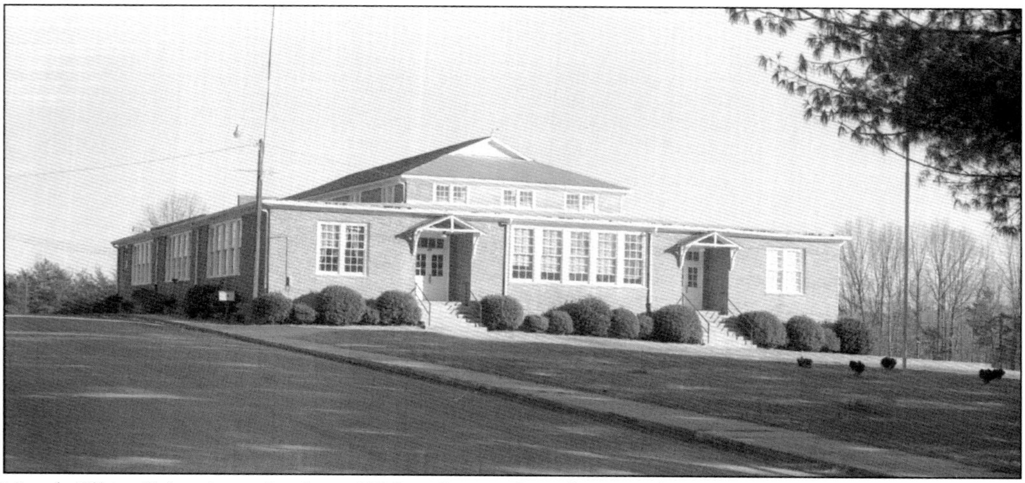

North Elkin School was built in 1926 and served grades one through seven for many years, with one classroom per grade. It was consolidated with Elkin Elementary School in 1960 and was converted to a middle school housing grades five through seven. It was located on old US Highway 21, North Elkin Drive, and was closed in 1992. Pictured here in 1981, it was destroyed by fire in 2002. (SJC, photograph by Randy Hedrick.)

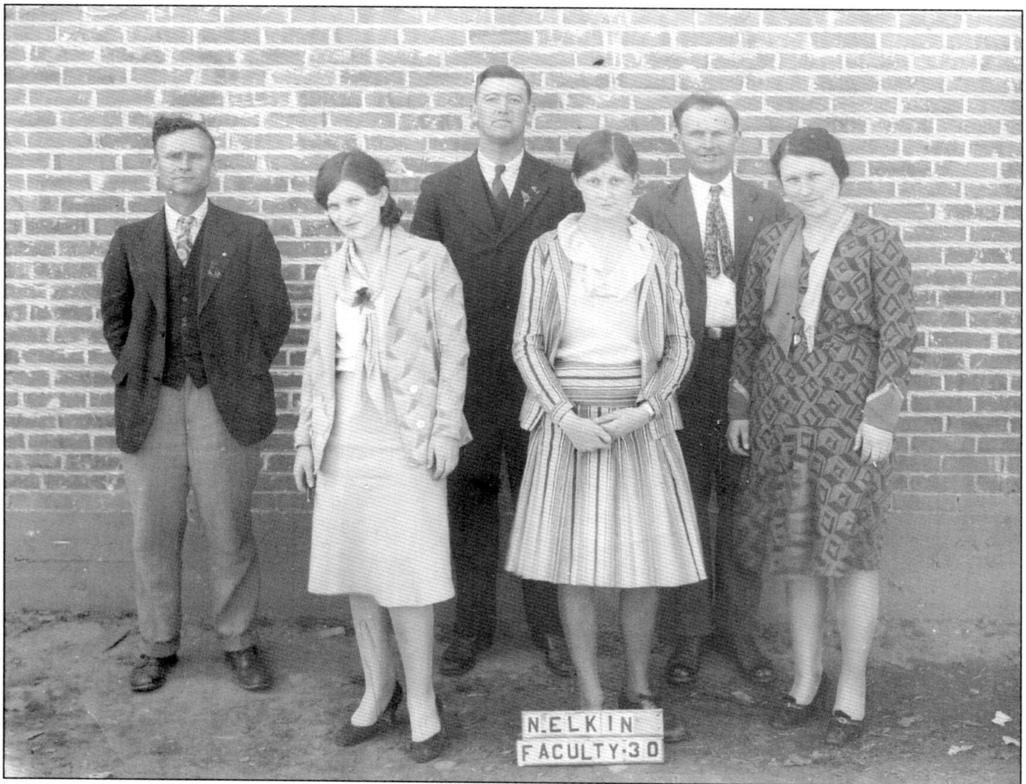

Faculty members of North Elkin Elementary School in 1930 are, from left to right, Robert Guyer, Ruth Sale, Claude Harris, Mary Brown, principal and teacher Don Cochrane, and Arlena Armfield. (KCS.)

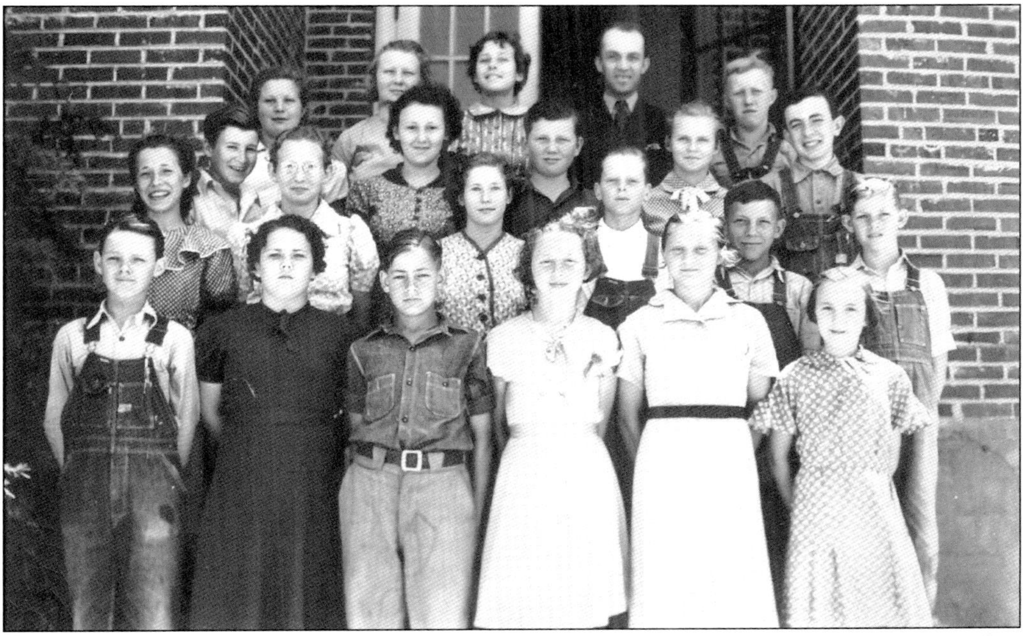

This photograph of the seventh-grade class and the school principal at North Elkin School in 1937 includes, from left to right, (first row) Roger Gentry, Violet Childress, Odell Collins, Connie Hinson, Marie Collins, and Mary Felts; (second row) Eva Johnson, Celia Guyer, Nell Carter, D.G. Guyer, Dewey Simmons, and Don Cochrane; (third row) Sam Foster, Dorothy Steele, Philip Yarborough, Margaret Carter, and George Felts; (fourth row) Doris Nixon, Susie Grace Hemric, Joy Darnell, principal Roy Blackwelder, and Joe Hayes. (MCH.)

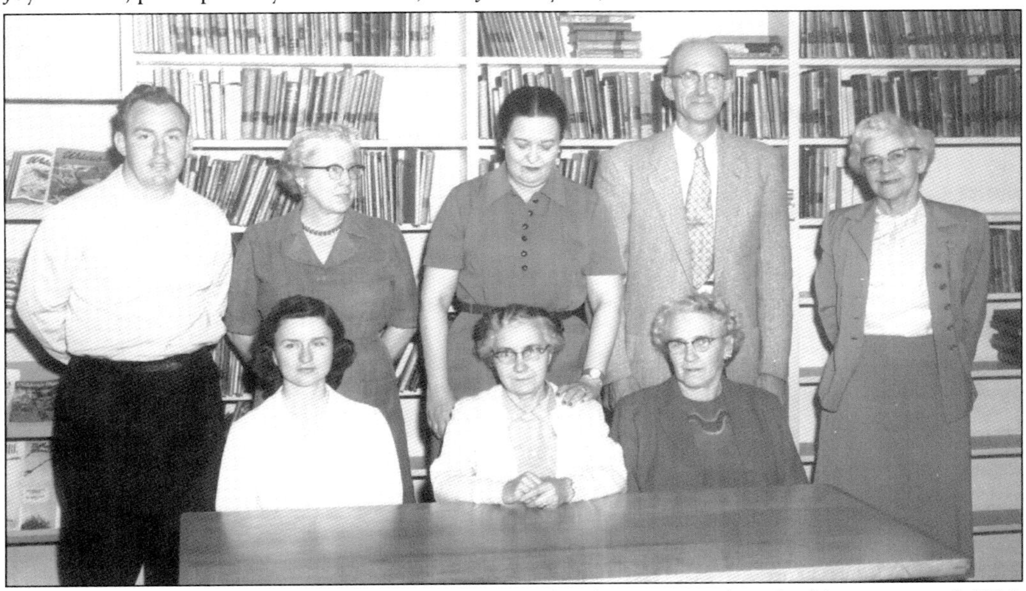

The faculty members of North Elkin Elementary School are pictured in the library around 1954. They are, from left to right, (first row) Kay Cheek Hurt, Esther Click, and Ethel DeJournette; (second row) Clyde Parker, Mary Bette Haymore, Annie Rowe Dixon, principal F.M. Matthews, and Mae Payne. (KCH.)

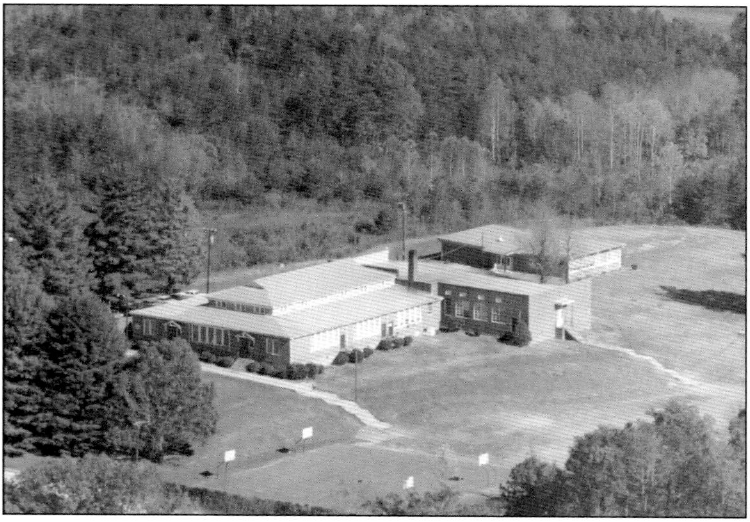

North Elkin School is pictured in the early 1970s in this aerial photograph by Henry DeWolf. The main building was constructed in 1926 and destroyed by fire in 2002. The cafeteria addition behind it was finished in 1949. The building in the back was completed in 1965 and contained three additional classrooms to house the seventh grade. (EHC.)

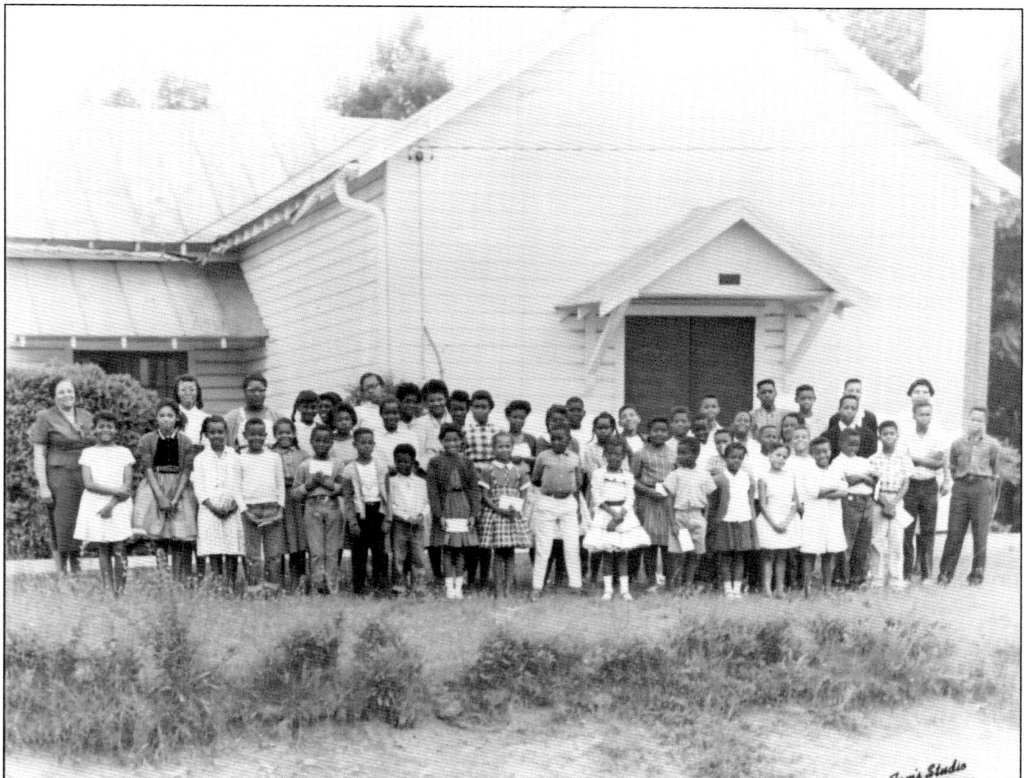

The students and teachers at Oak Grove Elementary School are pictured in this c. 1961 photograph taken by Tom Morrison. Teacher and principal Oressa Hauser is on the far left, and teacher Bernice Davenport is on the right side of the third row. Integration with North Elkin Middle School and Elkin Elementary School began in 1963. St. Home Baptist Church began using this building for services after the school closed in 1965. (PKG.)

Five

Artists, Writers, Musicians, and Founding Fathers

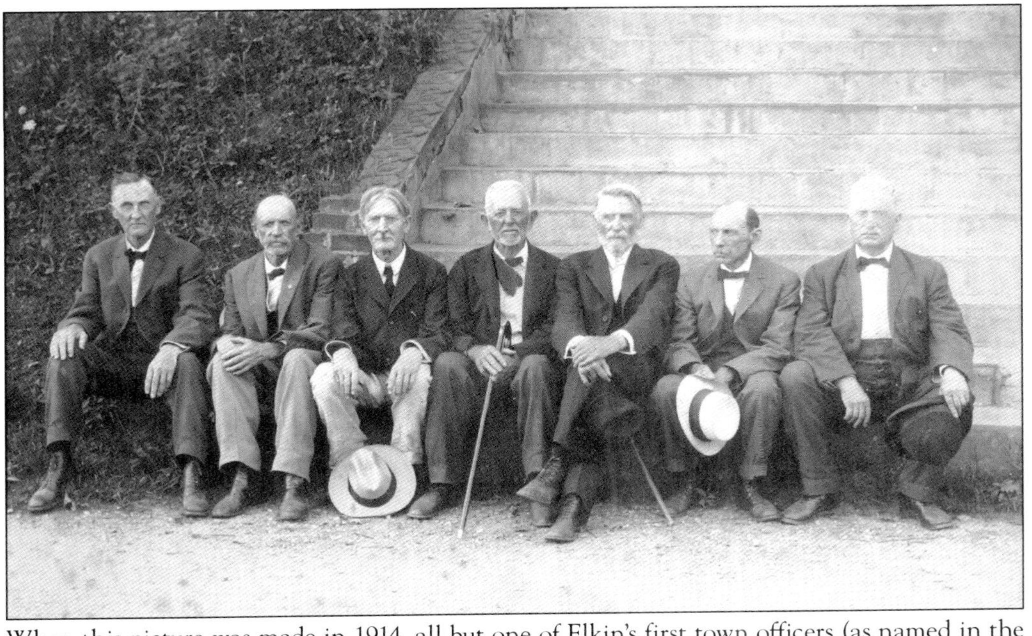

When this picture was made in 1914, all but one of Elkin's first town officers (as named in the original charter) were still living. Richard Ransome Gwyn died in 1894. Sitting on the steps of the Elk Inn are, from left to right, Abel Graham Click, constable Frank Tharp, treasurer and clerk J.S. Bell, former mayor Alexander Chatham, Thomas L. Gwyn, Gilvin T. Roth, and Dr. Joseph W. Ring. (RRB.)

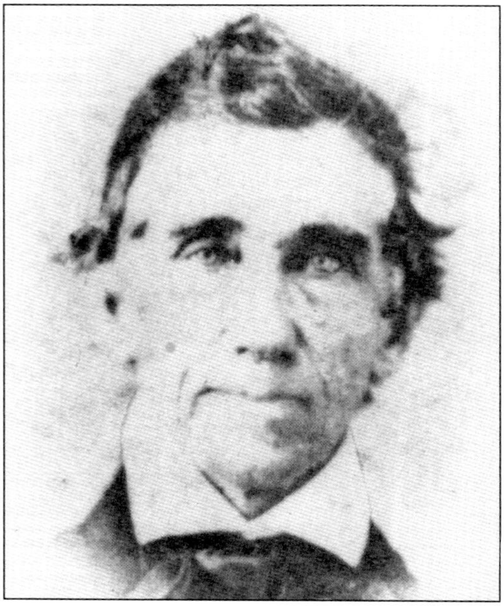

Richard Gwyn (1796–1881), the founding father of Elkin, owned approximately 6,000 acres of land, encompassing the Elkin area. In 1840, he built the first house in Elkin, known as Cedar Point. Gwyn was the first postmaster of Elkin, and he started the Elkin Manufacturing Company cotton mill on the Elkin Creek in 1847. In 1850, he built a one-room building to house the first school and church in the town. Gwyn is buried in Hollywood Cemetery in Elkin. (SJC.)

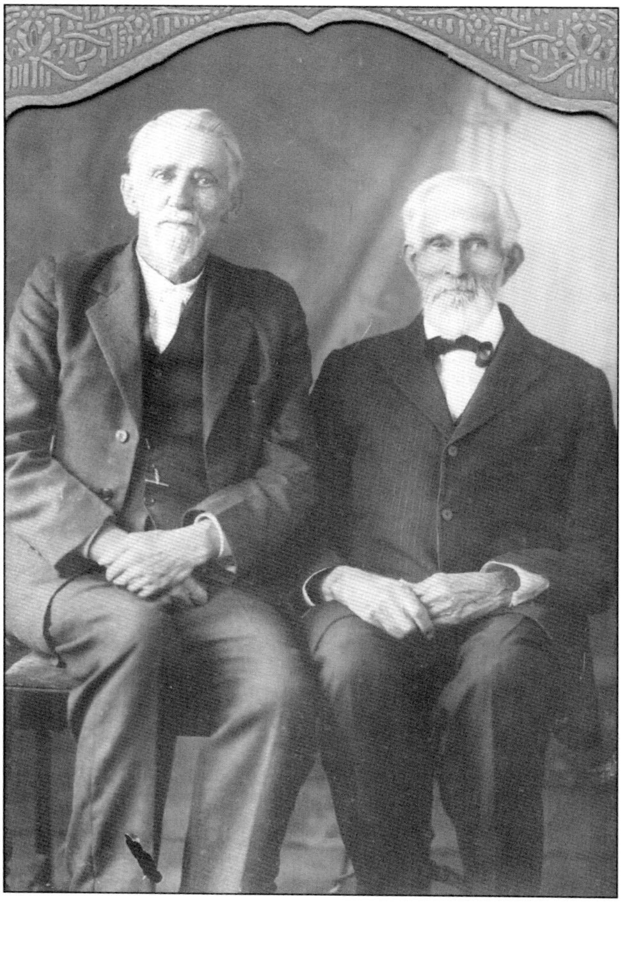

Thomas Lenoir Gwyn (1842–1934), pictured on the left, was the youngest son of Elkin founder Richard Gwyn. He, along with Alexander Chatham, started the Elkin Valley Woolen Mill in 1877. John C. Hurt (1845–1931), picture on the right, was a commissioner of Surry County and a justice of the peace. Gwyn and Hurt were Confederate Civil War veterans and were very close friends because of their shared war experience. (KCH.)

Dr. Miles Andrew Royall (1862–1952) was an eye, ear, nose, and throat doctor who began practicing in Elkin in 1913. While practicing medicine in Yadkinville in 1895, he performed the first successful appendectomy in the state of North Carolina on the dining room table in a patient's home. In 1892, he was elected to the state senate, and he served as mayor of Elkin from 1929 to 1935. His son George E. Royall owned Royall Drug and served as mayor from 1955 to 1961. (ER.)

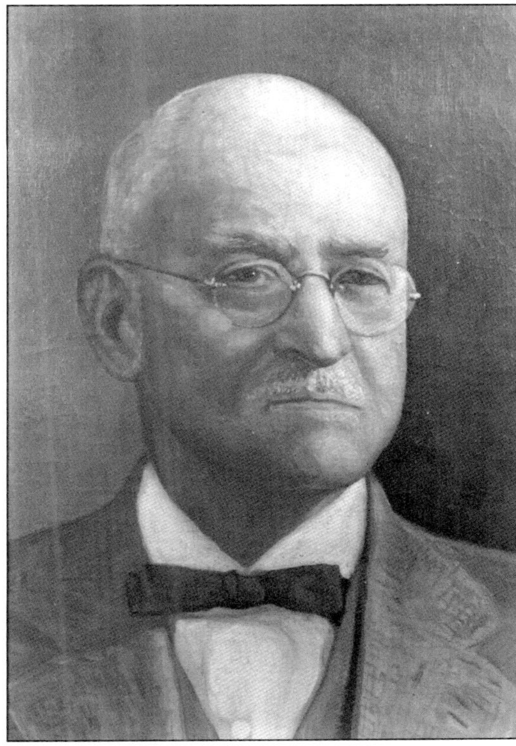

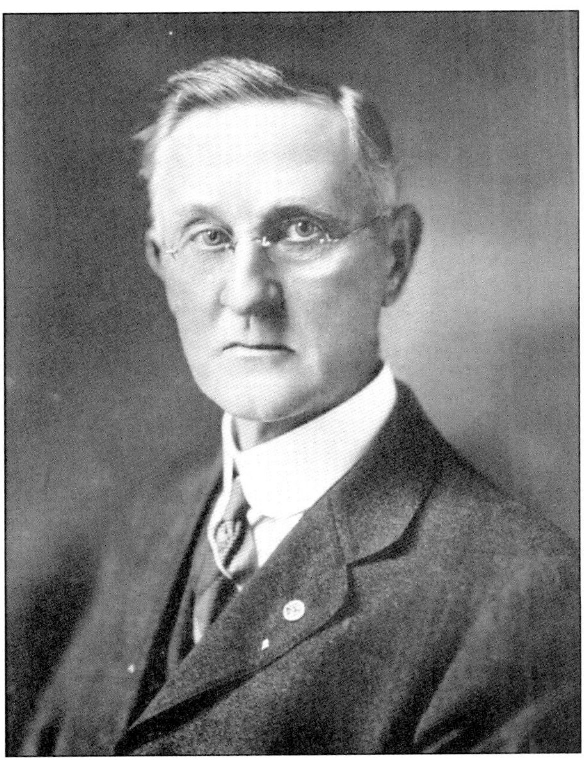

Abel Graham Click (1858–1931) wrote *Click's Veneer Tables* and started the successful dry goods business Click and Company, which was located on the southwest corner of Main and Bridge Streets. He became president of the Elkin Furniture Company in the late 1910s. Click was the father of dentist Dr. E.G. Click and artist J. Harold Click. (SJC.)

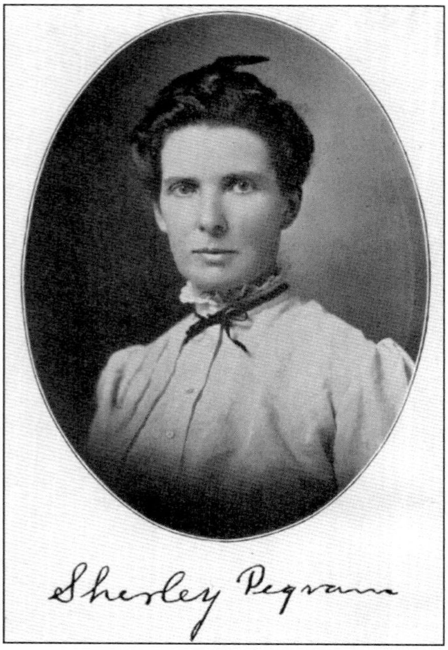

Sherley B. Pegram was born in 1863, the daughter of Robert Wesley Pegram and Phebe Ann Bryan. Known as Elkin's first poet, she wrote and privately published a book of poetry, entitled *Sherley, A Book of Poems Choice and Rare*, in 1911. Pegram never married and lived with two of her sisters, Molly and Aurora, on their farm, located at the present-day site of the Valleybrook community and Hugh Chatham Memorial Hospital. (SJC.)

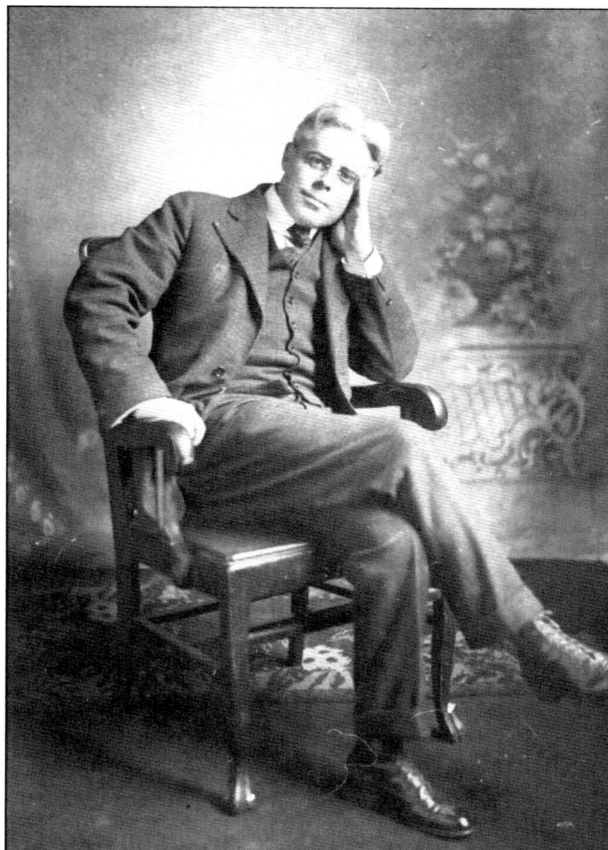

Dyckman Waldron Baily was born in 1871 in Mount Kisco, New York. He moved to Elkin around 1896 and started the Baily Manufacturing Company, makers of locust pins and cross arms. He was the mayor of Elkin for two years in the late 1890s. His family left Elkin in 1903. In 1915, he wrote a novel entitled *Heart of the Blue Ridge*, which was based on the Elkin and Stone Mountain communities and was later made into a silent film. Bailey also published three additional novels and an autobiography. (EHC.)

Walter Couch and the Wilkes Ramblers recorded four songs for RCA Victor in February 1937, and two 78-rpm records were released on the Bluebird label. This photograph was taken at the recording session at the Hotel Charlotte, which no longer exists. Pictured here are band members Bonson Couch (left), his brother Walter Couch (center), and their first cousin Kelly Couch. They performed for many local dances and also had a program on WAIR in Winston-Salem until August 1937. (SJC.)

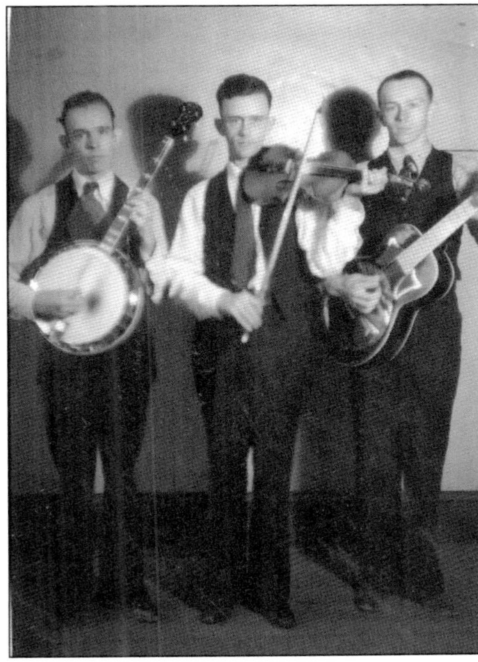

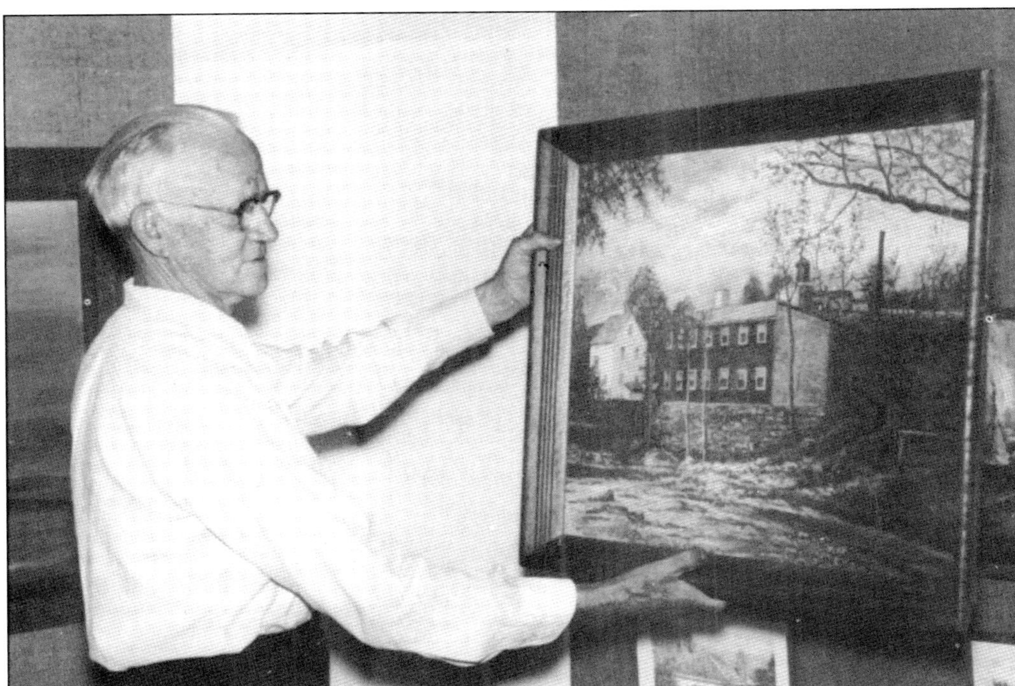

J. Harold Click (1896–1978), an Elkin native, studied art at the Pratt Institute in New York in 1922. He is pictured in 1969 with his painting of the Elkin Manufacturing Company, which was located near Elkin Creek at the present-day site of the Elkin Public Library. Click was well known for his oil and watercolor paintings of gamecocks, as well as scenic views of Elkin. He is buried in Hollywood Cemetery in Elkin. (SJC.)

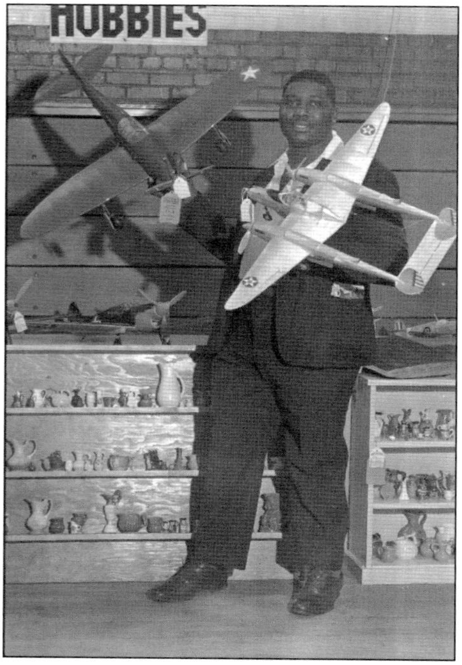

Clifford Morrison was well known in the Elkin community for his various types of folk art, including paintings and wood carvings. He is pictured in October 1944 at a Chatham Manufacturing employee fair, where he won a prize for his model airplanes. Morrison died in 1988, and the Foothills Arts Council in Elkin holds an annual juried art show in his memory. (SJC.)

In 1961, the *Elkin Tribune* celebrated its 50th anniversary with an eight-section, 64-page paper. Publisher Harvey Laffoon (left) and assistant publisher Alan Browning Jr. hold the section describing Elkin churches. Laffoon was the editor and publisher of the *Elkin Tribune* from 1926 until 1968. During his tenure, the paper won 60 state and national awards for excellence. Laffoon began his newspaper career working for the *Elkin Times* in 1913. (EHC.)

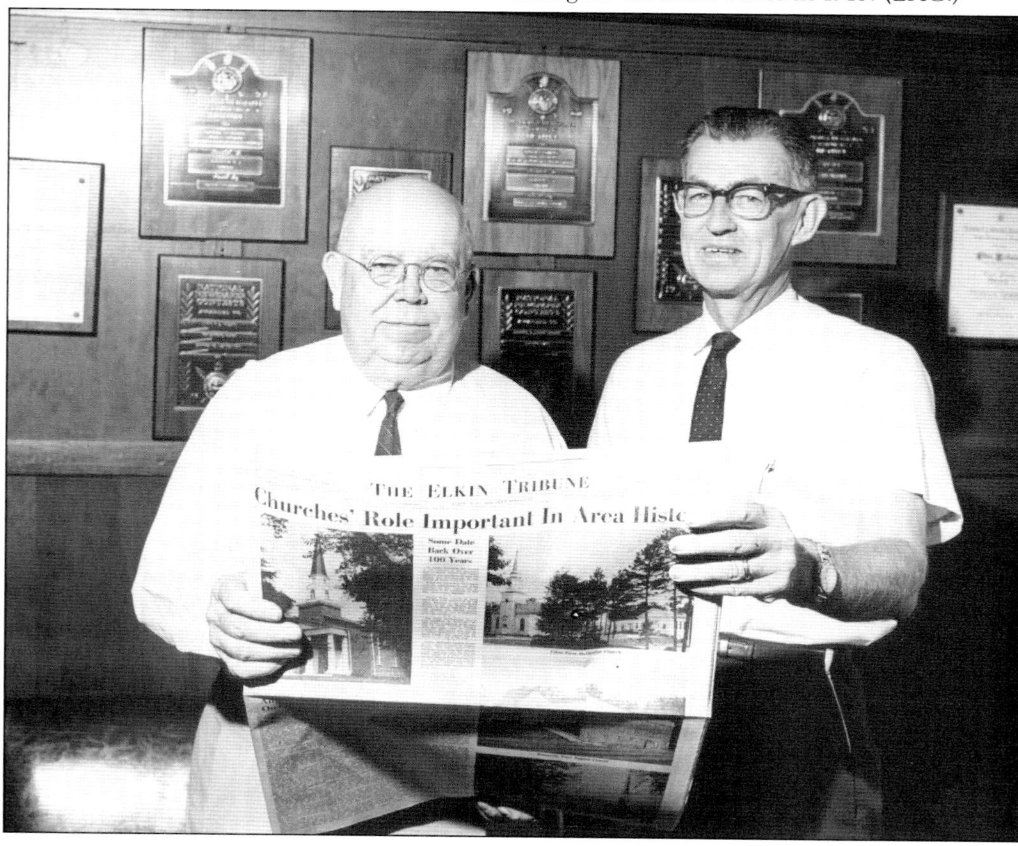

Six

The Elkin & Alleghany Railway

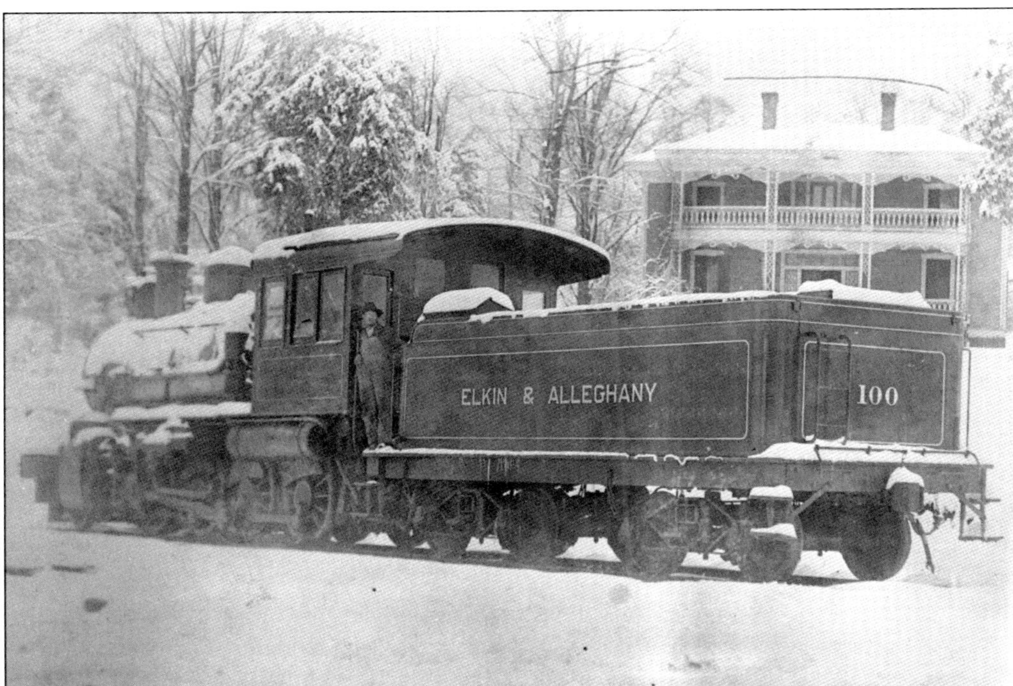

Engineer Dallas McCoin and the Elkin & Alleghany (E&A) Railway engine, a 2-8-0, cross West Main Street in front of the Richard Ransome Gwyn house on March 11, 1912. The E&A Railway Company was incorporated in 1907. Major supporters were Gov. Rufus A. Doughton and Hugh G. Chatham. The goal of the railway was to connect a line from Elkin to Jefferson, approximately 60 miles away. (JWP.)

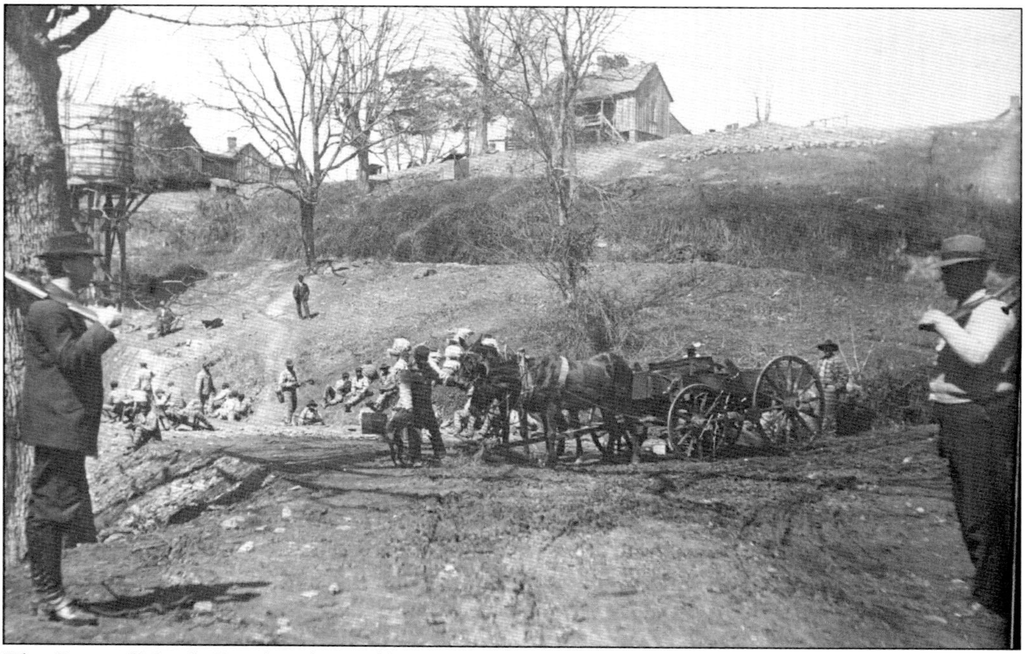

The State of North Carolina loaned between 50 and 100 prisoners to the railway for construction purposes in exchange for stock in the company. The convicts are shown working under guard in 1908 in the vicinity of the present-day location of the Elkin Public Library. Cotton Mill Hill is in the background, with houses overlooking Elkin Creek on the left. (JWP.)

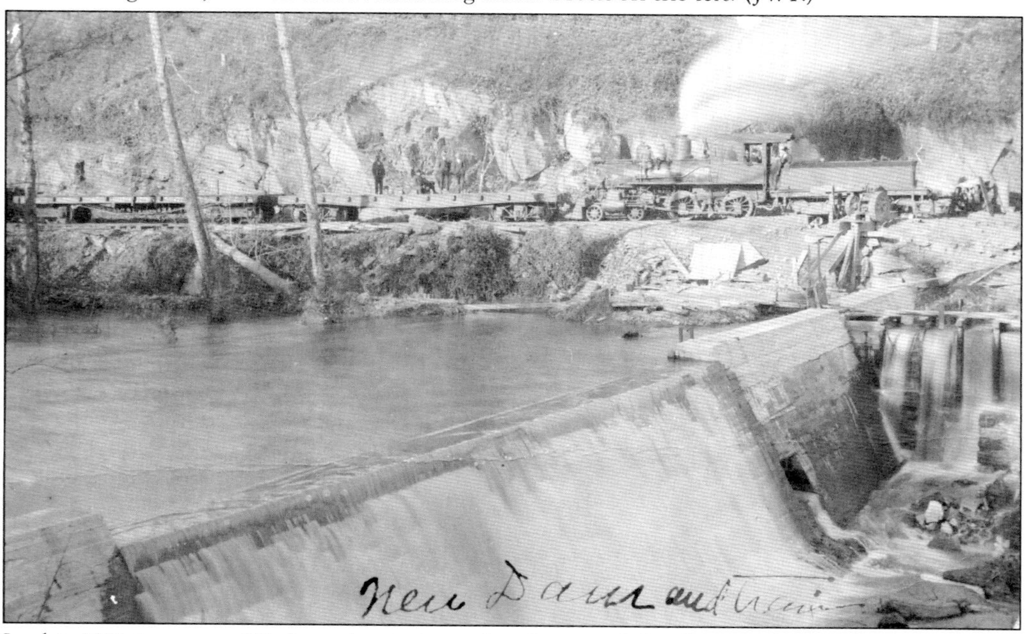

In this 1911 image, an E&A engine is shown heading north by the new dam at the former Elkin Manufacturing Company location. This was the second dam constructed in this area. Note the freshly blasted rock bank behind the train. Front Street currently covers this portion of the railway bed. (EHC.)

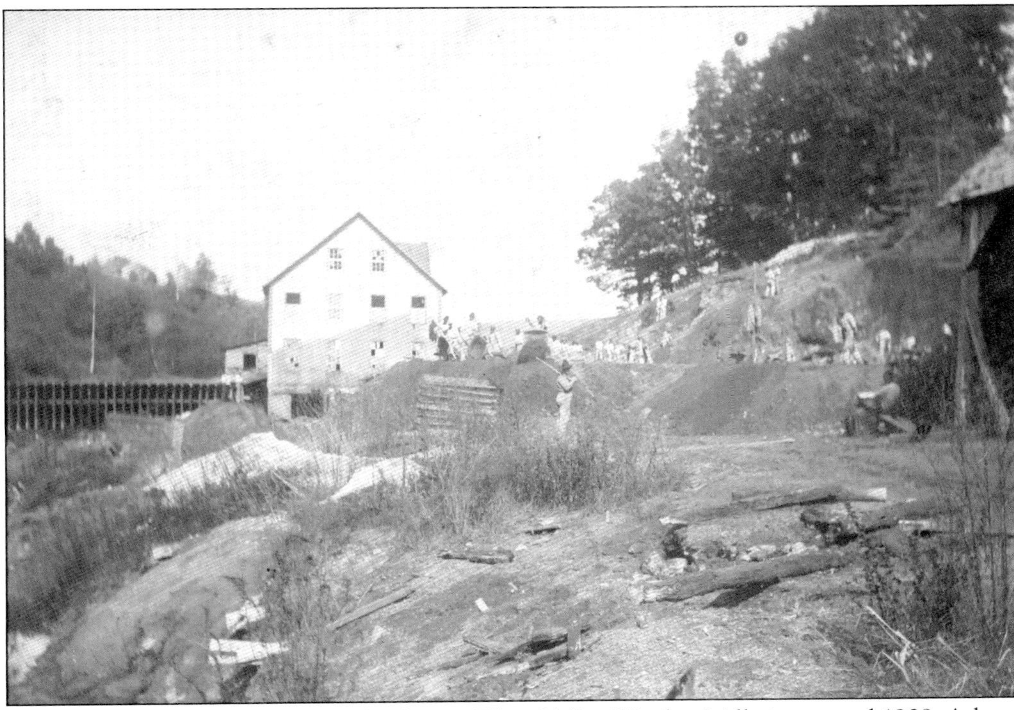

Convicts work on the railway at the former Elkin Valley Woolen Mill site around 1909. A large portion of this building had been demolished, as evidenced by the old roofline on the side of the mill. The railway crossed Elkin Creek north of the mill and continued on the west side for approximately one mile before crossing back to the east side of the creek. (JWP.)

One of the large railway cuts is pictured on the three-mile extension that branched off the main line of the E&A Railway. The main line ended at the community of Veneer. From here, logs were hauled to the Elkin Veneer Company in town, and bark was taken to the Elkin Tannery to be used in tanning leather for the Elkin Shoe Company. (JWP.)

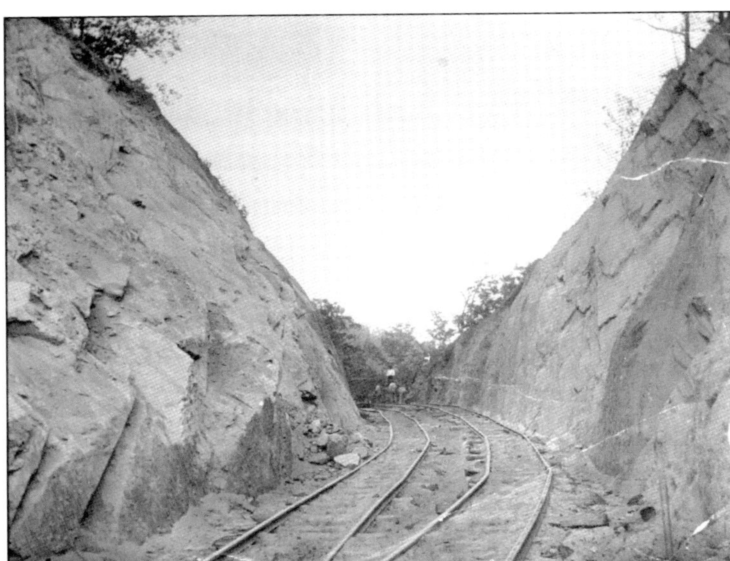

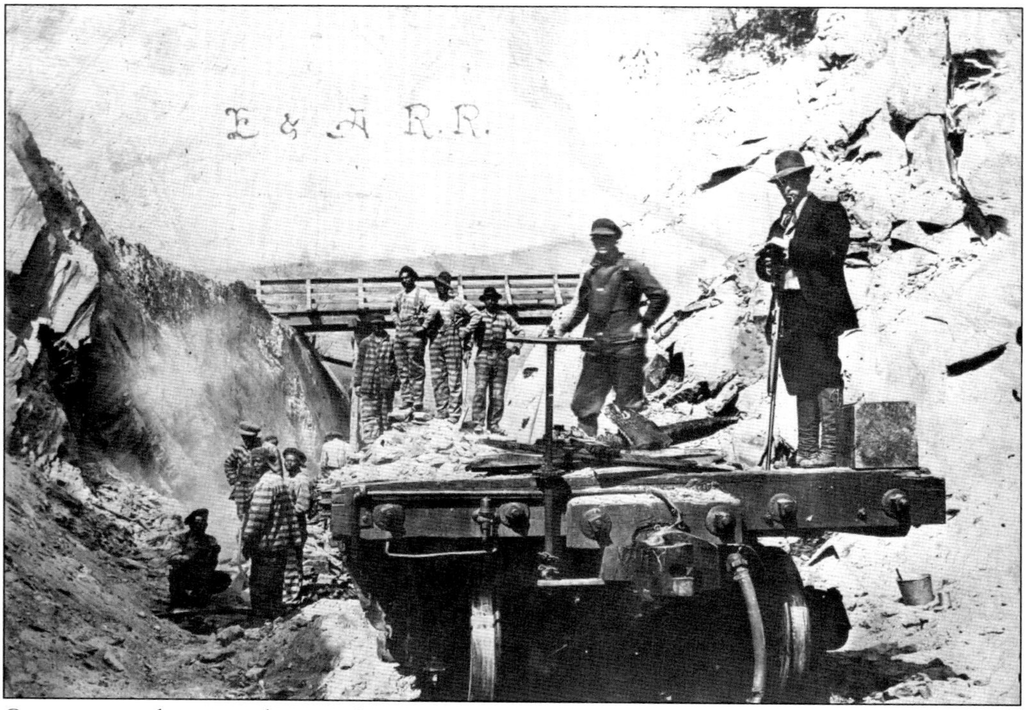

Convicts are shown working under guard on the three-mile extension intended to go through Roaring Gap on the way to Sparta. The bridge in the background was part of the old mountain road that led from the foot of the mountain to Roaring Gap. This road was the predecessor of Highway 26, later known as US Highway 21. (JWP.)

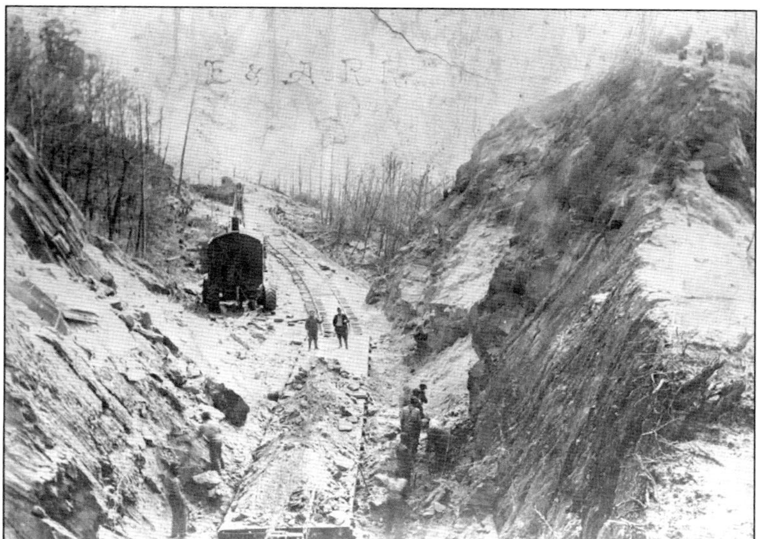

This picture was taken from the bridge in the previous photograph, looking north on the three-mile extension. Notice the steam shovel that was used to make huge cuts through the mountain. Dirt was piled onto flatcars and hauled away to fill the low places on the line. The railway fell short of its goal and never made it to Roaring Gap. (JWP.)

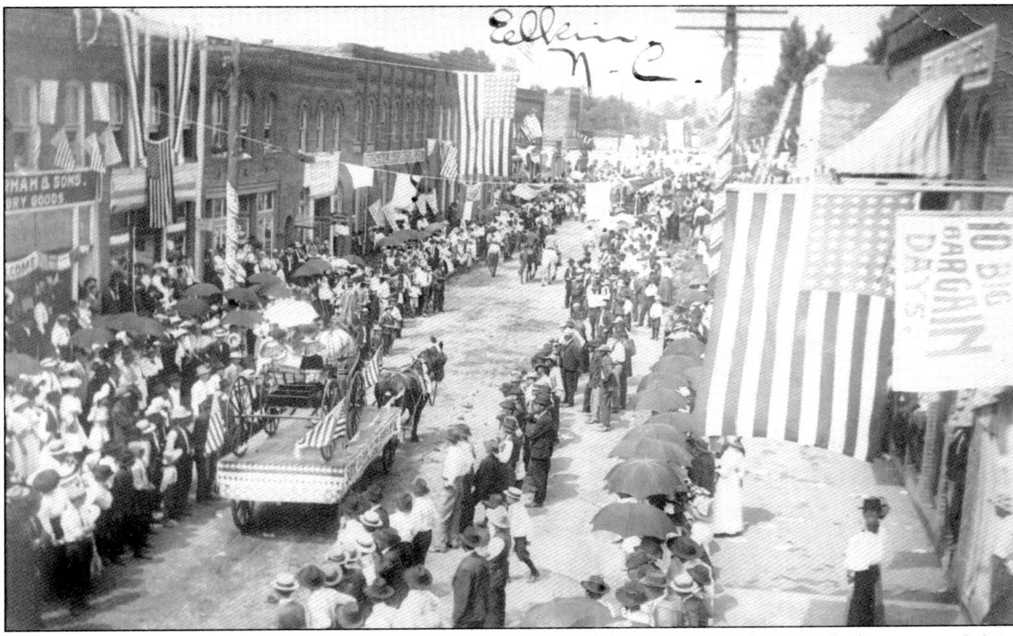

On the morning of July 4, 1911, the E&A Railway celebration parade traveled west on Main Street. The *Winston Journal* stated that 10,000 people attended. Professor Collins from Charlotte ascended in a hot-air balloon and then parachuted out, landing on Cotton Mill Hill near the school. Henry Ford, from Winston, prepared a huge barbecue lunch for the crowd. (RRB.)

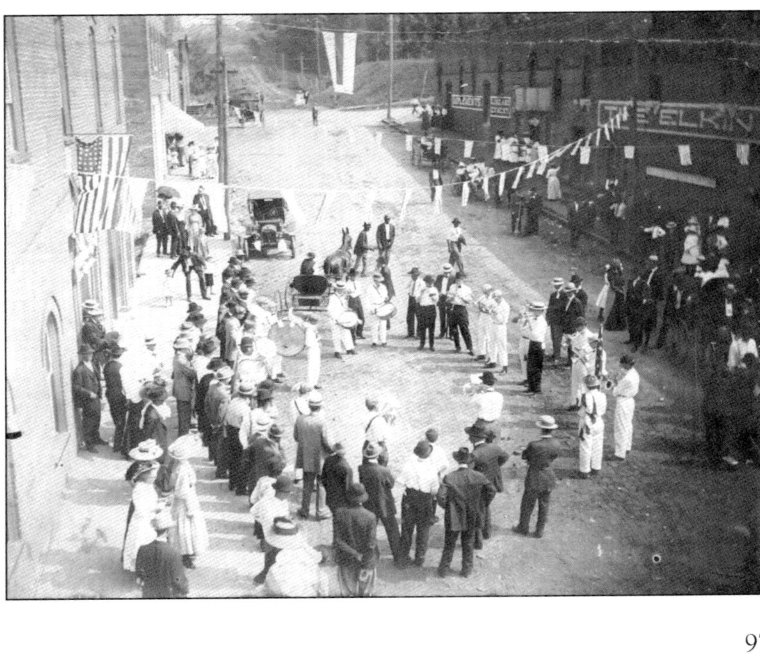

This view, looking north on Bridge Street, shows a band playing as part of the E&A Railway celebration on July 4, 1911. The Elkin Hardware Company is on the right, and the Elkin National Bank is on the left. An interesting feature is the narrow dirt road leading north from town, which became US Highway 21. (GWS.)

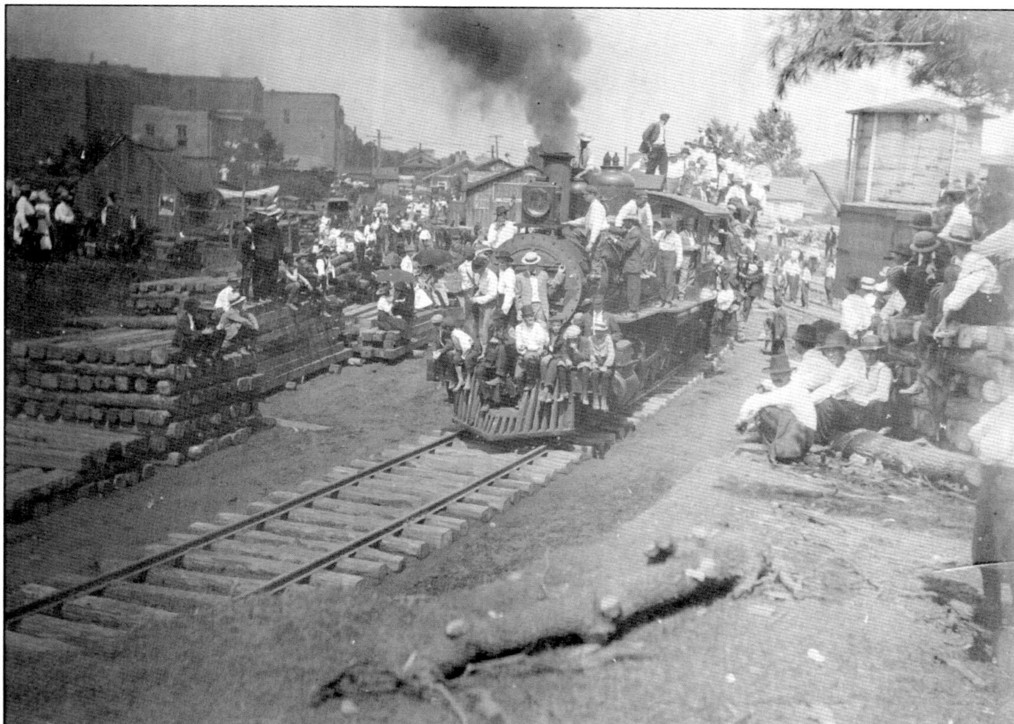

The first run of the train on the E&A Railway took place on July 4, 1911. The train ran northward along the east side of Elkin Creek, just past the shoe factory dam. The trestle across the creek had not been completed, so it ran in reverse back to town along the same route. As shown in the photograph, everyone wanted to be among the first to ride the new train. (GWS.)

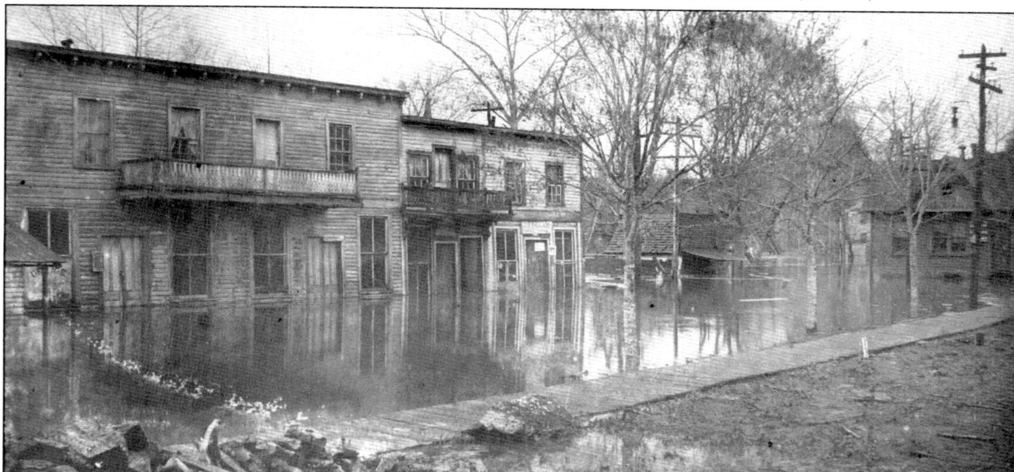

The office building for the Elkin Manufacturing Company, built around 1880, is shown in the far right of this photograph of Front Street during the 1898 flood. It was later used as offices for the E&A Railway. In 1931, the railway applied for abandonment. The rails were sold for scrap, and the crossties were sold for 10¢ each. Remnants of the rail bed can still be seen along the route from Elkin to Veneer. (RC.)

Seven

The Junction of Two Rivers

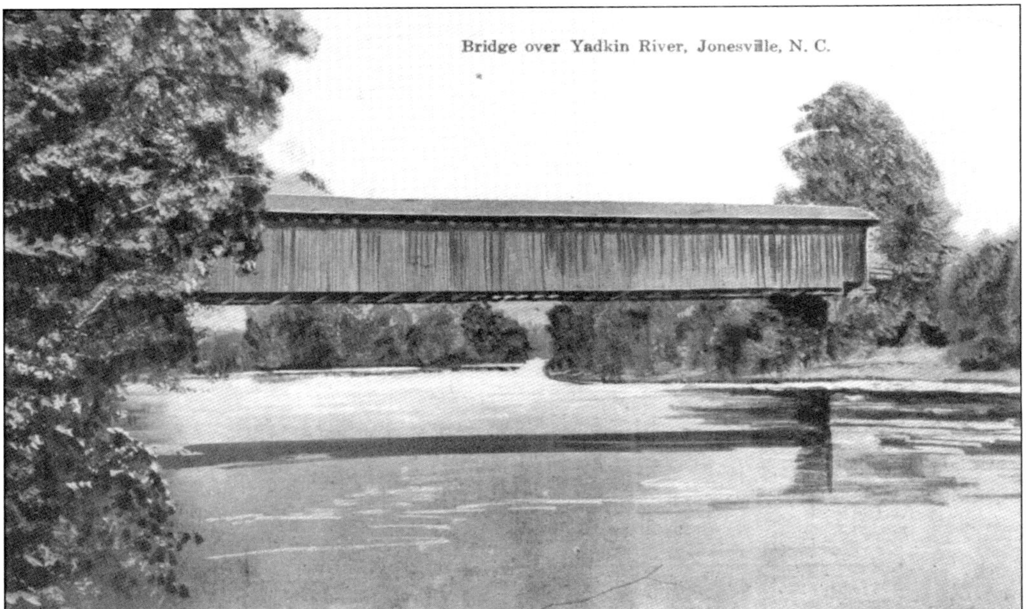

The covered bridge over the Yadkin River was the first bridge that joined the towns of Elkin and Jonesville. It was built by a Mr. Lindsay, from New England, and opened in May 1872. At that time, it was said to be the longest wooden suspension bridge in the world, with a span of 210 feet. It was initially operated as a toll bridge with a crossing fee of 5¢. (SJC.)

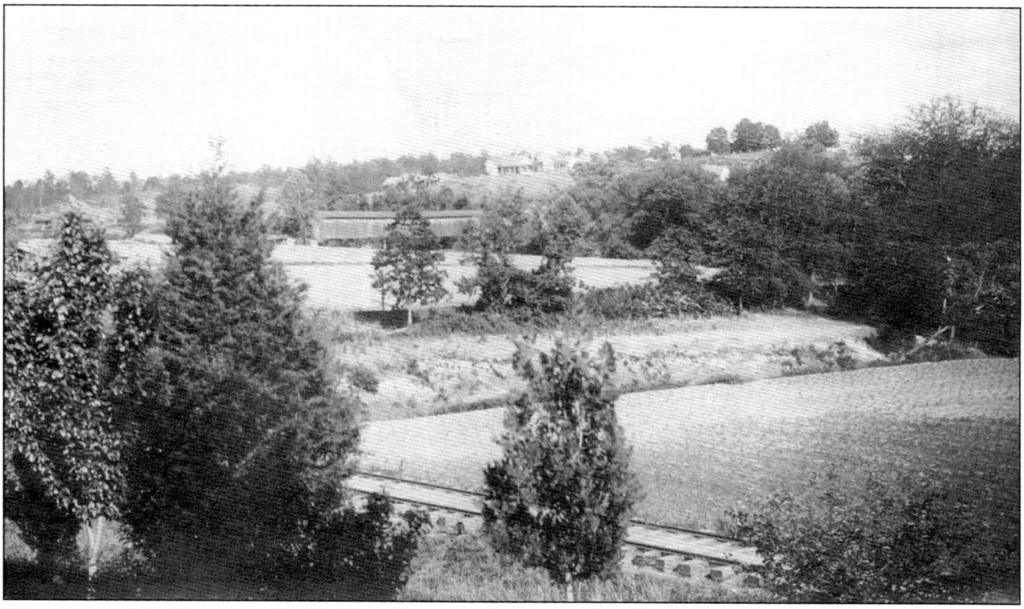

The covered bridge over the Yadkin River is shown in the distance. Before the bridge was built, the only way to get from Elkin to Jonesville was by ferry. The tracks of the Northwest North Carolina Railroad are in the foreground, and Elkin Creek is in the center. This photograph was taken around 1900 from the Gilvin Roth yard on Terrace Avenue, looking southeast across the fields toward the river. (RRB.)

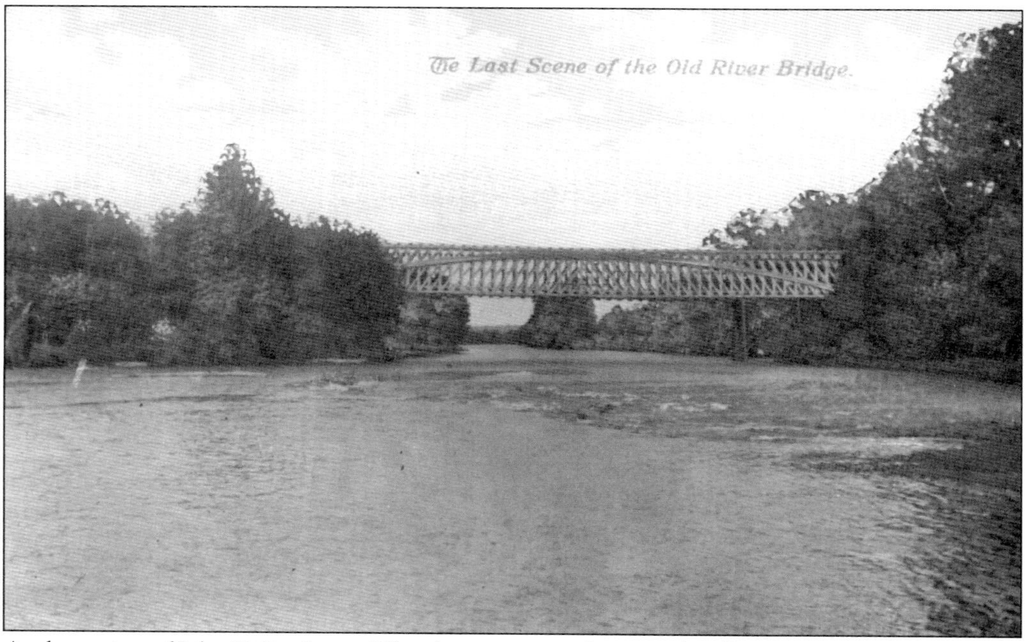

At the urging of John F. Cooke, an Elkin businessman, Surry and Yadkin Counties purchased the covered bridge in 1904, and the crossing became free. This postcard shows the wooden skeleton of the bridge, with the long arch extending to each end, as it was being dismantled in 1913. It was replaced with a steel bridge in 1914. (SJC.)

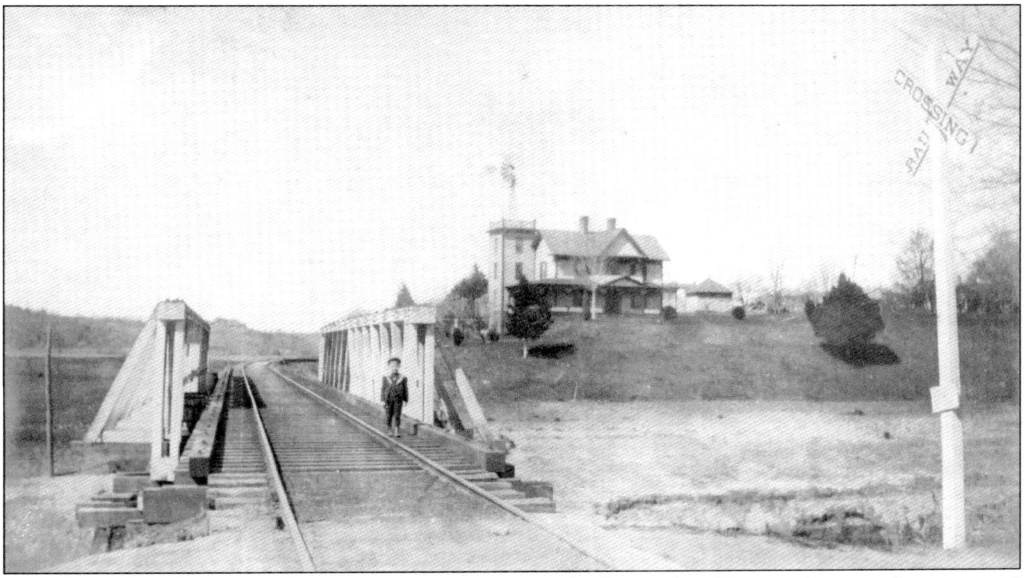

The Gilvin Theodore Roth house was built in 1880 and is located on Terrace Avenue. It is pictured around 1903 with the first train trestle that crossed Elkin Creek. An engineer by profession, Roth built a windmill to furnish running water for his home, which was the first house in Elkin with a working bathroom. The boy standing on the trestle is Roth's son William. (RRB.)

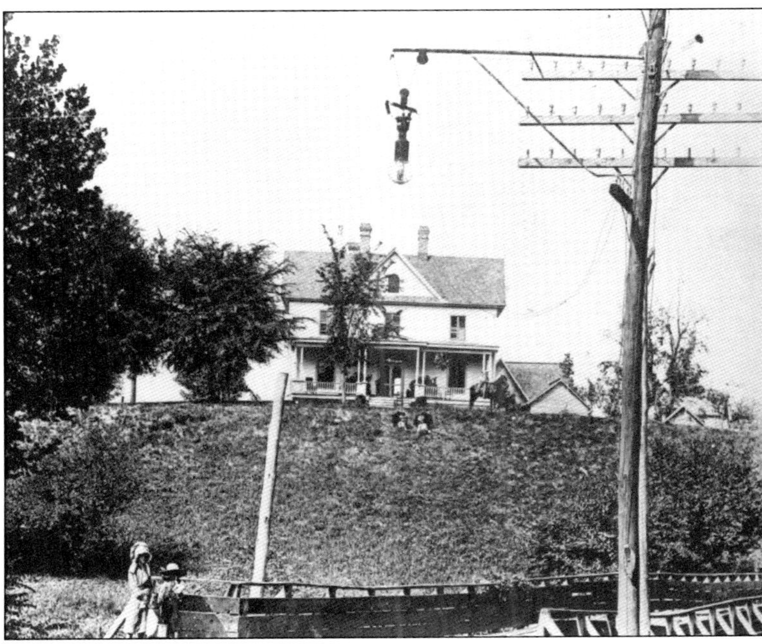

This c. 1898 image shows Dr. Joseph W. Ring's house on Terrace Avenue, overlooking the first bridge over Elkin Creek at West Main Street. Sometime before 1916, it was replaced with a steel bridge, which was replaced by a concrete bridge in 1923. Of note are the electric arc streetlight and the insulator pins and cross arms that were manufactured in Elkin. (EHC.)

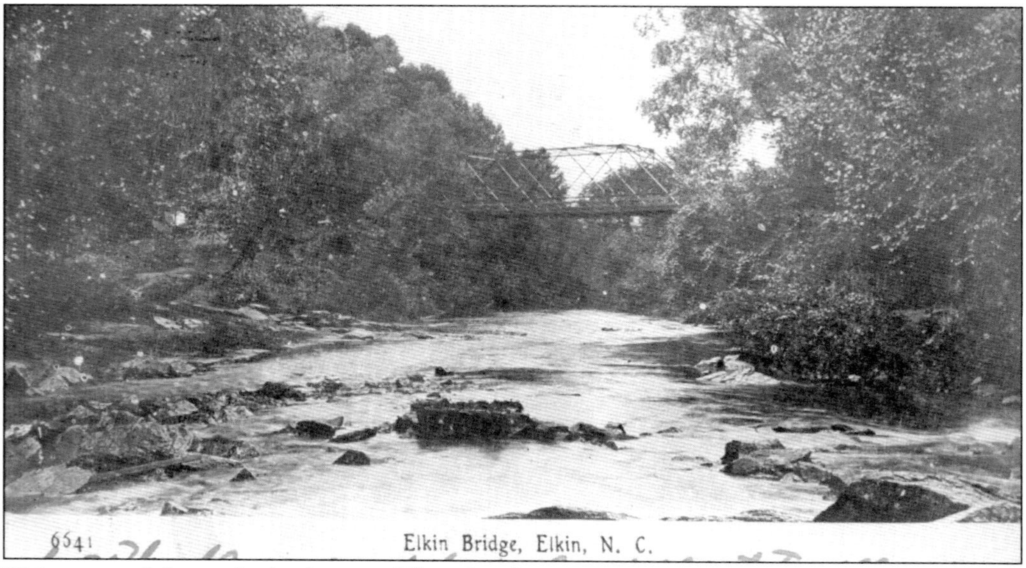

This postcard shows the bridge over Elkin Creek in 1909. It was located north of Highway 268, near the site of the Elkin Valley Woolen Mill and, later, the Elkin Shoe Company. The bridge no longer exists, but the rock bridge supports are still visible in the creek today. The earliest known record of the Elkin River, known locally as Big Elkin Creek, is on the 1770 map of North Carolina by John Colet. The town of Elkin was named after the river. (SJC.)

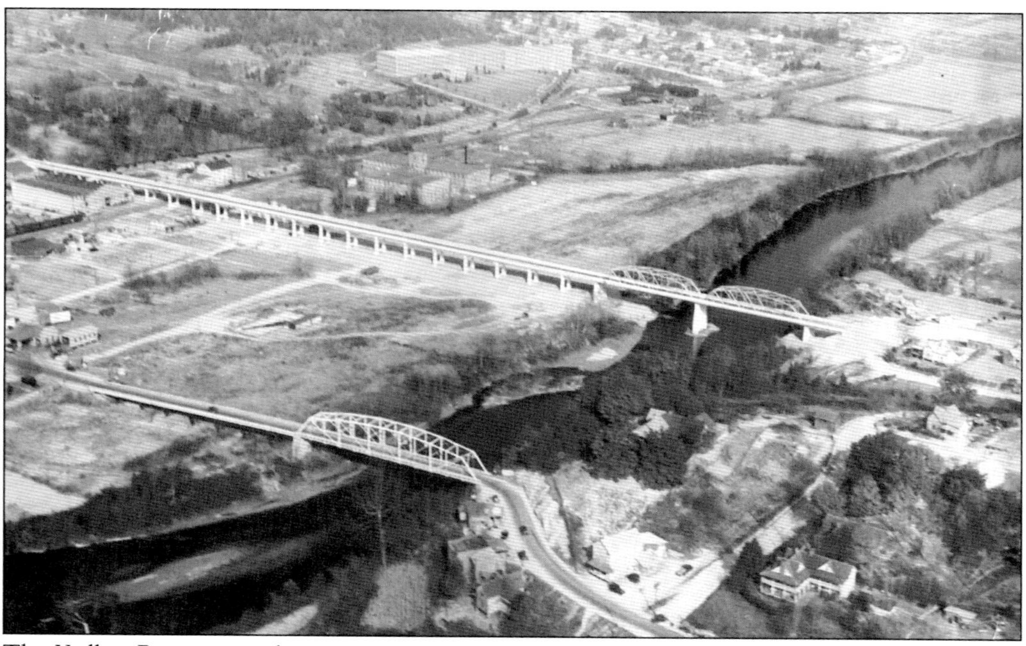

The Yadkin River not only separates Surry and Yadkin Counties, it also separates the towns of Elkin and Jonesville. This c. 1931 aerial view of the river shows the second steel bridge, built in 1917, in the foreground and the Hugh Chatham Bridge, built in 1931, in the background. The town of Elkin is to the left of the river, and Jonesville is to the right. (EHC.)

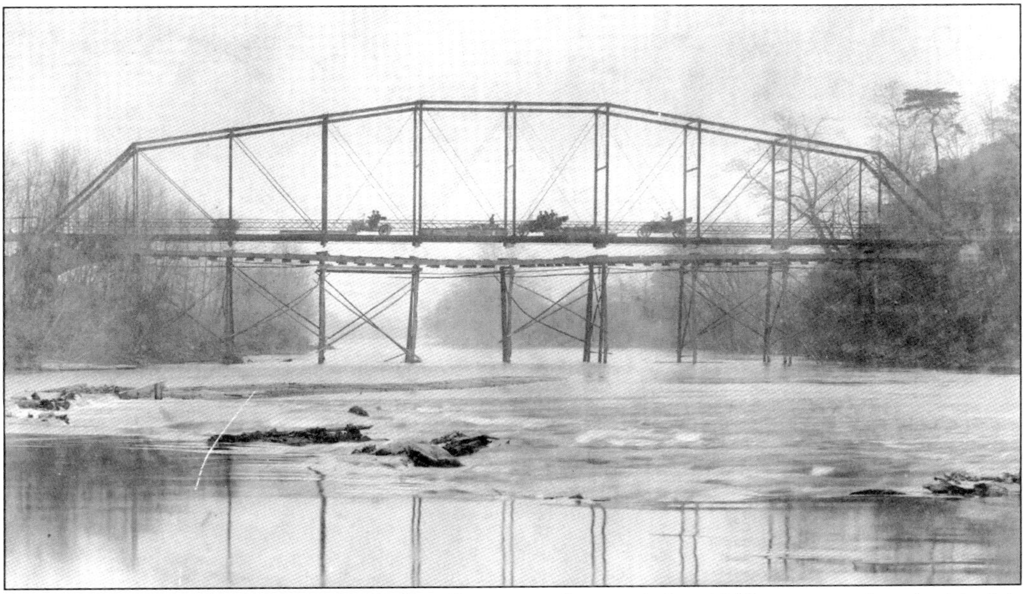

When the covered bridge over the Yadkin River was dismantled in 1913, it was replaced with this steel bridge. It was built by the Roanoke Bridge Company and cost taxpayers in Surry and Yadkin Counties $4,820. The construction scaffolding had not been taken down when this picture was taken. At normal water levels, this bridge stood about 30 feet above the river. During the 1916 flood, it was washed 100 yards downstream. (SJC.)

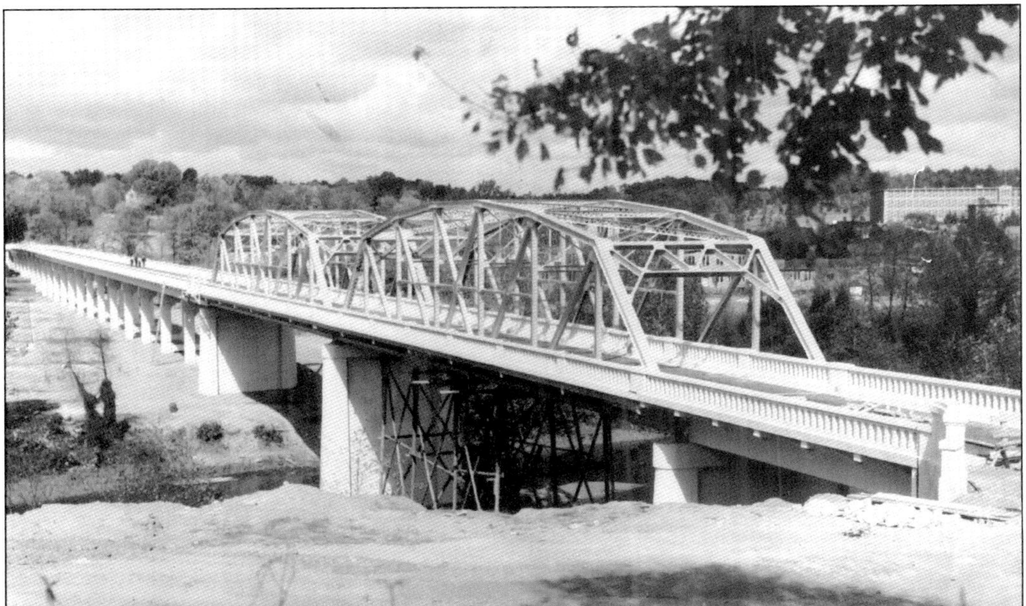

The Hugh G. Chatham Bridge was constructed between March and October 1931 and opened to motorists that November. It was part of a larger federal plan to build US Highway 67 from Winston-Salem to Elkin. The bridge was built by E. A. Wood and Company of Andrews, North Carolina, for $162,906. It was 1,508 feet long and spanned the Yadkin River as well as the railroad bed below. This bridge was torn down in 2010. (EHC.)

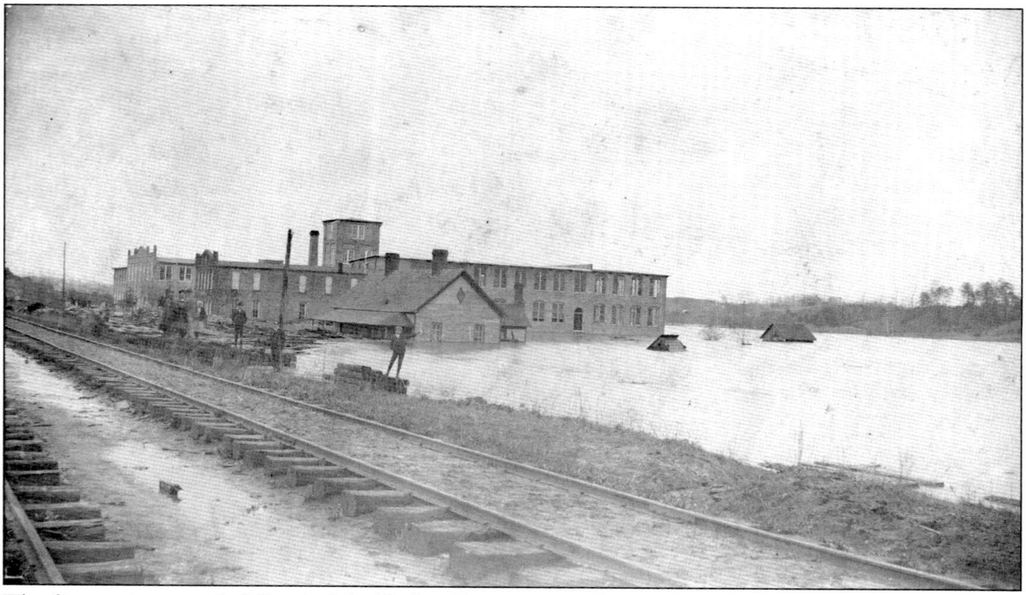

The first major recorded flood of the Yadkin River occurred on September 23, 1898. The floodwaters rose 32 feet above normal. Prior to this event, the highest recorded flood levels were 20 feet above normal, observed when the railroad bed was being originally surveyed. Built in 1893, the Chatham Manufacturing Company mill, located east of downtown Elkin and south of the railroad tracks, is pictured above. The image below, looking southeast from the west side of the Elkin Creek, shows the water level at the original wooden train trestle, built in 1890 over the creek. This trestle was replaced sometime before 1907 with a steel structure, possibly as a result of damage from this flood. The covered bridge is barely noticeable against the line of trees over the head of the man standing on the railroad tracks. The Baily Chair Company, owned by D. Waldron Baily, is visible at left. These images have been previously identified in other references as pictures of the 1916 flood, but they are actually from the flood of 1898. (Both, RC.)

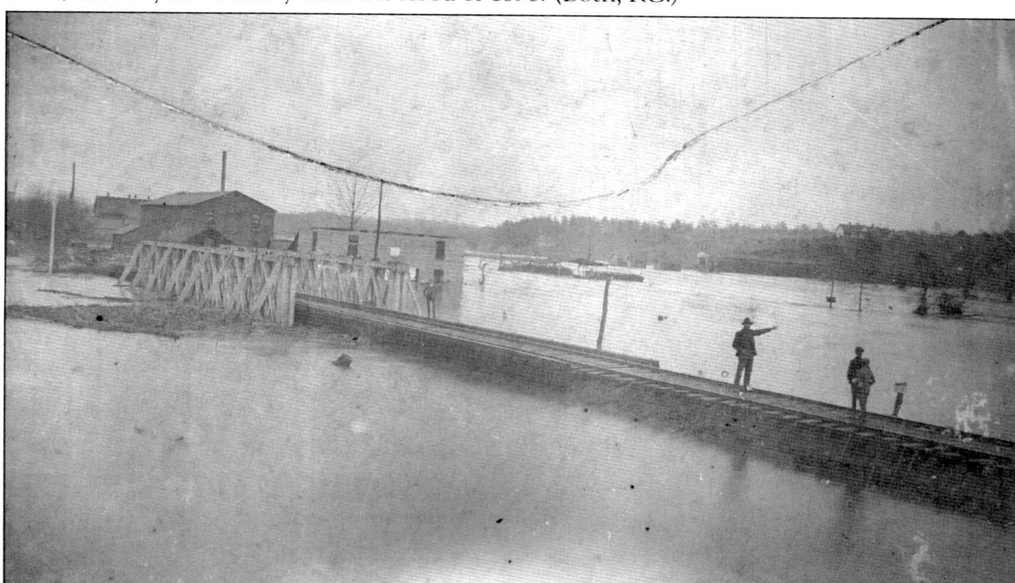

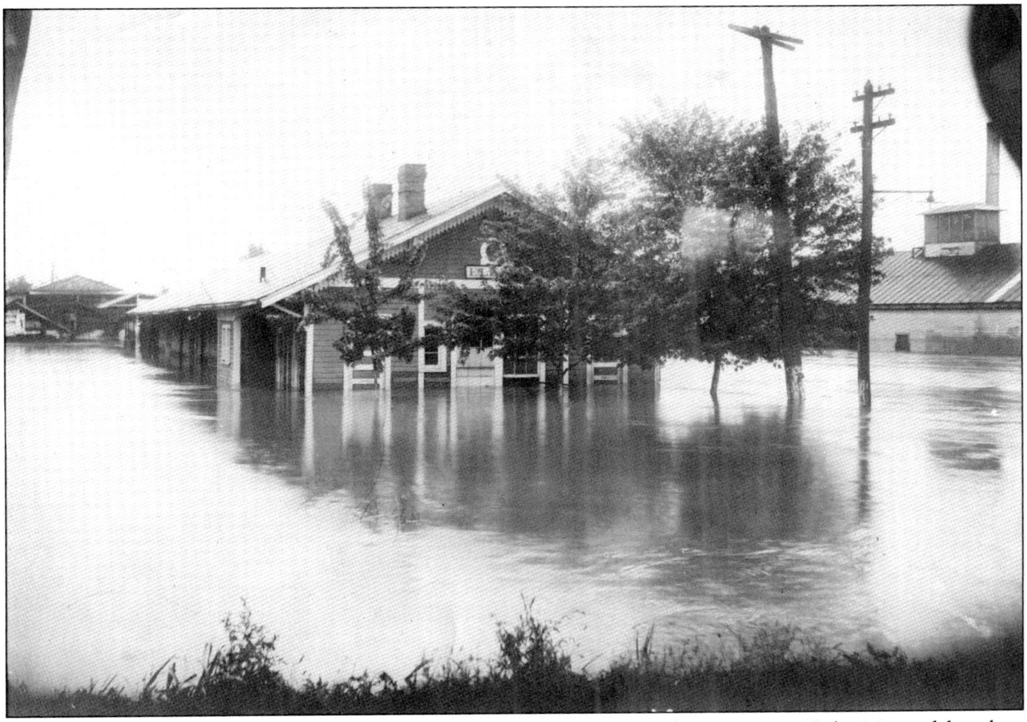

Rain began falling on Friday night July 13, 1916. It continued raining on July 14, and by that evening, the floodwaters of the Yadkin River were rising one foot every three minutes. The water crested at 40 feet above normal at 5:00 a.m. on July 15 and remained at that level for about one hour before it began receding. The high-water mark was about four feet over the Southern Depot platform pictured above. The image below, looking south on Bridge Street, shows the Holcomb Brothers Building on the left, with the Elkin Depot behind it. The Elkin Bottling Company is on the right in the old Hotel Myrtle building. The steel bridge over the Yadkin River, built in 1914, had already washed away. (Above, EHC; below, JWP.)

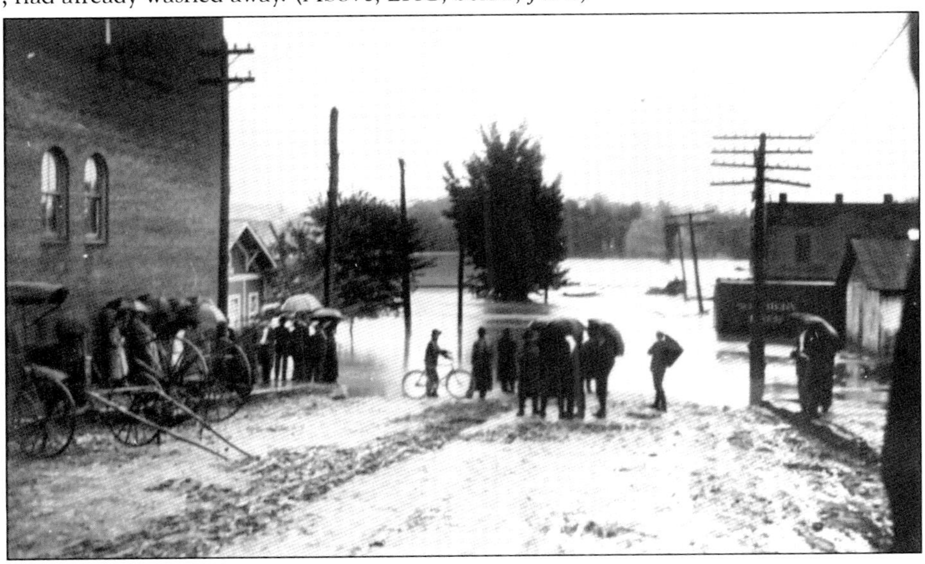

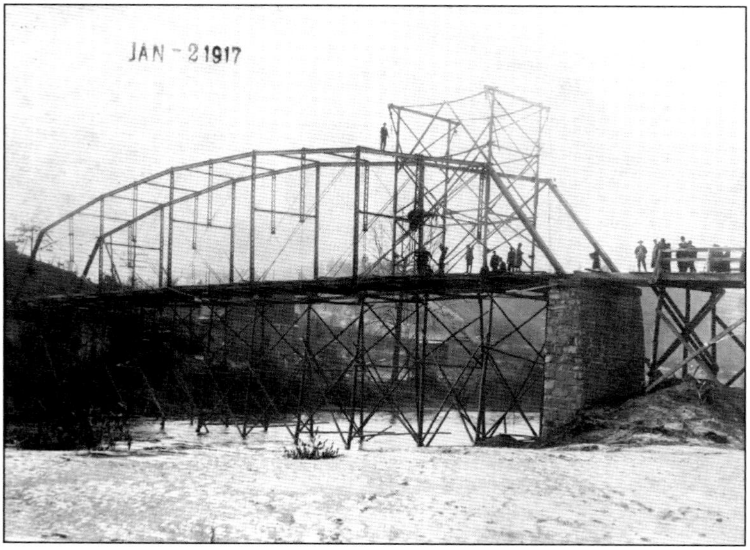

The construction of the second steel bridge over the Yadkin River is pictured on January 2, 1917. This span, which replaced the one destroyed by the 1916 flood, was 10 feet higher than the old bridge and 510 feet long, not including the approaches. Its cost was about $20,000. A ferry was used to cross the river until the new bridge was completed. (JWP.)

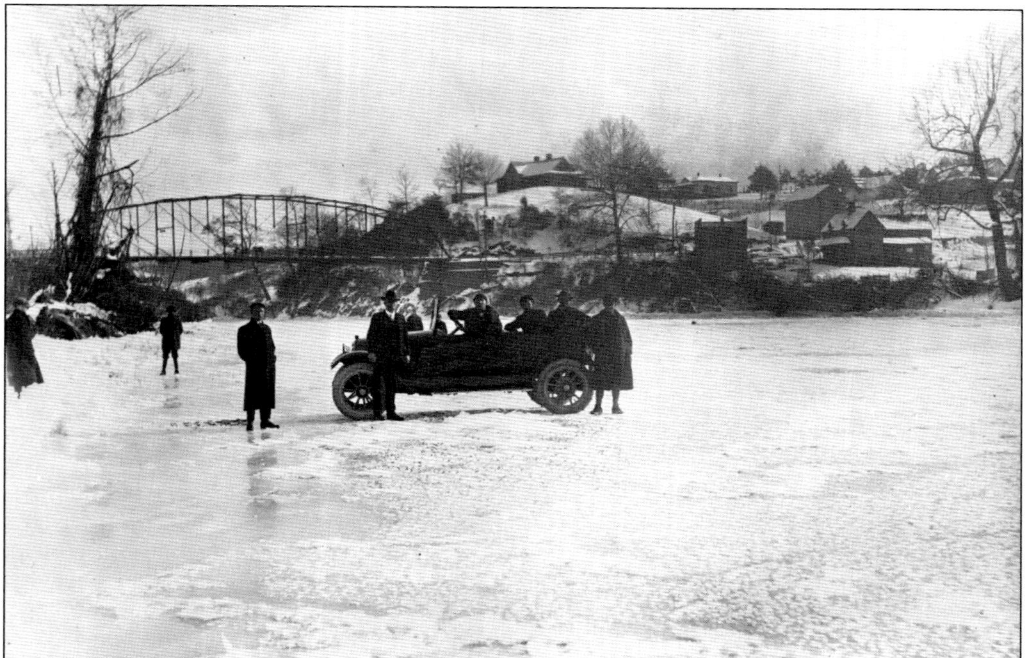

On December 17, 1917, the Yadkin River froze to a thickness of eight inches. Andrew Greenwood drove his car onto the ice with friends Grady Harris, Ernest Nichols, Grady Nichols, W.W. Whitaker, Paul Eidson, and photographer L.R. Combs. The new second steel bridge is in the background. (JWP.)

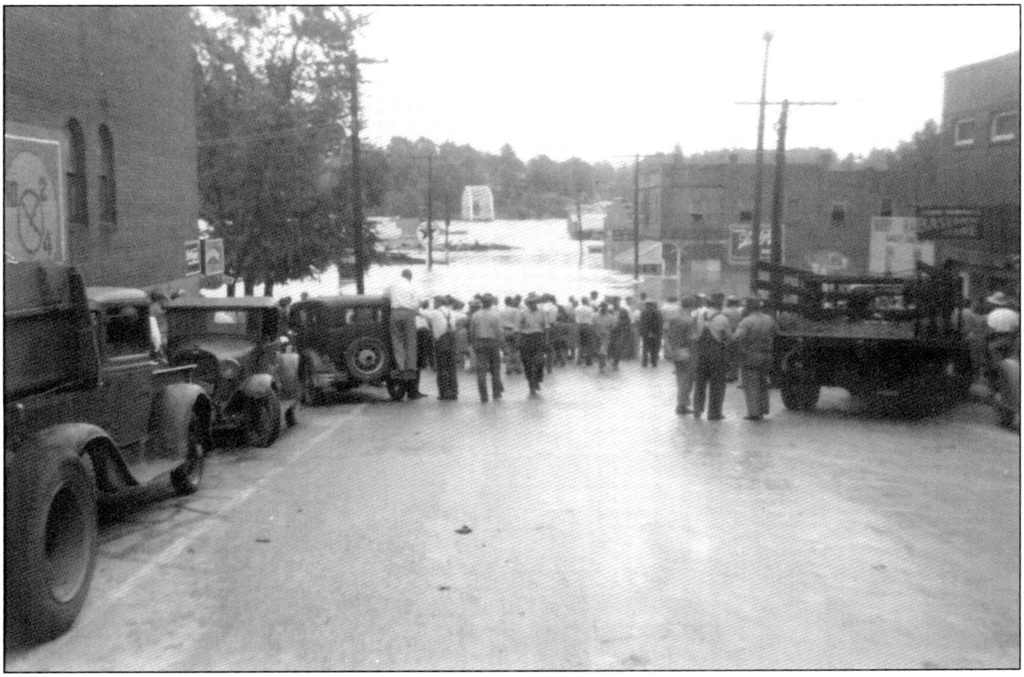

Early in the morning on Wednesday, August 14, 1940, the floodwaters of the Yadkin River began rising again. The waters crested around noon the same day, and by noon the next day, the river was practically back in its banks; however, damage to Elkin was estimated at $500,000. The above image shows South Bridge Street, looking toward the Yadkin River Bridge. Casstevens Hardware is on the left, and Sydnor-Spainhour's department store is on the right. Most of the buildings on the south side of Main Street had water in their basements. Boys from the Civilian Conservation Corps camp, located in North Elkin, worked tirelessly to assist citizens. The image below was taken from the steel bridge over the river on South Bridge Street looking north. The approach to the bridge was gone, and the river bottom lay in ruins. (Both, EHC.)

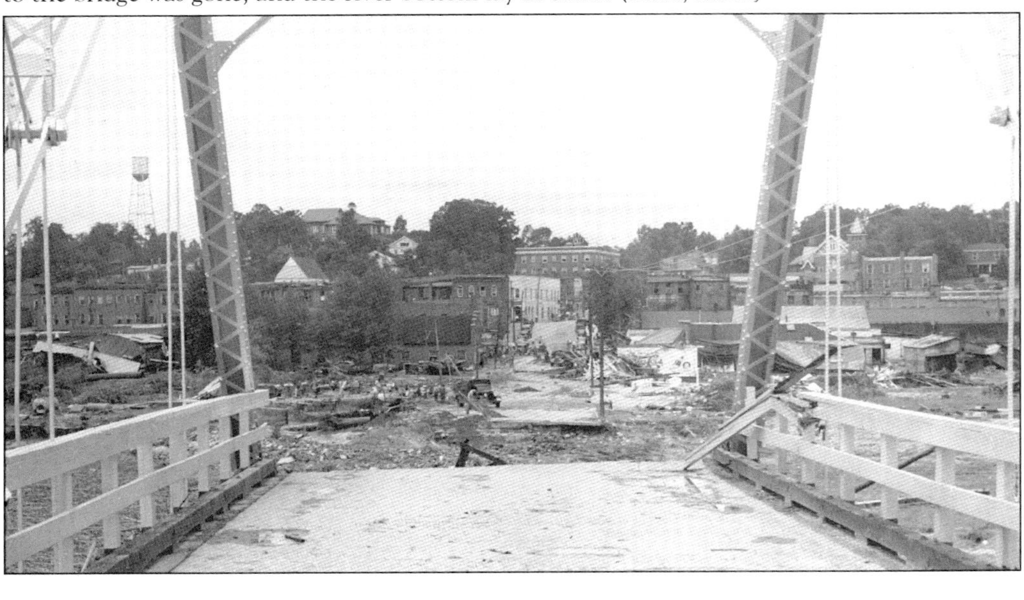

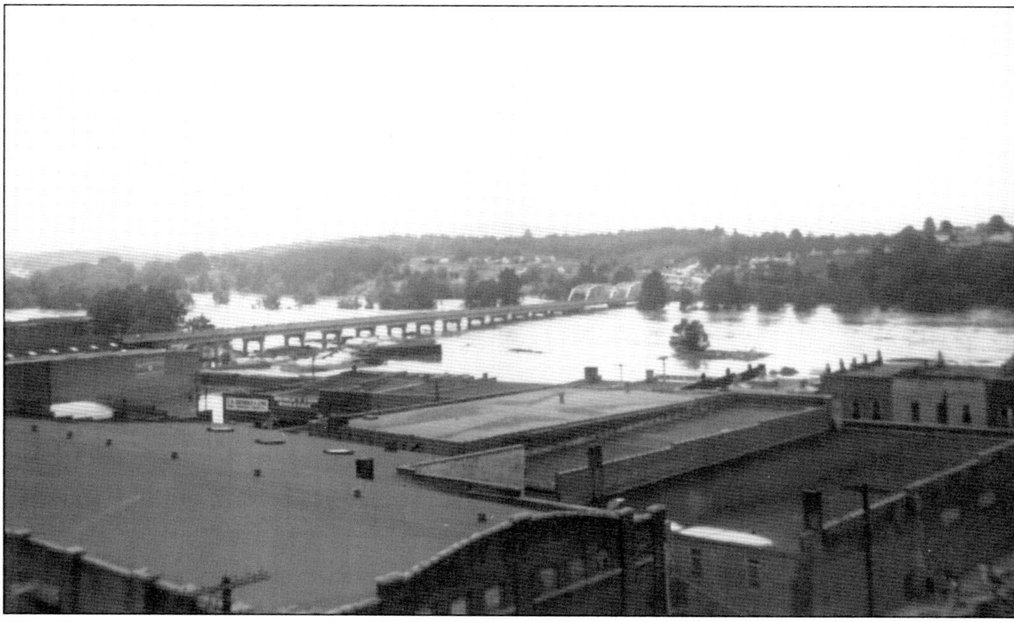

The flooded river bottom and the Hugh Chatham Bridge are pictured from atop the Hotel Elkin. The 1940 floodwaters were near their peak when water came within a few feet of the underside of the bridge; the water level crested between 18 and 24 inches higher than the flood of 1916. Numerous families with houses along the river bottom were made homeless. A large Texas Oil Company gasoline storage tank washed downriver, lodged against the grandstand at the Chatham baseball field, and exploded, burning the grandstand to the ground. Several other gas and oil tanks lodged against the bridge supports but did not cause any damage. The view below shows the Yadkin River Bridge, on South Bridge Street, in the distance. Numerous spectators parked along the roads and gathered between the buildings. The *Elkin Tribune* headline stated: "Elkin People Take Disaster in Stride as Flood Rolls On." (Above, EHC; below, JWP.)

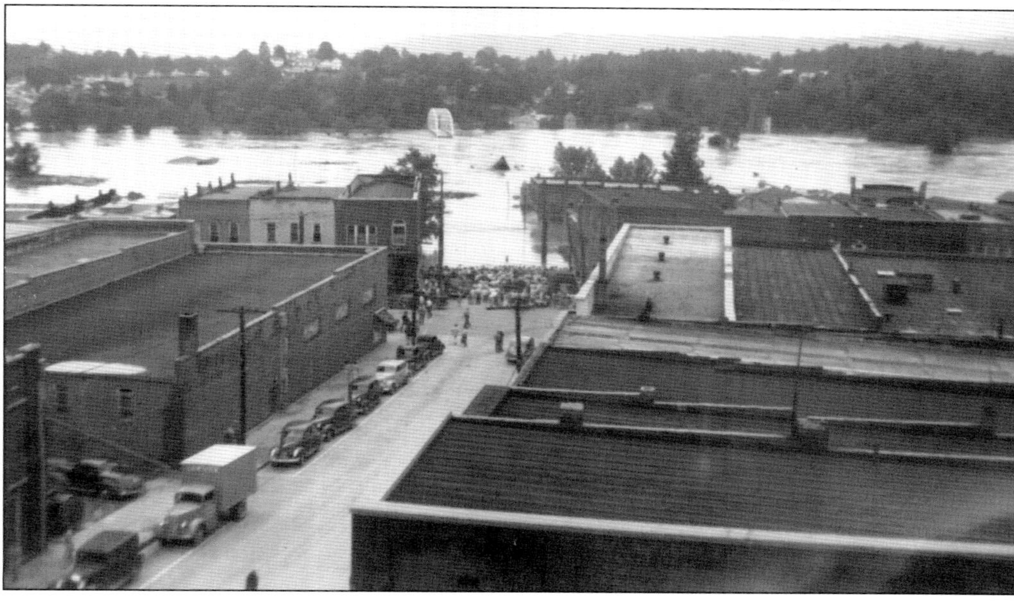

Eight

Chatham Manufacturing Company, "The Mill"

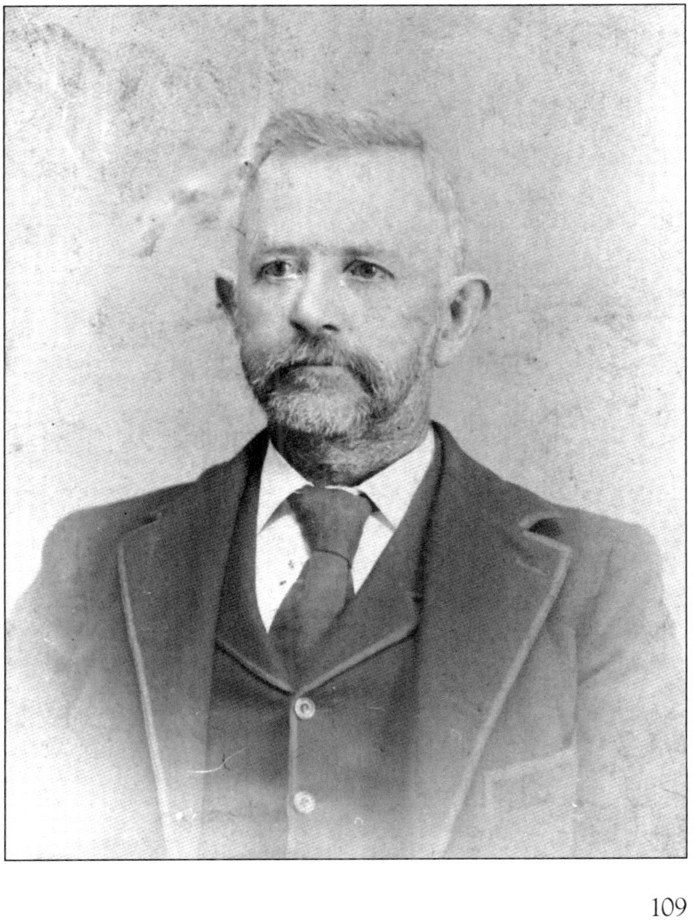

Alexander Chatham was the first mayor of Elkin, from 1889–1891, and one of the founders of the Elkin Valley Woolen Mill, which later became Chatham Manufacturing. He was the father of Hugh Gwyn Chatham, who would succeed him as president of the company. Alexander Chatham was born in Wilkes County in 1834, was a Confederate veteran, and died in 1920. He is buried in Hollywood Cemetery in Elkin. (EHC.)

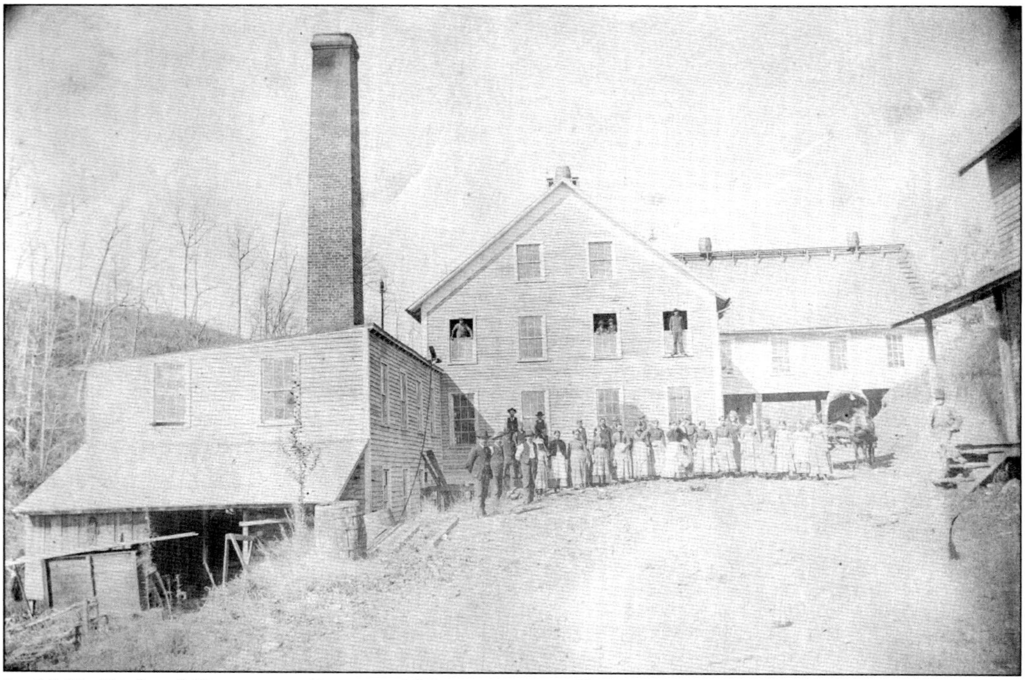

In 1866, Richard Ransome Gwyn sold his cotton mill to R.W. Foard and moved the gristmill operation one mile up the creek to the Elkin Valley. Gwyn's store and mill, shown above, were together called R.R. Gwyn & Company, were located on the east side of Elkin Creek at the upper dam (referred to as the "Shoe Factory Dam"). Gwyn bartered for wool in exchange for goods, and installed a wool-carding machine in a building adjoining the gristmill in the mid-1870s. In 1877, Alexander Chatham and Thomas L. Gwyn bought the business and renamed it the Elkin Valley Woolen Mill. The Elkin Shoe Company moved to this location in 1896, where it remained until 1909, when it moved to the west side of the creek. In the c. 1900 image below, an addition to the building is under construction. (Above, TR; below, JWP.)

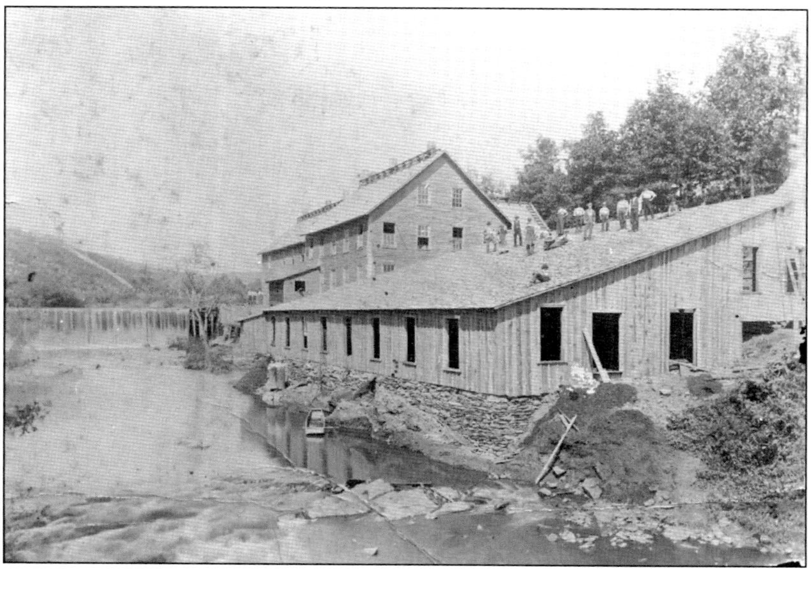

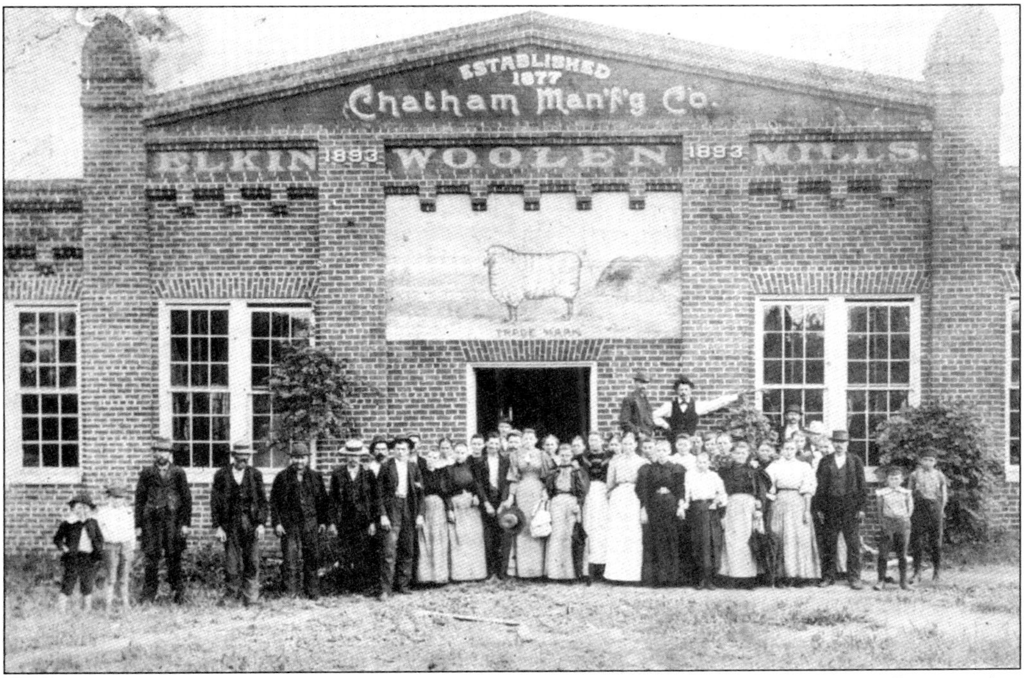

In 1890, Alexander Chatham bought Thomas L. Gwyn's interest in the Elkin Valley Woolen Mill, and it was reorganized as Chatham Manufacturing Company. The second Chatham plant was built in 1893 east of downtown Elkin alongside the railroad tracks; this enabled the company to take advantage of the new railway, which arrived in Elkin in 1890. A second story was added to this building in 1899. (SJC.)

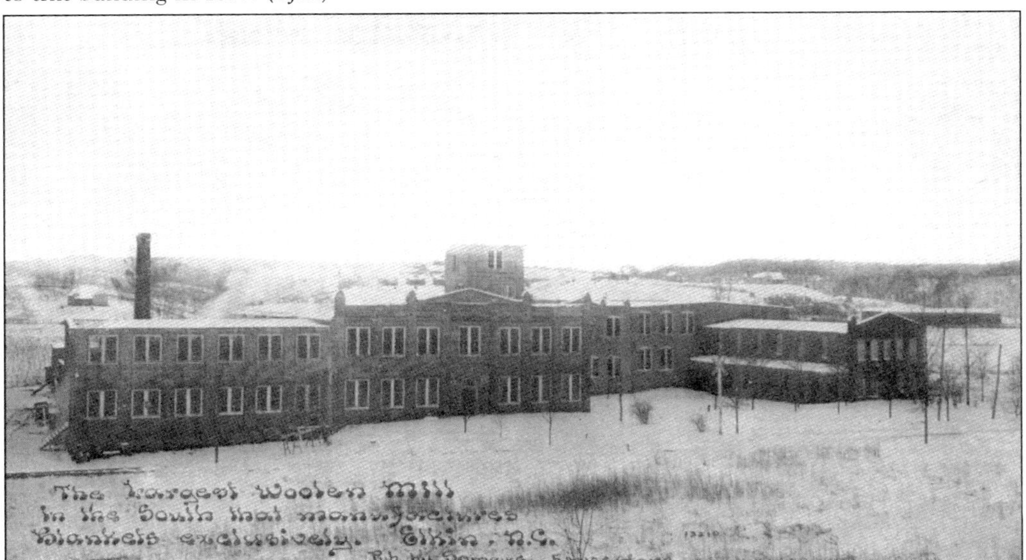

Snow covers the Chatham Manufacturing plant in this postcard from around 1910. At the time, it was the largest woolen blanket manufacturer in the South. It was badly damaged in the floods of 1898, 1916, and 1940, as well as a 1940 fire that destroyed more than half of the structure. The remainder of this building, affectionately referred to as the "old mill," was razed in 1974. (SJC.)

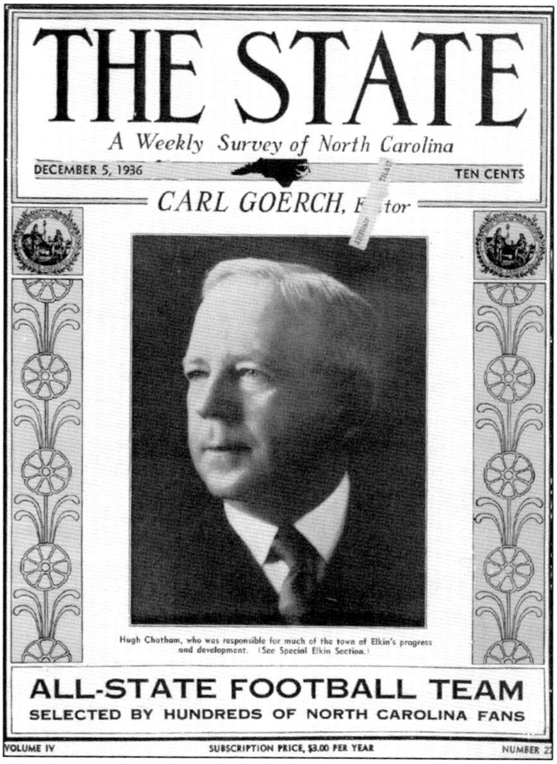

THE STATE

A Weekly Survey of North Carolina

DECEMBER 5, 1936 TEN CENTS

CARL GOERCH, E tor

Hugh Chatham, who was responsible for much of the town of Elkin's progress and development. (See Special Elkin Section.)

ALL-STATE FOOTBALL TEAM

SELECTED BY HUNDREDS OF NORTH CAROLINA FANS

VOLUME IV SUBSCRIPTION PRICE, $3.00 PER YEAR NUMBER 2

The December 5, 1936, issue of *The State* shows Hugh Gwyn Chatham on the cover. He was born in Elkin in 1864 and died in 1929. In 1890, he succeeded his father, Alexander Chatham, as president of Chatham Manufacturing Company. Hugh Chatham was a great statesman, businessman, father, and benefactor to the town of Elkin. The Hugh Chatham Memorial Hospital and the former Hugh Chatham Bridge were both named in his memory. (OSM.)

The waters of the flood that hit Elkin on July 15, 1916 surround the 1893 Chatham Mill. Floodwaters crested eight feet higher than during the flood of September 1898, and damage to the mill was estimated at $150,000. Eleven two-horse wagons and a crew of 100 men were used to move debris and equipment out of the old mill. Thankfully, Hugh Chatham decided to rebuild in Elkin rather than move the mill to Winston-Salem, where the finishing department was located. (EHC.)

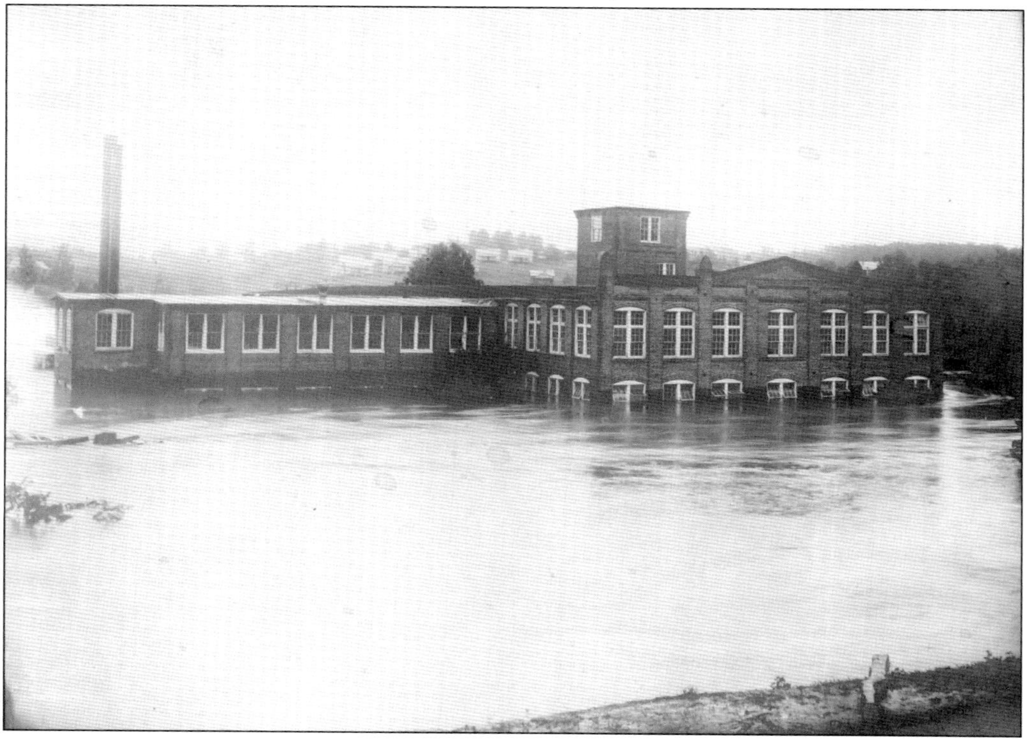

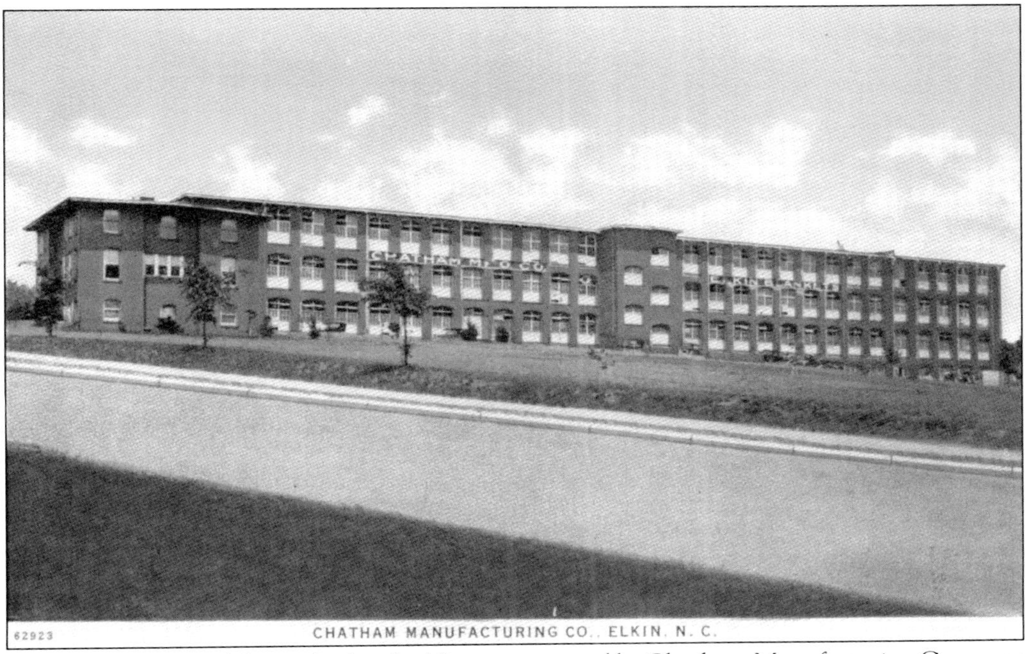

This c. 1925 postcard shows the first building constructed by Chatham Manufacturing Company on higher ground after the 1916 flood. This was the first of many structures at this location, where plant buildings still stand today; it was completed in 1919 and housed the weaving department. (SJC.)

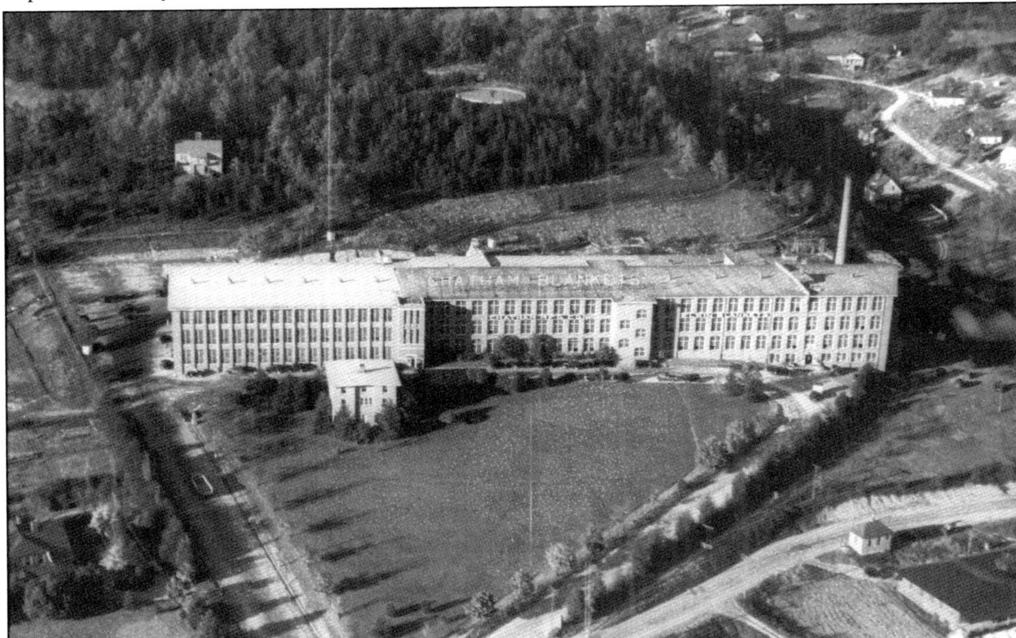

This aerial view of Chatham Manufacturing was photographed between 1935 and 1937. The Lucy Hanes Chatham Clubhouse is at top left. The right half of this structure was completed in 1919, and the left half, behind the small building in front, was completed in 1927. (SJC.)

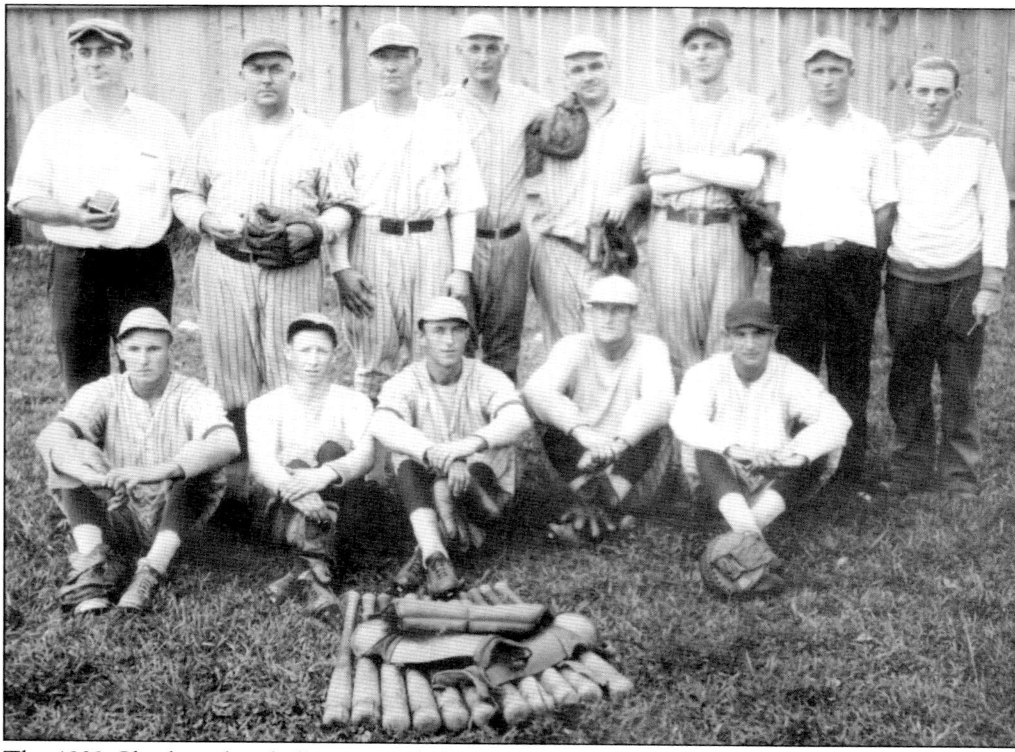

The 1929 Chatham baseball team includes, from left to right, (first row) Lakey Harkrader, Pat Osborne, Dewey York, M.D. Gross, and Herman Day; (second row) manager Ed DeBorde, Russ Powers, Johnnie Francis, Walter Barnette, Wade Lineberry, Clyde Day, umpire Charlie Long, and scorekeeper Jim Young. (SJC.)

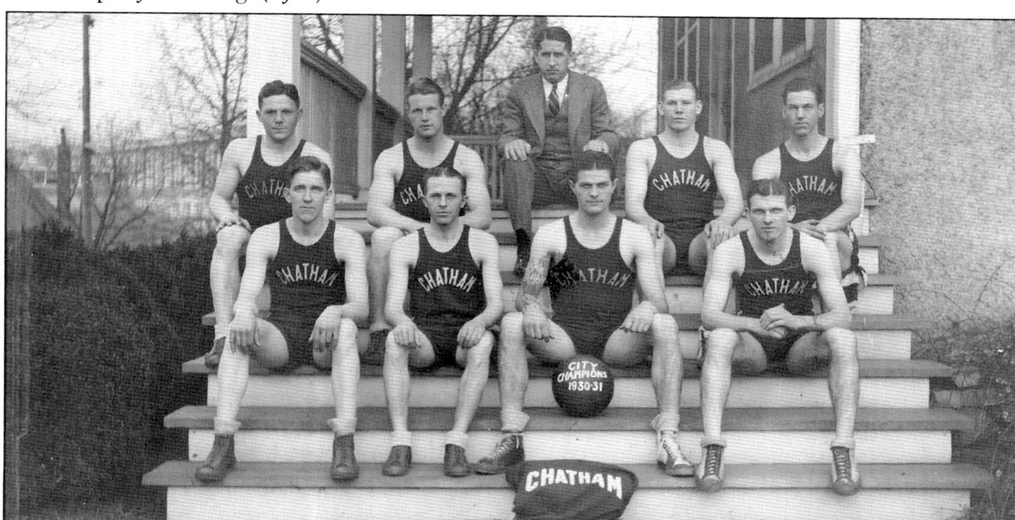

The Chatham men's basketball team won the city championship during the 1930–1931 season. Pictured here are, from left to right, (first row) "Foot-eye" Sampson, E.T. Shamel, John Sappenfield, and Stuber Flynt; (second row) "Beef" Boles, Worth McAlister, manager R.W. Harris, Bob Southern, and Bill Byrd. (EHC.)

Richard Thurmond Chatham was the son of Hugh Gwyn and Martha Lenoir Chatham. He was born in Elkin in 1896 and died in 1957. He was a veteran of both world wars, serving in the Navy and achieving the rank of commander. He was president of Chatham Manufacturing from 1929 to 1945, and he served in the US House of Representatives from 1948 to 1956. (CL.)

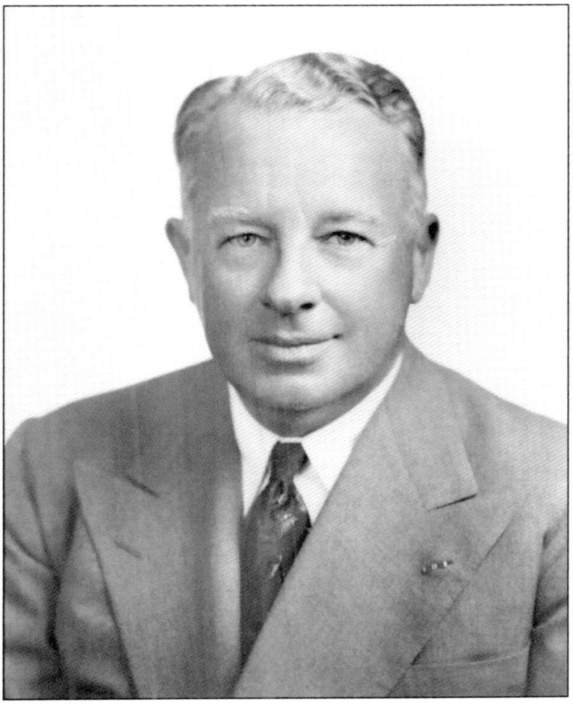

This aerial view of Chatham Manufacturing Company was taken in 1945 by employee Walt F. Burgiss. The Gilvin Roth YMCA, at lower left (with columns), opened in 1942. Chatham employed over 2,500 employees at the company's peak. Although Chatham originally made primarily woolen blankets, it also manufactured homespun for clothing, automobile upholstery, fiber-woven blankets, and other types of fabrics. (SJC.)

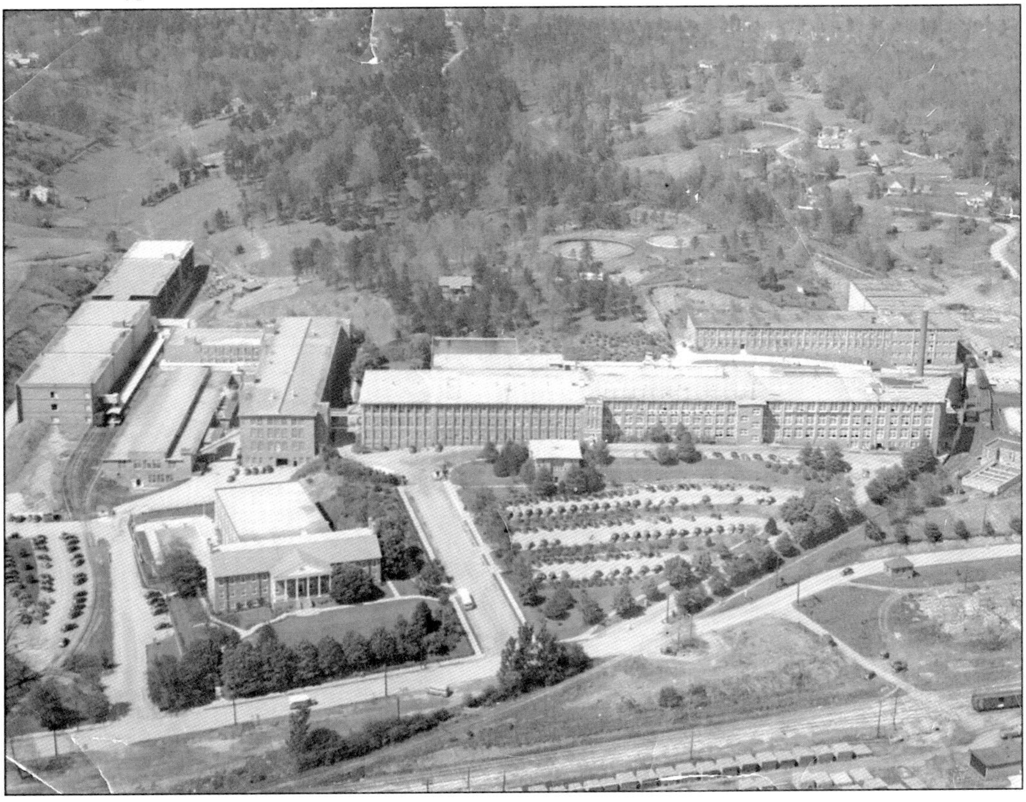

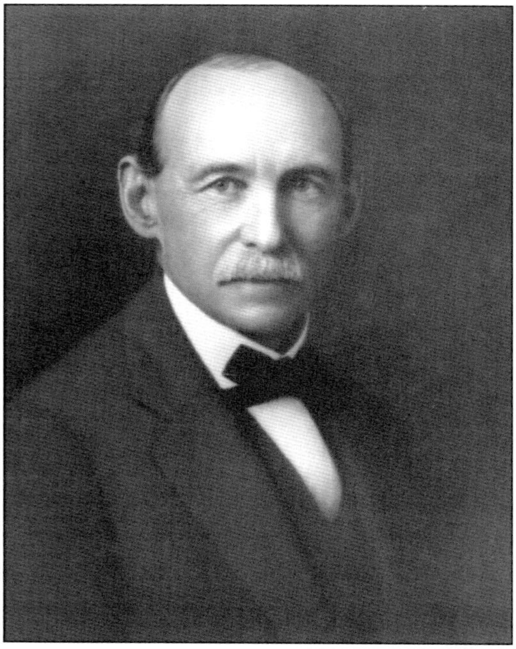

Gilvin T. Roth (1854–1927), an engineer by profession, came to Elkin from Pennsylvania in 1878 to assist in the installation of equipment and training of employees at the Elkin Valley Woolen Mill. He partnered with Alexander Chatham and Thomas L. Gwyn and was made general superintendent of the mill. The YMCA building, completed in 1942, was named in his memory. (SJC.)

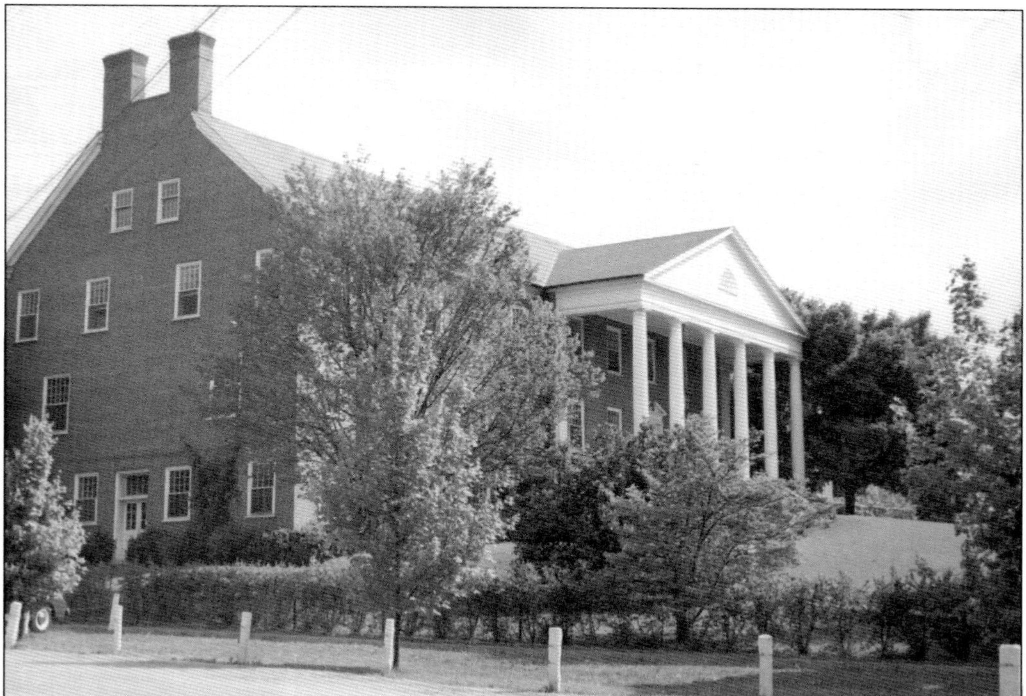

The Gilvin T. Roth YMCA was a gift to the Elkin community from Chatham Manufacturing Company and was formally dedicated on May 2, 1942. Complete with banquet facilities, a library, a bowling alley, an outdoor swimming pool, a gymnasium, and meeting rooms, it became a local center of activity. In 1973, because of declining interest and other issues, the pool was closed, new memberships ceased, and services were scaled back. (SJC.)

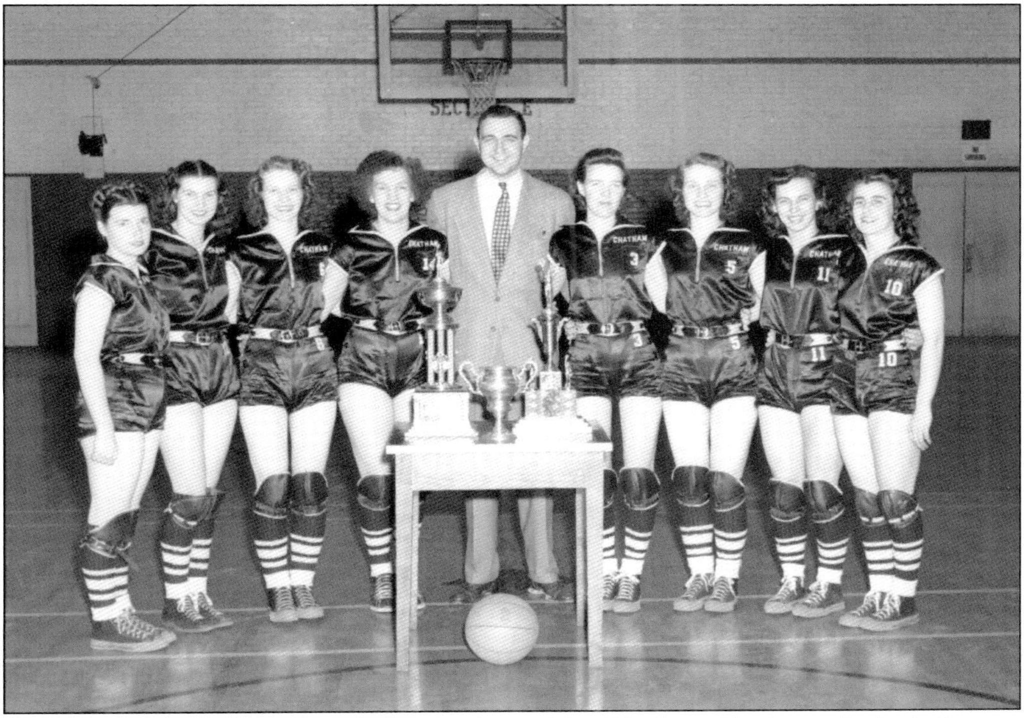

This April 1948 photograph includes members of the Chatham Blankettes basketball team. Pictured here are, from left to right, Reola Shore, Ruth Reich, Janie Sherrill, Doris Norman, coach Don Brock, Maurice Gordon, Jennie Sherrill, Betty Cope, and Francis McBride. Trophies for first place in the Southern Textile Tournament and for third place in the AAU National Tournament, held in St. Joseph, Missouri, are displayed on the table. (SJC.)

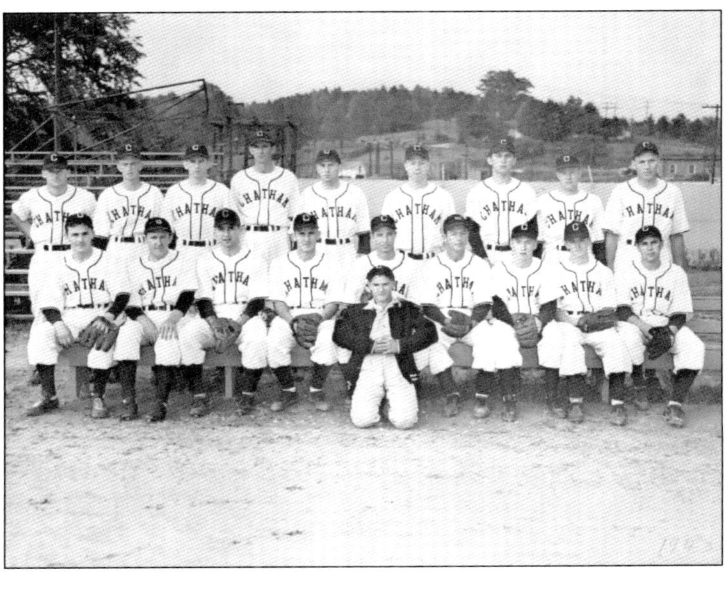

The 1948 Chatham Blanketeers baseball team includes, from left to right (first row) Tat Davis, Dick Mackie, Greg Collins, Bill Cross, Veo Story, Woody Mabry, Shorty Brown, Bill Smith, and Buck Hines; (second row) Bob Withrow, Sonny Blackburn, Red Powers, Jack Swift, Robert McCann, Cotton Harris, Jim Phillips, Gene Hampton, and manager Tige Harris. Bat boy Howard Hayes is front and center. (SJC.)

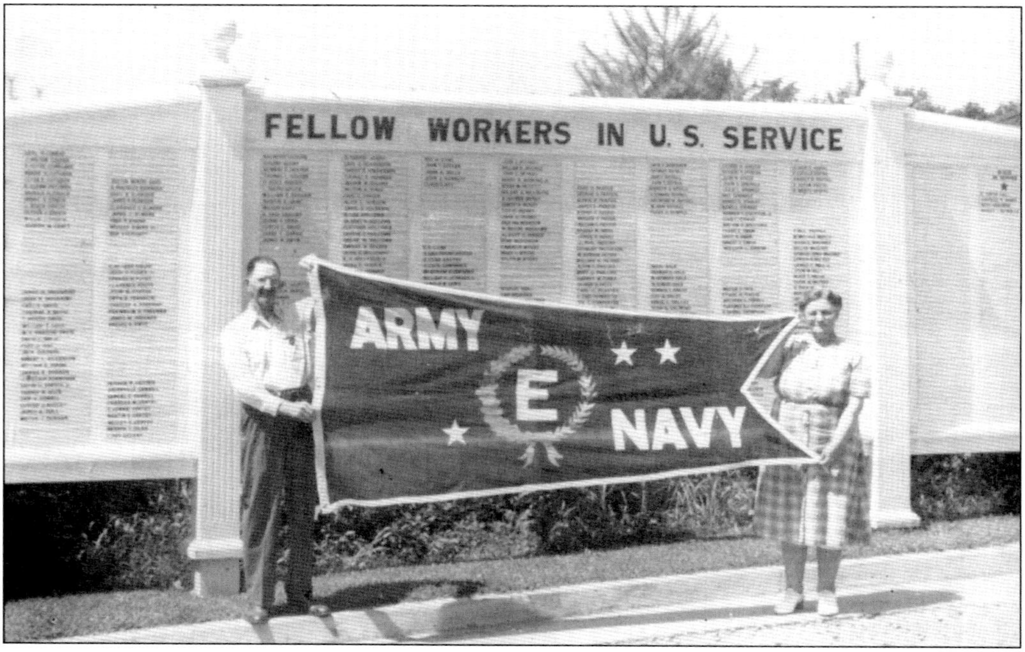

In August 1944, Dan Woodruff and Fanny Talley proudly displayed Chatham's Army-Navy award for excellence pennant, with three stars for outstanding wartime production. It was first given in August 1942. During both world wars, Chatham Manufacturing made millions of blankets for all branches of the armed forces. When this photograph was taken, these two employees had the most years of service, and neither had had a lost-time accident. (SJC.)

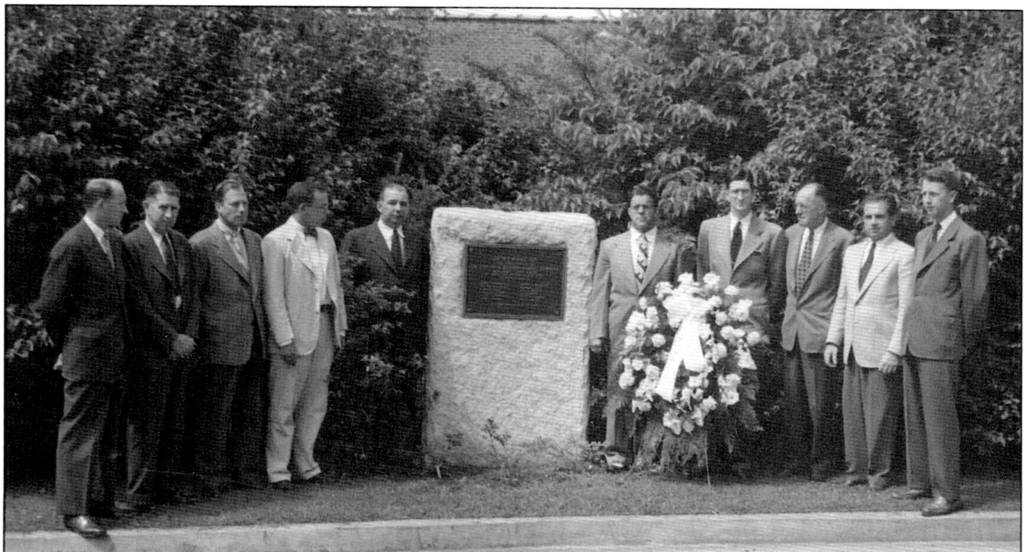

The Chatham World War II Memorial was dedicated in May 1947 to the 12 Chatham employees who died during the war. The bronze plaque was donated by the Thurmond Chatham Unity Club, and the Mount Airy granite shaft was purchased with employee donations. Pictured here in 1948 are, from left to right, Bill Butler, Raymond W. Harris, Harry Lassiter, Hugh Chatham II, Fred Neaves, Carl Plaster, Reece Gilliam, C.J. Hyslup, Lloyd Dudley, and Paul Kennedy. (SJC.)

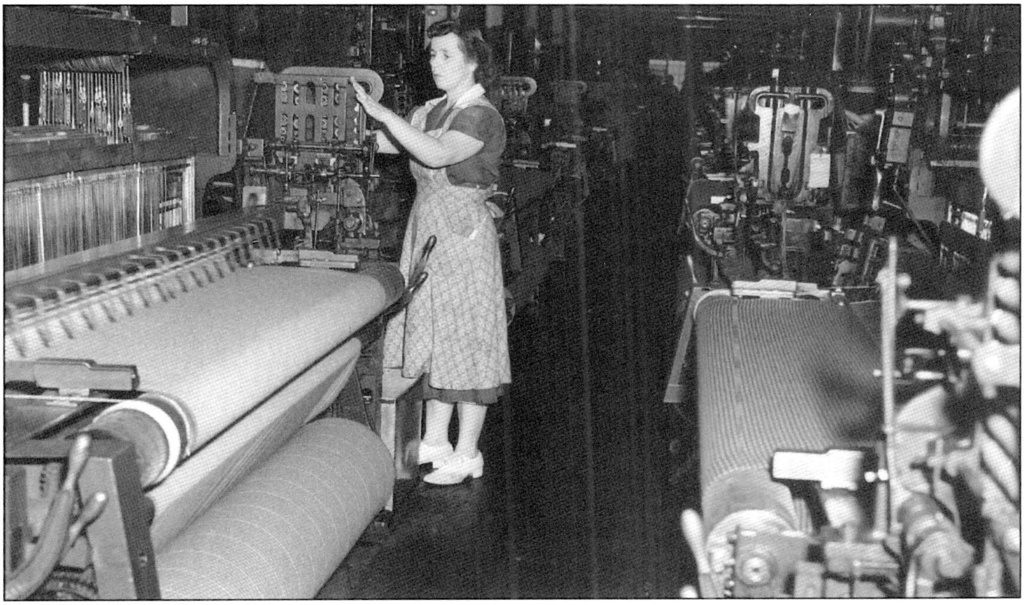

In this 1952 image, Ollie Benton Couch checks the bobbin magazine of one of the looms in the weave room. Couch retired from the mill in 1975 after 39 years of service; she was born in Yadkin County in 1914 and died in 2006. The looms were arranged so that one weaver could operate more than one loom at a time. (SJC.)

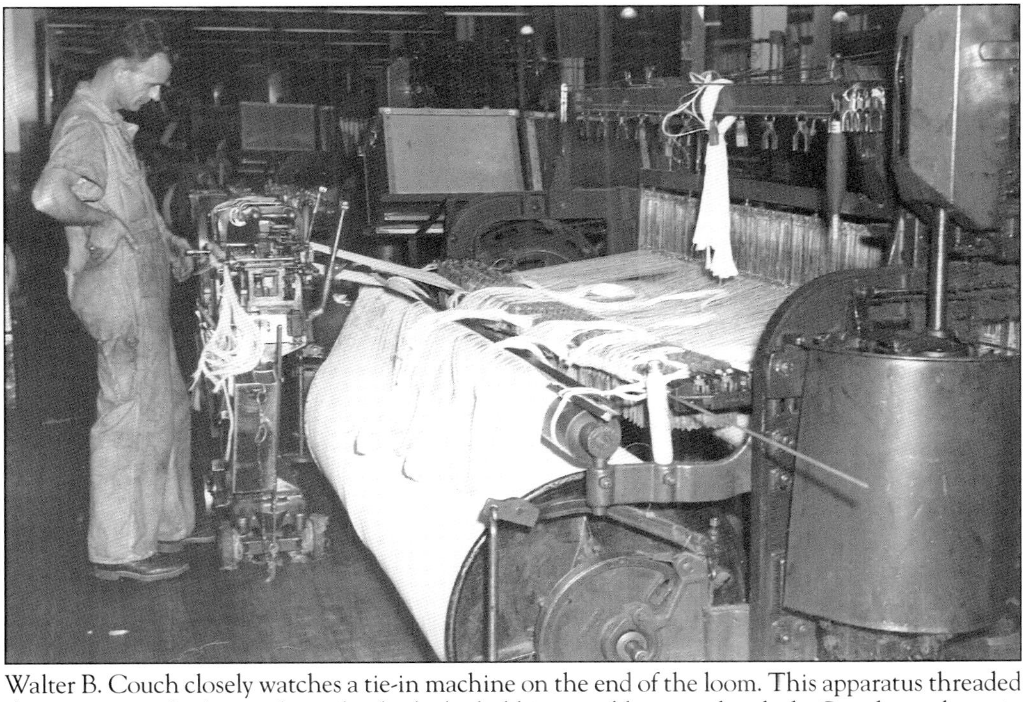

Walter B. Couch closely watches a tie-in machine on the end of the loom. This apparatus threaded the warp onto the loom, through which the bobbins would weave the cloth. Couch was born in the Pleasant Hill community, near Elkin, in 1912 and died in 1989. He worked in the weave room at Chatham from 1932 until he retired in 1974 after 42 years of service. (SJC.)

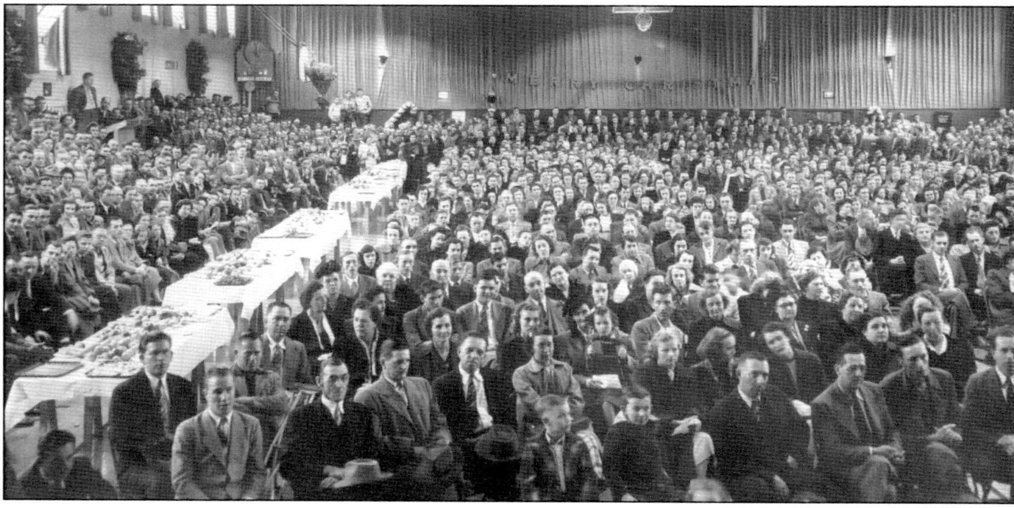

Over 2,000 employees attended the annual Chatham Christmas party in the YMCA gymnasium on December 23, 1949. Part of the crowd is pictured, along with the heavily laden refreshment tables. Christmas bonus checks were often distributed after these events. (SJC.)

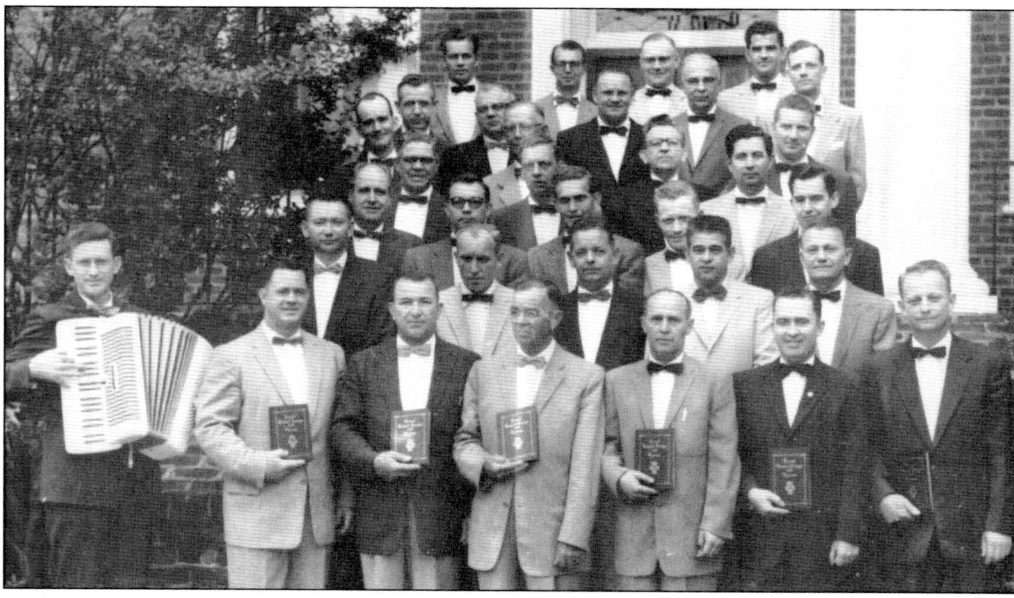

Walt Burgiss photographed the Chatham Male Chorus on the steps of the YMCA building in July 1957. Most of the members were fixers in the weave department. They are, from left to right, (first row) Grady Thomas, Dan Norman, Smith Collins, Arthur Harmon, Nelson Benton, Elmer Morrison, and director Everette Darnell; (second row) Paul Luffman, Robert Barker, U.D. Jolly, Roy Caudle, and Rastus Darnell; (third row) Carlie Layell, Oscar Holcomb, John Darnell, Everett Byrd, and James DeBorde; (fourth row) Free Calloway, Walter Flynn, Edwin Wall, and Charles Collins; (fifth row) Sam Spicer, Clarence Darnell, and Alex Carter; (sixth row) Phillip Ray, Lawrence Wall, Carmel Tucker, Roby Reece, and Roy Lawrence; (seventh row) David Darnell, Grady Day, Ernest Byrd, and D.A. Swaim Jr. Joseph Darnell, Fred Burcham, and Morrison Snow are not pictured. (SJC.)

Nine

Klondike Farm, the Model Guernsey Dairy

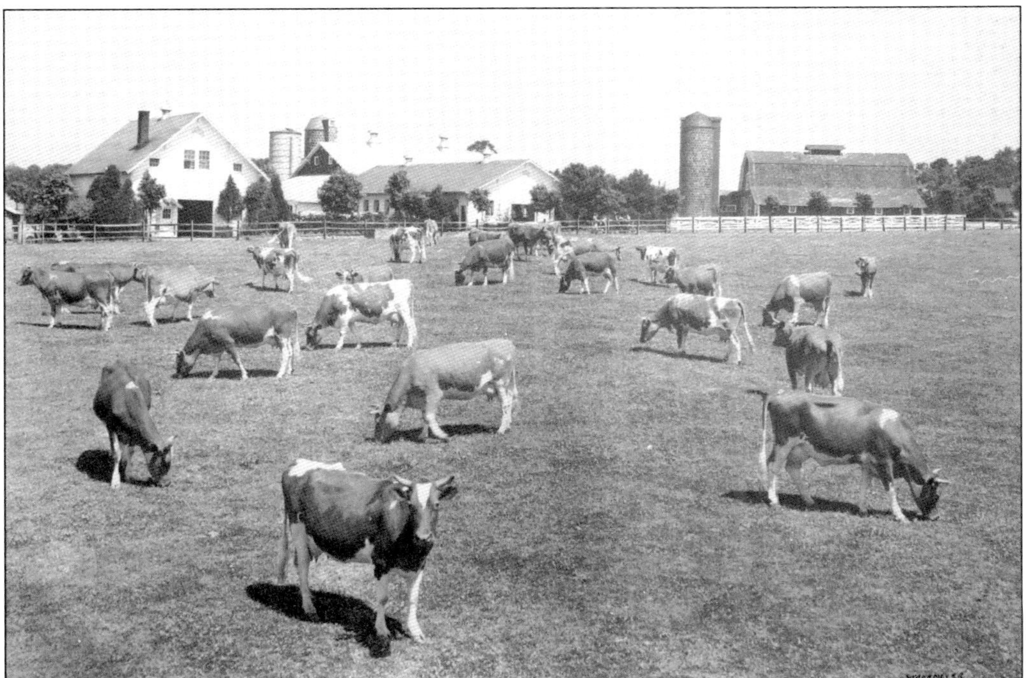

Klondike Farm was located four miles north of Elkin on Highway 26 (now old US Highway 21). In 1925, Thurmond Chatham purchased the farm from his father, Hugh G. Chatham, and his uncle Richard M. Chatham. The property encompassed more than 1,000 acres and was a model farm, raising Guernsey cattle, Berkshire hogs, Shropshire sheep, and Rhode Island Red chickens. This picture was taken in 1938 by Strohmeyer and Carpenter. (SJC.)

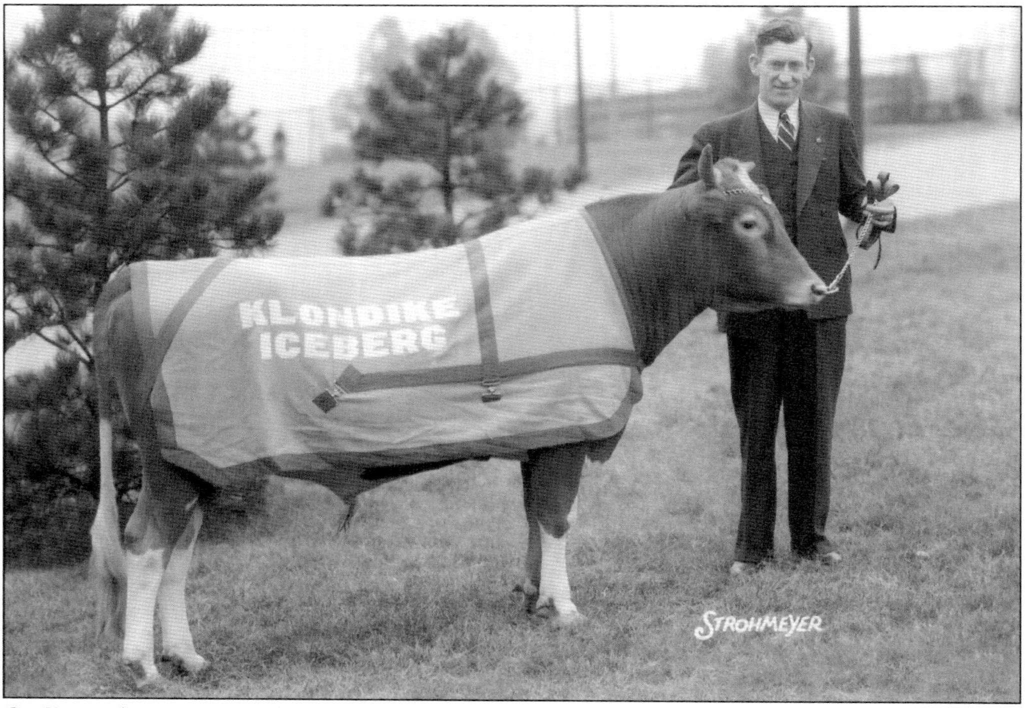

On December 19, 1933, Klondike Iceberg, the most famous cow in the world, was born 247 miles north of the Antarctic Circle. Iceberg is pictured here in 1935 with Edgar Cox, of the Byrd Expedition. His mother, Klondike Nira, was one of three cows sent on the second Richard E. Byrd expedition to the South Pole; she contracted frostbite and had to be put down. After much fanfare, Iceberg returned to Klondike Farm, where he resided until his death on August 16, 1945. (AG, photograph by Henry A. Strohmeyer.)

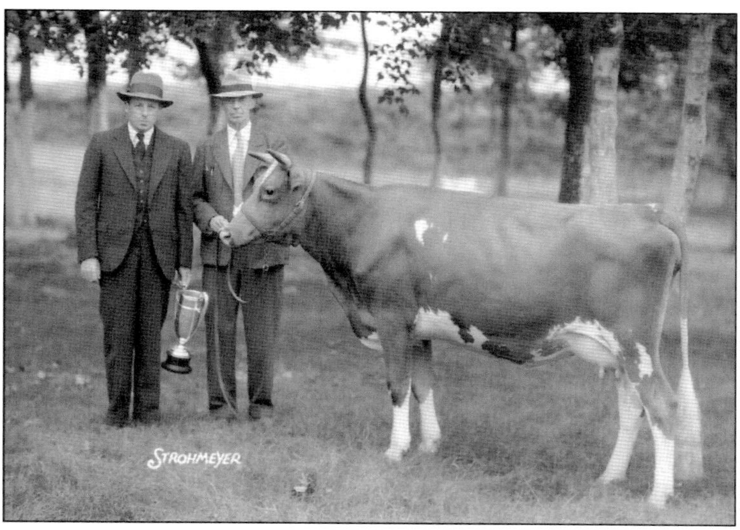

Thurmond Chatham (left) and Klondike Farm manager Ruohs Pyron are pictured here in 1934 with Klondike Gracious, the grand champion of the North Carolina Breeders Show. Pyron was hired as manager in 1925 and served until his death in 1938. Thomas F. Cooley then became the farm manager, serving until his death in 1964. (AG, photograph by Henry A. Strohmeyer.)

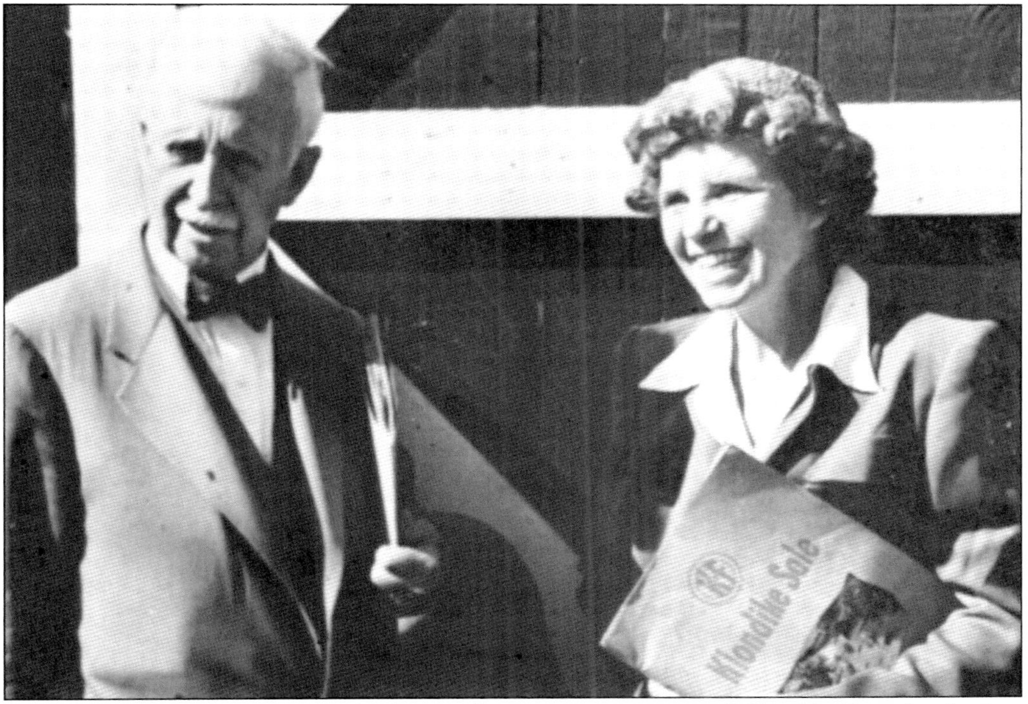

In 1943, J.C. Penney, founder of the famous department store, visited Klondike Farm for the first annual Guernsey cattle sale. Penney is pictured with Lucy Hanes Chatham, wife of Thurmond Chatham, the president of Chatham Manufacturing and owner of Klondike Farm. Cattle sales were held annually at Klondike, and people would come from across the country and pay thousands of dollars for purebred Guernsey cows. (SJC.)

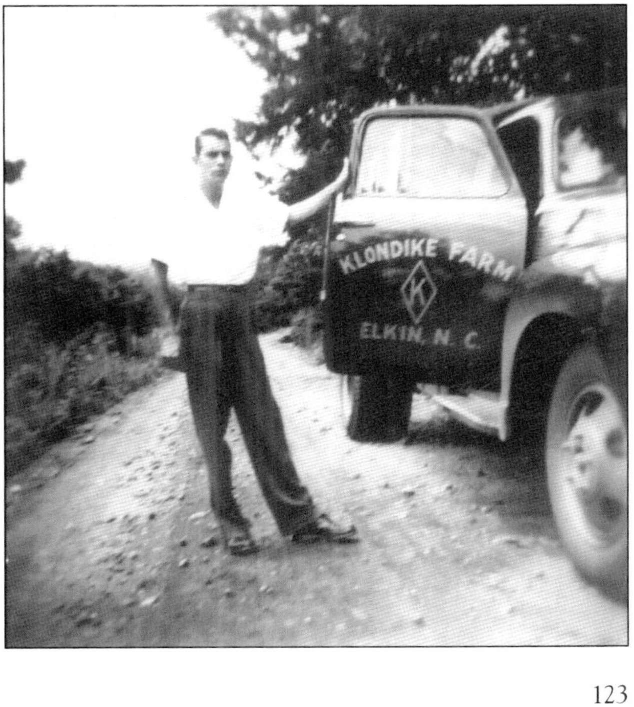

Gilmer Caudle was a milkman for Klondike Farm from 1948 until 1960. He then went to work at the Chatham mill, in the wet finish department, until his retirement in 1988. He is pictured with a 1949 Chevrolet non-refrigerated flatbed truck. Milk was loaded onto the bed of the truck and packed with ice to keep it cool while making deliveries. (GC.)

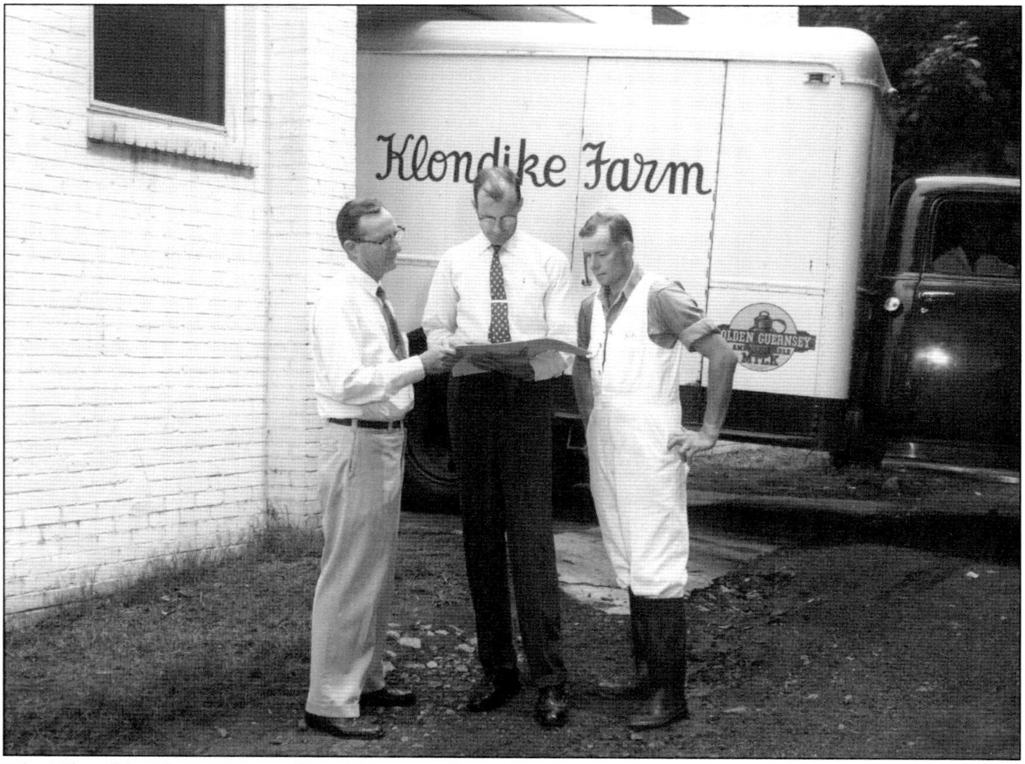

The Klondike Farm Dairy officially opened on May 30, 1927. It quickly became known for quality milk with a higher fat content from the purebred registered Guernsey herd. This early-1950s image shows Thomas F. Cooley (left), Klondike Farm manager for over 25 years, with ? Beeker (center), a salesman with Diversey Corporation, and creamery manager Brady Cothren. (CL.)

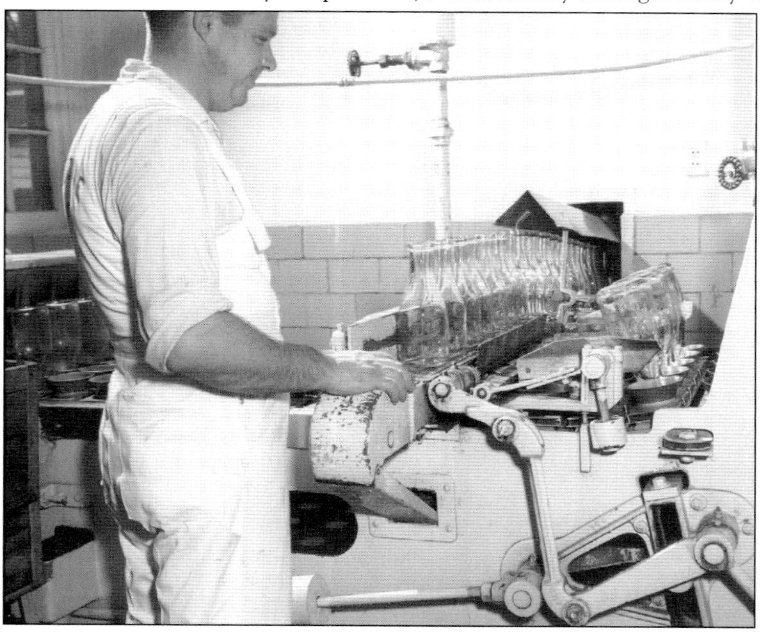

In this late-1950s photograph, Coolidge Layell watches the milk-bottle-washing machine send clean quart bottles into the filling room. Dirty bottles were loaded on the left side of the machine and run through a cycle, similar to that of a dishwasher, using Spec-Tak cleaner. Sparkling clean bottles came out of the right side and were flipped over onto the conveyor to proceed into the filling room. (CL.)

Creamery manager Brady Cothren loads the capping machine with caps, which were placed on the bottles after they were filled with milk by the filler. Klondike originally bottled milk in quart, pint, and half-pint bottles. In the mid-1940s, the company began using green pyroglazed bottles with the famous Klondike Farm logo. Local customers claimed that Klondike made the best chocolate milk in the world. (CL.)

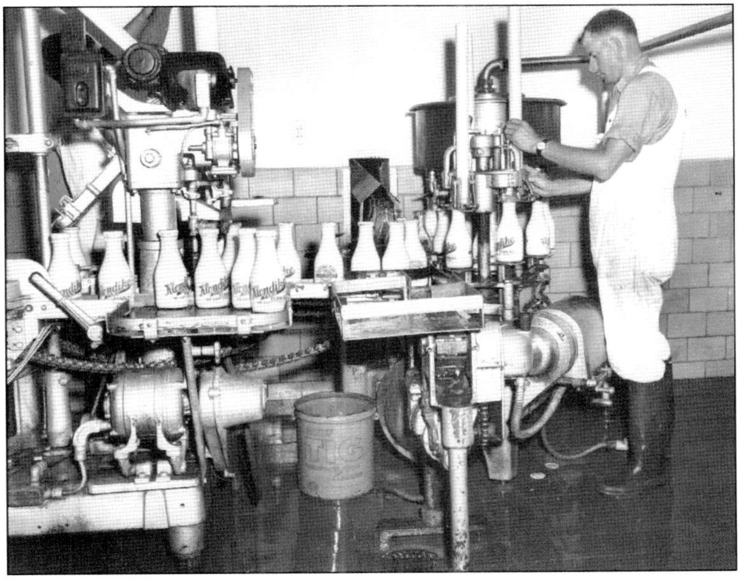

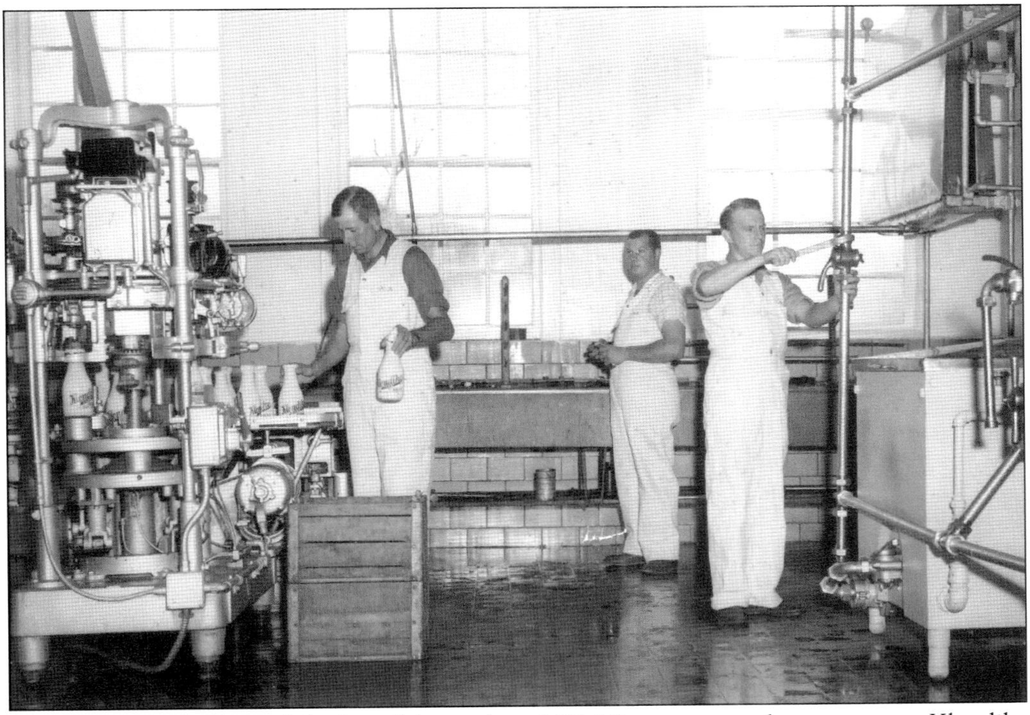

Brady Cothren (left), Coolidge Layell (center), and Gib Nixon operate the creamery at Klondike Farm in the 1950s with exceptional skill and cleanliness. The bottle-filling machine is at left, the milk vat is at right, and the pipe-washing sink is on the back wall. In August 1965, the Klondike herd was sold at auction, and all milk production ceased. (CL.)

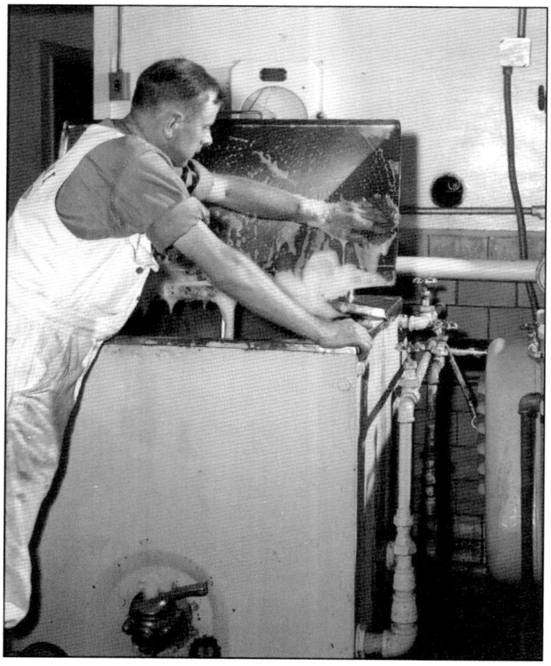

Creamery manager Brady Cothren cleans the milk vat with Tig, an industrial cleaner. The vat held 100 gallons of milk, which was cooked for 30 minutes at 143 degrees, allowed to cool, then bottled. The homogenizing machine is at right. In regular pasteurized milk, the cream would rise to the top of each bottle. To make homogenized milk, the machine broke up the fat cells, suspending them in the milk. (CL.)

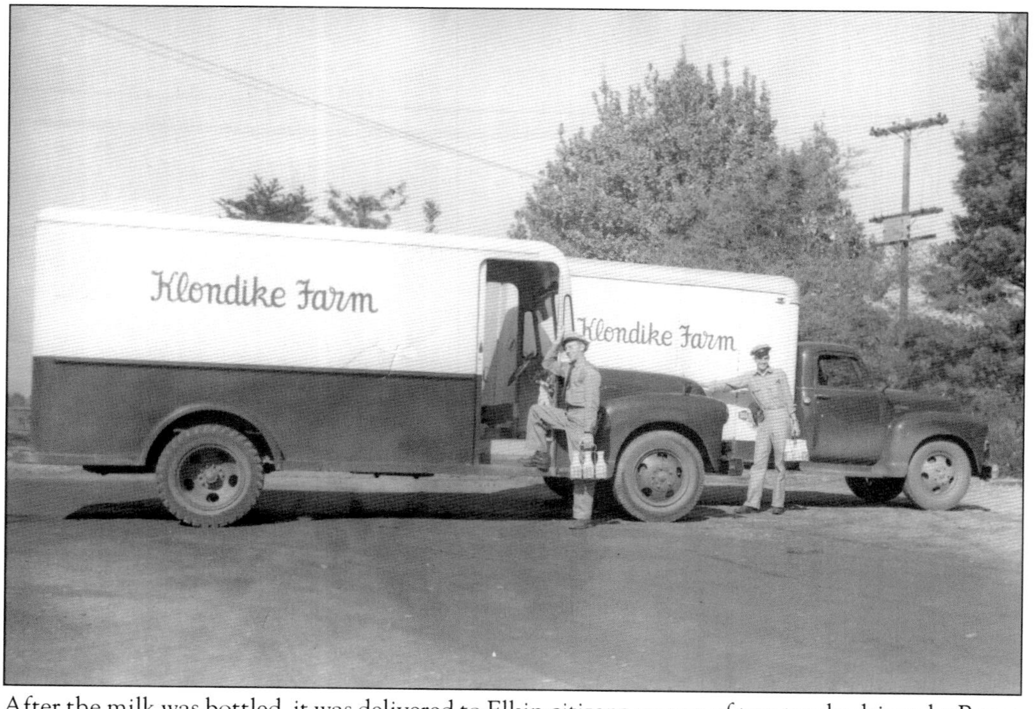

After the milk was bottled, it was delivered to Elkin citizens on one of two trucks driven by Reece Hemric (left) and Gilmer Caudle. Hemric drove the retail route to homes, and Caudle drove the wholesale route to grocery stores, Elkin and Jonesville schools, and the hospital. Klondike offered customers pasteurized milk, homogenized milk, chocolate milk, buttermilk, heavy cream, and even eggnog (at Christmas). (CL.)

BIBLIOGRAPHY

Baily, Waldron. *The Autobiography of Waldron Baily*. New York: Exposition, 1958.

Bell, W.M. *The North Carolina Flood: July 14, 15, 16, 1916*. Charlotte: W.M. Bell. 1916.

Bray, Dan R. Jr. *The Elkin & Alleghany Railway Company*. Traphill, NC: Norman Offset, 1979.

Byrd, Hazel. *First Century, A History of First Baptist Church of Elkin, North Carolina, 1889–1989.* Elkin, NC: Privately published, 1989.

Canipe, Ruby Bray. *Early Elkin-Jonesville History and Genealogy*. Jonesville, NC: Tarheel Graphics, 1981.

Chatham Manufacturing Company. *Chatham Blanketeer*. Elkin, NC: Chatham Print Shop, 1933–1965.

Town of Elkin Committee for the Collection of Historical Information. *Elkin 1889–1989: A Centennial History*. Charlotte: Delmar, 1989.

Elkin Tribune. 1914 Industrial Edition. Elkin, NC: Elk Printing, 1914.

———. Golden Anniversary Edition, 1911–1961. Elkin, NC: Elk Printing, 1961.

Hickerson, Thomas Felix. *Happy Valley: History and Genealogy*. Chapel Hill, NC: Privately published, 1940.

Jackson, Hester Bartlett, ed. *The Heritage of Surry County North Carolina, Vol. 1*. Winston-Salem: Hunter, 1983.

Norman, Mary H. *Elkin Baptist Association, One Hundred Years 1879–1979*. Jonesville, NC: Tarheel Graphics, 1981.

Pegram, Sherley. *Sherley, Book of Poems Choice and Rare*. Richmond: Hermitage Press, 1911.